DISSECTING "*ANATOMY O.*

THE AUTHOR, THE CRIME,

THE NOVEL, AND THE FILM

Eugene R. Milhizer

AVE MARIA SCHOOL OF LAW PRESS.

ISBN: 9780578920948

Images Courtesy of:
Central Peninsula & NMU Archives
Frederick Baker Jr.
Eugene R. Milhizer
Ernest "Woody" Woods

Saul Bass inspired book cover design created by
Rob Oliver III
www.roboliver3.com

Printed in the
United States of America.

Ave Maria School of Law Press, Inc.

Naples, Florida 2019

To my wife Dianna, who inspires me to be a better man.

TABLE OF CONTENTS

ACKNOWLEDGEMENTS

The author is grateful for the generous time and invaluable assistance provided by a wide array of people and institutions in Michigan, Florida, and elsewhere.

In Michigan, the author extends thanks to Marcus Robyns, University Archivist, and Eliza Compton, Arrangement & Description Specialist, both at Central Upper Peninsula and Northern Michigan University Archives, Northern Michigan University ("NMU"), the repository of the Voelker Papers Collection. Dr. Robyns and Ms. Compton afforded unencumbered access to the Voelker Collection, and cheerfully provided prompt and thorough follow-up support.

The author also would like to thank the Voelker family, who granted the author full access to restricted materials in the NMU archives. The author is especially grateful to Voelker's daughters Julie Voelker Cohen and Gracie Voelker Woods, and Gracie's husband Ernest ("Woody") Woods. Gracie and Woody graciously invited me to a dinner with Julie in John Voelker's country home, and Woody took me to the famous Uncle Tom's Cabin on Frenchman's Pond, Voelker's sanctuary and secret fishing hole. All of this extraordinary access and support provided a deep, detailed, and intimate window into John Voelker's life, times, thinking, and beliefs. It also allowed me to make some wonderful new friends.

The author is indebted to Elizabeth Delene, who generously shared her master's thesis on John Voelker with me. It was a rich resource, especially for the thoughts and insights of Voelker family members and contemporaries whom she interviewed, many in great depth.

The author appreciates the assistance of The John D. Voelker Foundation, and its President Richard F. Vander Veen, III, for his insights and personal recollections about John Voelker.

Other thanks for support in Michigan are extended to Jack Borgeois, the owner and proprietor of the Lumberjack Tavern in Big Bay, Michigan, where the shooting in the Peterson murder case occurred; Kurt Gronvell and Stacey Willey of Globe Printing in Ishpeming, Michigan, for providing a tour and information about the iconic "Autograph Wall," and especially to Kurt for allowing me to take photographs of the Wall and use them in this book; Robert Dossetto, Circuit Court Bailiff, Marquette, Michigan, for his tour of the Marquette County Courthouse and the wealth of inside information he provided; the staff of Marquette's Peter White Public Library and the Marquette Historical Society; Scott Holman, the owner and proprietor of the Mount Shasta Lodge in Michigamme, Michigan; Gary Walker, former Prosecuting Attorney for Marquette County; Danny Abbott, an extra in the film *Anatomy of a Murder*, who is one of the few surviving cast members; the staff at Ishpeming's Carnegie Library, Congress Pizza, and Tee Pee Bar; the staff of the Landmark Hotel in Marquette; the staff of the Thunder Bay Inn and Perkins Trailer Park in Big Bay; John (Tom) Burke, a resident of Ishpeming; John Wirtanen, former owner of the Wonder Bar, in Ishpeming; Jim Hebbard; Roy Peterson; and many others too numerous to mention.

For their assistance in Florida, the author would like to thank Mr. Rob Oliver for the cover art, and the Ave Maria School of Law Library Staff, especially Associate Professor and Library Director Ulysses Jaen, Technical Services Librarian Val Oliver, Circulation Supervisor Rachel Hocott, and Foreign and Comparative Law Librarian Asli Karaevli. The author is also grateful to Professor Brian Scarnecchia and Professor Kevin Govern, colleagues at Ave Maria School of Law, and Professor Ronald Rychlak, University of Mississippi School of Law, for their thoughtful comments about an early draft of this book.

The author is grateful for the institutional and financial support provided by Ave Maria School of Law, and in particular to its President and Dean, Kevin Cieply, who approved launching the Ave Maria School of Law Press with this book as its inaugural publication, and Elizabeth

Westhoff, for promoting this effort. The author is again grateful to Professor Jaen for his invaluable assistance and guidance in transforming the author's research and law review article draft into this book.

The author would like to thank his research assistants, Evelyn Hildebrand, Alicia Henry, Marina Moussa, Andrew Hocott, and Cherish Fuller, for their remarkable work on this project.

Last, and certainly not least, the author is most grateful to Frederick M. Baker, Jr., Secretary-Treasurer of the John D. Voelker Foundation, and a good friend of John Voelker. Mr. Baker's support and contributions were invaluable. The author is especially grateful for his personal accounts of John Voelker and his superb editing of this book. I treasure his support and friendship, and I am in his debt.

FOREWORD

Most American males of a certain generation, including mine, and certainly including John Voelker's, were raised according to an unwritten "Male Code." Robert Garfield describes this Code as a set of rigid, but unwritten, guidelines equating masculinity with stoicism, silence, and strength, and defining manliness in a way that leaves little room for the emotional intimacy that friendship requires.[1] As a result, as men grow older, and the close friends of their youth (when the Male Code did not yet fully apply) recede in time, distance, and intimacy, or disappear entirely, in death, men often find themselves with dozens of acquaintances, but few close friends with whom they share a deep emotional connection. But men who live by that Code do not stop craving the closeness of friendship; indeed, men, much more than women,[2] are likely to experience feelings of depression and anger as their isolation increases with age, accentuated by changes in technology, social organization, and our work lives.[3]

One of the many traits that made John Voelker so remarkable was his complete rejection of the isolation the Male Code inflicts, a theme that runs like a golden thread through most of John's work was his hatred of "the City" and the awful isolation and anonymity it imposes on the individual. His returns to the Upper Peninsula, with his bride in the 1930s, after a gallant attempt to subordinate himself to his love for Grace by following the traditional route to "success" in a large Chicago firm, and in 1961, from Lansing, where his appointment to the Michigan Supreme Court had obliged him to spend too much of his precious "stream time," were each acts of rebellion against isolation, anonymity, and the world of the Male Code.

John had many intimate friends, and he made new ones throughout his life. He was unafraid of intimacy, I think, at least partly because life in the U.P.'s small communities is an intimate affair. One example of John's ability to form deep bonds throughout his life is the one that grew between him and his friend Gigs Gagliardi, the owner of the Roosevelt Bar, where *Anatomy's* cast watered during location filming in Ishpeming and Marquette. Gigs could not have been more unlike John, in most respects. John was a member of the "gentry," a professional with an excellent education and extensive knowledge of history, literature, and the larger world. Gigs had little education and moved in the stratum of Ishpeming society that seized opportunity when it presented itself, surviving and prospering on his native wit and his toughness. Gigs could keep order in his bar when men twice his size acted up, and he could recall meeting Al Capone when he was a boy, accompanying a relative on a run to Chicago for "hootch" during Prohibition. So far as I know,

John's only fight was the hilarious one in which he ended up rolling down the stairs of the University of Michigan's Law Library locked in a furious embrace with his opponent, defending her honor on his first date with Grace. But John and Gigs formed a close bond as grown men that centered around fishing (before John taught Gigs to flyfish he had always "drowned worms"), a fondness for Old Fashioneds, a shared love of the U.P. and its people, the joy of telling stories about shared friends and acquaintances, and the mutual respect the two had for each other. After John died, Gigs refused to play cribbage with anyone, because it was "their" game.

John made friends because he was comfortable in his skin; he lived life as he chose to live it. If the quality and material comfort of that life was enhanced by his sudden success, at the age of 53, with the publication and filming of *Anatomy*, the ease of living life on his own terms after that success does nothing to disprove the point: John also did what he chose to do for 53 years before that improbable success occurred. The lure of wealth, success, and power, the putative rewards of adhering to the Male Code, could not induce John to compromise his values, or his openness to friendships with men he encountered along his way through life. Friends were more important than "success." John was in many ways a private man, and inhabited a writer's mind, one that never ceased examining, learning, and fabricating from what occurred around him, but it was his openness to and appreciation for other men and their accomplishments, as if they were characters in the novel of his life, that allowed John to command such loyalty and even devotion from his friends.

And so, it was with me and my friend Rich Vander Veen when, as young "lads" from below the bridge, we had the great good luck to meet and eventually, in the last eight years of his life, become friends not only with John, but with some of his dearest friends. Gigs became a beloved figure and contributed much to the success of the eponymous Foundation we established with John to create a fishing fiction writing award and provide law school scholarships to Native Americans. John's dear friend "Jim White" (so-called in one of John's stories), who recovered while living in a teepee he built at John's Pond (which still stands today) from the soul-crushing effects of white civilization, joined with us under the name he reassumed after spending nearly a year there, James Washinawatok. With John's quiet encouragement, Jim regained his pride in his Native American heritage after he collected himself at Frenchman's, and became a tribal elder and a tribal judge, esteemed and honored by his Ho-Chunk people. No two men could have been more different, but John and Jim were the same in this respect: they lived life as they thought it should be lived, and not by any "code" that interfered with their humanity and their capacity for brotherhood.

I could describe many other examples, such as artist Paul Grant, restauranteur and chef Ted Bogden, television personality Charles Kuralt, jurist Damon Keith, to mention only a few. All were numbered among the legion of fiercely loyal and devoted friends John made throughouthis life.

A foreword should be brief, and I do not wish to outwear my welcome, so I will provide only two more examples: John so impressed Rich Vander Veen and I that we have grown old as volunteers doing a few good things in his name, in service of the two causes he chose for his Foundation.

The remarkable thing about John was that, both through his writing, and what was written about him, he could inspire a sort of "reverence," even in men who had not met him. And when I have encountered men like these, who, in John's honor, include the Old Fashioned as an ornament to their spiritous life; who play (or learn to play) cribbage; who have read John's books, been inspired by them, and enjoy talking about them and him; and who, given some instruction (or already possessing the touch), can cast from 10 o'clock to 2, if shown the way to Frenchman's Pond, I have discovered another gift that flows from having known and admired John: I, too, made a new friend, The Code be damned.

So now I invite you to meet my new friend Gene, who has performed a worthwhile scholarly task. He has not merely researched, organized, and distilled an enormous amount of information, discovered and uncovered through diligent and imaginative sourcing. He has also thoughtfully analyzed John, both as a person and as a writer, and the meaning of John's greatest novel, *Anatomy*. Despite John's genuine humility, he was far more than the mere "spinner of yarns" he often called himself.

Anatomy tells a story gleaned from an examined life, drawn from experience in one of the central arenas in which truth, or what passes for it in an imperfect world, is exposed or obscured, the courtroom. Gene understands this better than anyone I have read who has written critically about John's work. So, what you have in your hands is a serious addition to the body of work by and about this elusive, attractive, and endlessly interesting trout of a man and author. Oyez, oyez, draw near and give your attention.

Frederick Baker, Jr.
Lansing, Michigan
February 2021

PREFACE

Most lawyers enjoy a good courtroom war story. They delight in hearing one and luxuriate in telling one. They happily spin yarns about their brilliant courtroom exploits and the odd or sinister behavior of their opponents, judges, clients, and witnesses. *Anatomy of a Murder*[1] is a lawyer's war story, told on the grandest scale, with inspired mastery. In fact, it is probably the best lawyer war story ever told. It is engaging and titillating. It is profound and challenging. It is a rare combination of sizzle and steak.

Ironically, those most acquainted with real war are generally least willing to recount, and thereby relive, their battlefield experiences. They avoid "war stories" because they have seen first-hand the lives lost, the pain inflicted, and the destruction wrought; what they endured in combat taught them to abhor war. Retelling and reliving such scenes can be sorrowful and traumatic. Some things are better left unspoken.

With the obvious exception of capital cases in execution jurisdictions, lawyers fight a different, bloodless type of battle. Serious though the stakes may be, in the end, all trials are a game of wits, and lawyers—especially those who have won that game—tend to have a far different attitude about telling their "war stories." Where a combat veteran might prefer deterring war to prevailing in the field, trial litigators, who relish the stylized combat of a trial, from which they emerge, like a trout from a barbless hook, with "nothing hurt but their feelings,"[5] often take equal pleasure in describing it, especially "after an old-fashioned," as John Voelker once famously remarked on national television.[6]

Indeed, given their competitive spirit, litigators may prefer a courtroom triumph over a quiet settlement that may serve their client equally well. A litigator's attraction to the arena is as much about the battle as it is about the outcome. A litigator who revels in jousting and feinting with opposing counsel and the judge embraces a contested trial's test of will, intellect, stamina, and courage. One suspects that they are affirmed by the spectacle, the ritual pageant, and, yes—the attention.

Good litigators immerse themselves in trial preparation. They seek to exploit advantages and shore up weaknesses. They plan and plot. They anticipate and prepare for what Donald Rumsfeld was once described as "known unknowns" and "unknown unknowns,"[7] constructing intricate decision trees and fallback plans. And when the time comes and the trial begins, they merrily joust. They thrust and parry, wielding law and procedure like swords and shields. They spar with witnesses and play to jurors. They juggle several balls while dancing on their feet.

The competition is challenging and exhilarating. It tests their mettle and validates their worth. When the trial is over, litigators celebrate their triumph or lick their wounds. In either case, it is an occasion for the serious litigator to take stock and reflect upon his performance. The trial is replayed in their mind's eyes with the detail of a video recording. Litigators relive leveraged openings and missed opportunities, second-guess cross-examination strategies, and re-evaluate questions asked, arguments made, objections raised, and a myriad of other choices and decisions. And, humanly, some may deflect blame to others, sometimes unfairly and for self- serving reasons, when those choices go awry, while crediting themselves when they succeed.

It is during this critical period of self-evaluation that war stories about the trial begin to emerge and take shape. This creative process can be cathartic, even therapeutic. It provides an opportunity for the storyteller to re-write and even to un-write history. It allows him to justify and explain his actions, smoothing over rough patches as needed to shore up self-esteem. The process can be soothing and sustaining. It facilitates recovery for the next battle.

Every first-class legal war story shares several common attributes. First, the storyteller must properly set the scene. How did he get involved in the case? What was at stake? What obstacles were apparent? What challenges were faced?

Next, the storyteller must define the characters. What were the important players' traits and attributes? The cast will include major characters (opposing counsel, the judge, the client) and players with smaller parts (assistants, witnesses, and others). They may lend support, act as foils, or merely provide comic relief, but the accomplished storyteller will reveal some of their backstories to add interest and insight into their actions: had the storyteller crossed swords with any of the characters before? Were they ethical and trustworthy? Were they scoundrels? What advantages did they enjoy? What weaknesses did they exhibit or exploit?

With all of this as prelude, the storyteller can present the story's central dilemma, the fulcrum upon which the narrative turns. It could be the decision on a vital pretrial motion, an objection that must be sustained or overruled, a critical witness who must be prepared for direct examination or eviscerated on cross, managing a vexing client, or finding a way to suppress or obtain a crucial piece of evidence. Grandest of all, it could be a jury verdict in a hotly contested murder trial. Regardless of the particulars, the storyteller's ultimate success invariably turns on out-foxing opposing counsel, persuading a hostile or unreceptive judge, or convincing a skeptical jury. Stratagems are explained in asides to the "fourth wall," and dialogue is recounted to add drama and authenticity. And while a modicum of self-deprecation is encouraged, to confirm the storyteller's self-awareness and bolster his credibility, the tale inevitably concludes with the storyteller prevailing, or at least unfairly cheated out of the victory that should have been.

As time passes, the story evolves. On each occasion it is retold, the storyteller becomes slightly more eloquent and his intellect a bit keener. This propensity to embellish is not unique to litigators. It is human nature. The broken-field touchdown run at a high school homecoming game becomes more spectacular each time it is recounted, just as the second-shot three iron on a par five inches closer to the cup with each iteration. The storyteller is unencumbered in burnishing his tale, because the details about what actually happened are unlikely to be verifiable by independent evidence. The evolution of a war story is limited by little more than the storyteller's conscience and imagination.

To be sure, a savvy listener neither expects nor requires complete historical fidelity, or even independent corroboration. It is, after all, a war story, and accepted (and enjoyed) as such. Indeed, the listener welcomes a little puffery if it adds interest. The joy of a war story is in being regaled by and listening to it, and it is not dependent on its *precise* accuracy, so long as the narrative leads to the suspension of disbelief that lies at the heart of every successful story. The best war stories are experienced by the listener like virtual reality, where virtually anything can and does happen. And they are told with absolute conviction.

Anatomy of a Murder is such a war story writ large. The storyteller is John Voelker, who assumes the pen name Robert Traver to recount a fictionalized version of *People v. Peterson,*[5] a hotly contested murder trial in Michigan's remote Upper Peninsula in the 1950s.

In the actual Peterson trial, Voelker was the defense counsel who prevailed, winning a jury verdict of not guilty based on the defendant's temporary insanity. Voelker's novel has all the attributes of a good lawyers' tale: an evocative background, strong and diverse characters, a central dilemma that must be addressed, and the storyteller prevailing in the end. More than this, Voelker's account pushes nearly every hot button: murder, rape, spousal abuse, adultery, jealousy, betrayal, revenge, redemption, vindication, and validation.

But unlike most courtroom war stories, the authenticity of Voelker's tale can be verified by independent evidence. As this book concludes, Voelker's fictionalized rendition of the Peterson trial is remarkably true to the original. Often it is spot on.

But to dismiss *Anatomy of Murder* as a fact-based and entertaining lawyer story would unfairly diminish its significance and impact. It would be akin to referring to *War and Peace* as a realistic Russian yarn about the Napoleonic invasion. *Anatomy of a Murder* is much grander than typical war story fare; indeed, it is in many ways exceptional. Voelker's novel became a record-setting best seller. It launched a new genre of realistic courtroom trial fiction. Decades after its publication, it is still used as a teaching tool in law schools around the country. It remains a catalyst for legal academics to examine topics involving courtroom ethics, trial advocacy, and professional responsibility. It is also a great read.

The movie is no less extraordinary. It was a box office smash and a critical success. It was produced and directed by the renowned filmmaker Otto Preminger. It starred a Hollywood legend, Jimmy Stewart, and featured a distinguished cast. It garnered a slew of prestigious awards and award nominations, including winning the first Grammy awards for a jazz musical score and for a musical score composed by an African American, Duke Ellington. It was the first major movie production filmed entirely on location. It starred the nation's most famous real-life lawyer, Joseph Welch, who attained celebrity status through his prominent role in the McCarthy anti-communist Senate hearings. Sixty years after its debut in 1959, the film remains relevant, edgy, highly entertaining, and watched.

Measured by its commercial success, critical acclaim, and unique distinctions, *Anatomy of a Murder* is both an enduring literary classic and a cinematic triumph. But appraising *Anatomy of a Murder* solely by tallying profits, awards, and achievements overlooks its broader significance, complexity, and depth. The book and movie realistically and unapologetically tackle foundational concepts of justice, truth, ethics, and community standards. Both challenge settled conventions and scrutinize some of our most basic assumptions, in part because of the accuracy with which they depict the law, the role of legal counsel, and the conduct of criminal trials. They authentically expose the moral inadequacies of the criminal justice system and prompt thoughtful readers or viewers to reflect upon their own values and judgments.

This book explores—it dissects, if you will—*Anatomy of a Murder* in considerable detail. It tells the fascinating story of its author, John Voelker. It chronicles the actual, high-profile murder trial, in which he served as defense counsel. It explains how he adapted this real-life trial into a fictional form as a great novel. And it looks back on the production of the groundbreaking film that his novel inspired.

In addition to this largely historical assessment, this book considers several discrete legal and ethical issues the novel and film raise, including the implications of a criminal attorney "explaining the law" to a client in a manner that may "suggest" a dubious defense. It also reflects upon broader questions, such as the proper role of jury and the impact of community standards in a criminal trial. Finally, it evaluates the capacity of the criminal justice system to achieve true justice within the context of what Voelker called the "settled procedures and ancient rules" of the law.[6]

In order to fully appreciate the novel and film, one must begin by coming to know the author, John Voelker, who is, after all, both his protagonist's creator and alter ego. His life's journey is remarkable, repeatedly shaped by deep contradictions and reluctant compromise. Indeed, *Anatomy of Murder* is an autobiographical lawyer's war story about the warrior storyteller, John Voelker. It is a story about a well-educated and gifted lawyer who seeks sanctuary in remote woods and trout streams. It is a story about a brilliant trial litigator who performs his ethical duty by zealously defending an unlikeable client whom he sincerely believes is guilty. It is a story about a lawyer who at once champions the criminal justice system and laments its many flaws and shortcomings. It is a story about the inevitable contradiction between realism and idealism, and one man's way of coping with the dissonance. It is a story about pivotal choices and their consequences. It is the greatest legal war story ever told, and one told by "the closest thing to a great man"[7] that most of us are ever likely to know.

PART I

BEFORE THE MURDER

CHAPTER 1 – SETTING THE STAGE

Voelker was poised on the cusp of a transformative change of his fortunes. Though he could not foresee how profoundly, he understood that the next few days of trial would alter the trajectory of his career.

In narrow and immediate terms, he knew he was about to defend his first murder trial and that his professional life would be forever altered. On the other hand, he could never have foreseen the wildly improbable, even breathtaking, repercussions of the steps he would take in the next week to defend his client's liberty and, at the same time, salvage his obscure private practice in Michigan's remote Upper Peninsula. No one could have.

Voelker, of course, was fully aware that the trial would be hotly contested and highly publicized. Even at the time, he referred to it as a "five alarm murder case,"[1] and the stakes were nearly as high for Voelker as for his client. Preparing for the trial had been his singular focus for about two months. Voelker knew that if he could somehow obtain an acquittal for his client, his professional, financial, and personal circumstances would improve greatly.

What Voelker did not know—and could not have imagined in his wildest dreams—was that this trial, its aftermath, and its fictionalized legacy, would dramatically change not only virtually every facet of his personal, professional, and family life, but also have profound legal, literary, and cinematic consequences. But as the trial was about to begin, Voelker's thoughts were immediate and simple—to defend his client and win an acquittal.

A few months earlier, Voelker's client, Army First Lieutenant Coleman Peterson, had fatally shot a local tavern owner. Depending on which account one believed, the deceased had either just raped Peterson's wife or had consensual sex with her and then brazenly bragged about it.

Had the shooting occurred the previous year, Voelker would have been prosecuting the case instead of defending Peterson. But he had been narrowly defeated in his re-election bid for an eighth term as Marquette County Prosecuting Attorney, so when the crime occurred and the case was tried, Voelker had been a criminal defense attorney for only a few months. Though he had successfully represented several criminal defendants in his career, Voelker had never defended at a murder case. He knew that his performance during the Peterson trial, which would be followed closely in the media, and an acquittal, should he obtain one, would go far in establishing his bonefides in his new role as a defense counsel.

But the stakes were even higher than this for Voelker. He was financially strapped, with a family to support, a mortgage to pay, and a law office to run. If he did not win an acquittal, his client would never be able to pay his legal fees. A conviction would also tarnish Voelker's reputation as a litigator, which rested largely on his work as a prosecutor, thereby discouraging potential clients from retaining his defense services in the future. He also had a personal interest to vindicate: the young prosecutor who had ousted Voelker in the last election would oppose him in the Peterson case. Voelker always maintained that the new prosecutor had run a dishonorable campaign, so the Peterson trial was an opportunity not only for retribution, but also to show the voters that they had chosen unwisely. Finally, Voelker, like any successful litigator, took pride in his courtroom skills and legal acumen. Victory would be personally gratifying and affirming; defeat would be yet another tarnish on his recently battered self-image.

Beyond all personal interests, however, Voelker had a genuine sense of professional duty to his client. Voelker knew that Lieutenant Peterson was almost certainly guilty of premeditated murder under most readings of the letter of the law. But given the extenuating and mitigating circumstances in the case, Voelker had no legal or moral qualms about presenting a zealous defense and seeking an acquittal.

Beyond his narrow obligation to the client, Voelker also

3

passionately believed in our adversarial criminal justice system, in which the outcome is determined through a robust duel between advocates, played out before a jury. The decision of a jury, the official arbiter of the community's standards, offered the best promise of justice for defendants and society alike. For the adversarial criminal justice process to function properly and achieve justice, Voelker understood and believed that opposing counsel must clash with full force, vigor, and imagination. Voelker embraced this system and his role in it as an aggressive advocate obligated to challenge the prosecutor on his client's behalf whenever he could. Voelker performed this professional and institutional obligation not only out of a sense of duty, but with a personal conviction that he executed with aplomb.

To accomplish these objectives in his defense of Lieutenant Peterson, Voelker had to confront a variety of legal issues and moral uncertainties. Given the factual posture of the case, in which his client indisputably committed the fatal shooting, Voelker reasoned that Peterson's only hope of acquittal depended upon jury nullification premised on a highly vulnerable theory of temporary insanity. No other option was even remotely available.

Obtaining an acquittal of murder based on an insanity defense, sometimes called the "defense of last resort," especially in cases involving matters of honor, was a long shot under best of circumstances. In Peterson's case, the chances of success seemed especially remote, for several reasons. To begin with, Peterson did not believe he was insane, and the facts of the case suggested that his assessment was correct. It was nonetheless apparent to Voelker that, to obtain an acquittal, his client would have to set aside his belief in his sanity and help Voelker develop a plausible factual predicate for an insanity defense. More challenging than this, however, was the particular factual predicate required: Peterson would have to assist in constructing the intricate groundwork for a claim of *temporary* insanity based on *irresistible impulse,* a rare variation of the insanity defense still recognized at the time, and the only variation of that defense that held any hope of an acquittal.

Legal ethics prohibited Voelker from instructing his client on what to say about the facts on which the issue of his sanity would turn, or even to suggest overtly to his client a narrative that supported such a defense. The rules governing defense counsel's professional and ethical conduct required then, as they do now and always have, that the factual predicate for any defense, and certainly for an insanity claim, must emanate from the defendant's lips, unprompted by any suggestion of defense counsel.

Voelker creatively embraced the challenge of presenting the

temporary insanity defense in a manner consistent with his professional obligations. By carefully confining his counsel to the requirements of the law, on which it was his ethical responsibility to instruct Lieutenant Peterson, he was able to elicit from Peterson, without suggesting it directly, the factual basis for an insanity defense, using only means carefully crafted and confined within the bounds of legal ethics. Voelker had now obtained the ammunition he needed to raise the defense and possibly secure Peterson's acquittal at trial.

Voelker was well aware of all of these immediate ethical, tactical, and strategic considerations and complications. He prepared for them, addressed each as well as circumstances permitted, and navigated them skillfully. What Voelker did not know—and could not have known—were the larger implications and consequences of his defense of Lieutenant Peterson. Voelker had long been a gifted but commercially unsuccessful writer. Nothing in his own account of events surrounding the trial, and certainly nothing in the pedestrian details reflected in the record of the proceedings, suggests that Voelker ever imagined at the time that he would weave from the experience the novel he later wrote, nor that it would achieve record-setting sales, establish a new literary genre, and inspire a great movie. Nothing suggests that even this imaginative, aspiring uranium prospector envisioned that, as a result of defending Lieutenant Peterson as doggedly and creatively as he could, he would become both financially secure and a national celebrity. Certainly, he could not have foretold that but a few years hence he would trade quips with Johnny Carson on the Tonight Show or share a tin cup of bourbon with actress Lee Remick during a secluded Jeep ride on the outskirts of Marquette. Nor could he have conceived that he would be appointed to the Michigan Supreme Court and then later resign his office because of the competing demands on his time given his new-found celebrity status and financial security.

Certainly, none of these thoughts crossed Voelker's mind in July 1952, as the Peterson trial was about to begin in a packed courtroom in Marquette, Michigan. Voelker's focus and energy were directed solely toward zealously representing his client and obtaining an acquittal. To this undertaking he brought a store of training and experience, values and motivations, and needs and desires acquired during a lifetime that, with the perfect vision of hindsight, seems to have been laid by for the singular purpose of defending Peterson successfully. Voelker would prove to be as fully up to his task as defense counsel as he later proved to be uniquely qualified to write a great novel about the trial.

To understand Voelker, then, and how he obtained the acquittal that allowed him to fulfill his destiny, one must begin at the beginning—

with the man and the influences that shaped him.

CHAPTER 2 – VOELKER'S EARLY YEARS

Each person is unique, a product of an infinite combination of genetics, background, and experience. In pursuit of fulfilment, each person invariably encounters obstacles. When hopes and expectations do not materialize, immediate needs sometimes dictate compromise. But compromise often entails the terrible price of abandoning one's dreams. Though some resist compromise more than others, in the end, nearly everyone compromises. The differences in outcome, and the degree of compromise, are in each case attributable to any number of variables: the strength of one's character and resolve, the limitations of one's actual abilities, the reasons for continuing the struggle, and the extent to which one is subject to obligations to others that must be honored. For each individual, it is the vector of these forces that determines exactly where the line is drawn between compromise and standing one's ground. For John Voelker, whose dreams were perhaps larger than those of most men, it was the tension of this struggle between his dreams and the forces of compromise that defined the first five decades of his life.

John Donaldson Voelker was born on June 29, 1903, in the small Michigan town of Ishpeming, the Chippewa word for "heaven" or "high place."[1] The town was established a few miles west of Marquette, in the state's rustic Upper Peninsula.[2] This was iron and timber territory, still populated by Native Americans, but by then dominated by immigrant miners, lumberjacks, and those who catered to them. At the height of its prosperity, turn of the century Ishpeming was a bustling boomtown of over thirteen thousand residents, which boasted more saloons than churches. Ben Gazzara, who played the defendant in the film *Anatomy of a Murder*, said that when he first walked around the town during filming in 1958, he was surprised to see "about five bars on every street" that were packed with people drinking.[3] While most of the saloons have managed to survive to the present, Ishpeming's population has declined by about one-half from its glory days.[4]

Voelker grew up on West Barnum Street, in a neighborhood known as Kitchie Hill located a block west of the town's Main Street, in a two-story, clapboard house built in 1878.[5] Situated on a corner lot, the house was within earshot of the incessant percussion of the railroad switching yard,[6] which was punctuated like clockwork at 7:00 am and 3:00 pm by blasting at the mine, which routinely rattled glassware and dislodged pictures throughout the neighborhood.[7] West Barnum Street "rest[ed] above the cavernous Cliffs Shaft underground mine . . . which stretched under most of Ishpeming."[8] It is no exaggeration to say that Ishpeming was built, literally and figuratively, on iron ore mining.

Voelker was the youngest of six boys and the "baby of the

family."[9] His mother, Annie Voelker (née Traver), was a music teacher and a librarian at Ishpeming's Carnegie Public Library. George Voelker, John's father, worked a variety of jobs before purchasing and managing a saloon on South Main Street.[10] Both the library and his father's saloon were located within easy walking distance from the family home.

John's mother, Annie, married George, then a widower with three sons, in 1895.[11] George's first wife, Mary, had passed away seven years earlier. George's second marriage to Annie produced four children: Robert, Paul, Margaret, and John.[12] John had an especially close relationship with his mother, in part because his sister Margaret died at eight months. The loss caused Annie to become "overconcerned about the welfare of her next child."[13] She doted on John and, when he began to display signs of intellectual inclination and talent, she encouraged him to read and study the piano.

Annie urged George to invest in John's education, but he disapproved, pronouncing "higher education . . . a useless frill."[14] When John raised the subject of college, George dismissed the idea: "Lookit, Johnny, I haven't done so bad. College! Bah!"[15] John later mused that he "wanted to point out to my father . . . that certain dreary laws of economics, if not of personal taste, prevented every citizen from becoming a prosperous saloonkeeper. But I did not. For my father was not one to discuss his views with any man. He simply announced them."[16] Annie prevailed, however, and ultimately George agreed to provide financial support for John's college studies. This assistance was one of the few kindnesses George showed his son.

George Voelker was a product of his harsh and unforgiving times. John described his father as a "tall man with a bad temper and . . . [big] hands."[17] George was stern and gruff, and he "seldom got excited unless he was drunk or mad."[18] Unsurprisingly, he was not one to spoil, or even nurture his children. George enjoyed fishing and was a woodsman, a common characteristic of Voelker males. As a young man, he attended the University of Notre Dame for less than a year when, by his account, he was sent home in disgrace after punching a priest and complaining about the food.[19] George tried multiple business ventures including running a mercantile store, but he found the most success in owning and operating a saloon.[20]

As a child, Voelker listened intently to the stories that his mother regularly read to him, and, as a youth, split his time between his father's saloon and his mother's library. John said that as a boy his mother taught him to "go to the library and read, read, read . . ."[21] Friends have remarked, with perhaps some exaggeration, that John read nearly every book on its shelves.[22] John especially enjoyed the Horatio Alger and Tom

Swift books.[23] They told tales about boys rising from poverty and achieving success through good deeds, impressing upon his eager mind the value of moral integrity.

At the saloon, John performed tasks set for him by his father while listening to the conversation of its patrons and absorbing their colorful dialects. He swept the floor, but he also learned the delights of cribbage and sour mash bourbon.[24] Owing to the meager financial circumstances of his youth, in his later years, John preferred a bargain-brand bourbon, Evan Williams, rather than pricier alternatives, choosing taste over prestigious labels and catchy advertising slogans.[25] "Quality," he remarked more than once, "is in the bottle, not the label." In fact, Voelker's personal journals reflect that he struggled with a drinking problem for years. He tried to quit several times, but his abstinence would last only a few weeks or months. Voelker wrote in his journal that "[w]hen you start calling a bartender by his first name it is time to change bars."[26] It takes a moment to realize that his rue was mixed with wry.

Later in life, Polly's Rainbow Bar became Voelker's favorite cribbage hangout.[27] This was a no-frills, "all-man" bar, devoid of finer accoutrements, including stools—it was a "belly up to the bar" sort of place, and if a newcomer dared to ask if he served food, Polly would reply, "Where do you think you are, Burger King?"[28] Voelker spent many afternoons there drinking, smoking Italian cigars, and playing cribbage. Friends said Voelker was "one of the greatest cardplayers . . . [who] had a mind that would retain everything he played . . . and what might be left and what you could do with it . . . He was almost always the winner."[29] He proudly displayed a sign above the entrance to his famous Uncle Tom's Cabin ("Uncle's" for short)—his trout fishing sanctuary—proclaiming it the "Home of the U. P. Cribbage Champ."[30] Voelker loved the game and said he would often "play cribbage all night long."[31]

But as a young man, Voelker's saloon experience was mostly limited to his father's establishment. The place was a classic American melting pot where Finnish, Italian, Cornish, Swedish and other immigrants attracted by the Upper Peninsula's mining and timber industries mingled with local townspeople. Voelker became enamored of the rhythm and sounds of these foreign dialects,[32] learning to mimic them in speech, and later recording them masterfully and affectionately in his writing.

> Local characters have always fascinated me . . . Perhaps my natural curiosity was aided by the privileged advantage of often being able to study them in a special research laboratory usually denied lads of my age, namely, the inner precincts of my father's busy saloon on downtown Main Street, especially on pay days.[33]

Voelker's association with all manner of people in various states of inebriation surely enhanced his understanding of every stratum of the community. The ease with people of all backgrounds he acquired in youth explains his informality and disdain for pretension as an adult. He thought nothing of granting a request to autograph a copy of one of his books during breaks between arguments when he served as an Associate Justice of the Michigan Supreme Court.

George would often escape into the wilderness, to his family's relief. He owned three fishing camps and would regularly venture into the woods, sometimes for days, without farewell or explanation.[34] Elizabeth Delene, who interviewed John's wife and daughters extensively, concluded that, "life was much smoother when the temperamental George Voelker was in the woods."[35] When at home, George physically and emotionally abused his older children. On more than one occasion, John witnessed his father mete out crude parental discipline by pushing his half-brothers down the stairs.

Delene writes that "John suffered a different kind of abuse at the hands of his father," who inflicted emotional pain that left him with a "sense of emptiness that would stay with him throughout his lifetime."[36] One of John's earliest memories was when "his father threw him in the lake to teach him how to swim and then stood and watched as his son struggled to stay afloat."[37] As a result of the this episode, "John feared water, to the extent that he preferred to flyfish from a platform or fish 'gin clear water' to that of a fast moving stream."[38]

John Voelker never understood his parent's marriage, which appeared to him to be an irreconcilable contradiction. By any standard, George and Annie were very different people. Their union was likely as much a product of convenience as affection or attraction. George was a busy widower with three small sons. Annie, who moved to Ishpeming from downstate to teach music, was single and twenty-eight years of age, a spinster by late 19th century standards. In Annie, George saw a mature, substantial, and respectable woman who could maintain his home and care for his sons. For Annie's part, she knew George was a successful businessman with his own house, who could satisfy the imperatives of her biological clock. Before the couple wed, and as a condition for marrying George, Annie insisted that he quit the saloon business and take a respectable job. As a teacher and a proper pillar of the community, Annie could not abide being married to a bar owner. Initially, George acceded to her demand, managing a mercantile store for two years before reneging on his promise and resuming his saloonkeeper occupation.[39]

The couple's contrasting personalities and personas had a predictably confusing impact on their children, especially John. In his early (unpublished) novella, *The Burning Earth*, Voelker expresses this confusion through the character of a young man named Paul Biegler, who first appears here as Voelker's alter ego. Biegler often reappears in his personal journals and early published writings before emerging, fully developed, as the protagonist of *Anatomy of a Murder*.[40]

Voelker worked on *The Burning Earth* for over ten years, from the late 1930s through the 40s. It tells the story of brothers who ran away from home and headed West to escape their hateful and hated father.[41] Voelker does little to mask that the fictional family in *The Burning Earth* is closely patterned after his own. Voelker was cast as his alter ego, Biegler. Biegler's mother, Belle, is unmistakably Voelker's mother, Annie, whose middle name was Isabelle. Oliver, Biegler's father, closely resembles Voelker's father, George, whose middle name was Oliver. The original title was *Oliver's Boy*, and the story includes other striking similarities toVoelker's family, such as the death of Oliver's first wife, the presence of Biegler's three stepbrothers, and Belle's bout with breast cancer.[42]

In *The Burning Earth*, Voelker portrays Oliver in the most unforgiving terms. He writes "Kate Donovan who . . . was chief among Belle's appointed saviors . . . said, 'Don't marry that man, Belle! No good can come out of it. Those Bieglers is all crazy. He's a pup he is.'"[43] Later in the story, Voelker writes, again in Donovan's voice, " 'I tell you Belle, he's nothing but the keeper of a low dive. He cheats at cards, he chases fast women – and he beats them too. And – he's not even your own religion.' "[44]

Young Biegler echoes Donovan's scornful opinion of Oliver when he wonders, "Why on earth did mama ever marry such a crabby vile-tempered man? One who never played games with his children like other fathers?"[45] Mournfully, Biegler ponders, "Why couldn't my father have been anything but a saloon keeper?"[46] The import of *The Burning Earth* is unmistakable: through his alter ego Biegler, Voelker reflected upon and perhaps sought to resolve his life-long conflict with his father, posing questions that he never satisfactorily answered, which probably explains why he never completed the book.

George Voelker was a pervasive and powerful influence on his son's writing. Delene observes that "[a]ll of John Voelker's autobiographical works have a common thread: the father is a mean and nasty man, incapable of compassion. In many stories, the narrator ponders his relationship with this father he does not understand."[47] In the initial drafts of Voelker's many works, the protagonist is referred to in the first person as "I," which in later drafts changes to a third person, Paul Biegler (Voelker's alter ego). The father figure, initially called, in the first person, "my father," is subsequently referred to as Nicholas (his grandfather's name) or Oliver (his father's middle name).[48] In his "D.A. book," *Troubleshooter*, Voelker recalled "the many times I had wished to grow up quickly so that I could thrash this man,"[49] referring to his father. From George Voelker, his son John derived the enduring archetype of a temperamental, abusive, and emotionally distant father figure.

With his mother's support, Voelker survived his father's disinterest and abuse. Annie was a constant source of solace and resolve for the young Voelker, who responded eagerly to her appreciation for his intellect and loving nature. Voelker especially cherished the occasions when his mother read to him. One of his earliest happy memories was the "almost daily trotting" to the Carnegie library, not a block from his home, where he found his mother and the love of reading that she imparted to him.[50] She avidly supported Voelker's scholarly pursuits and missed no opportunity to encourage him. Through Annie, Voelker discovered and developed his intellectual independence.

Early in life, Voelker's burgeoning sense of self imparted a corresponding awareness of his modest circumstances. He enjoyed a good steak but could afford this luxury only if he won a bet, most likely at cribbage. Voelker soon realized that he would have to work hard to enjoy the lifestyle he desired. His first real job was to remove potato bugs from vegetables at a nearby farm. Local elites would ride by and look down upon him from their high horses while he picked the pests off of the plants by hand. Reflecting on this episode, Delene writes that Voelker:

> … felt inferior as these high society people stared at him. Although he was only eleven or twelve years of age, he came to the conclusion that there was no future in this type of work, so he dumped his pail of potato bugs, demanded his pay, and quit his job. He wanted a job in which people would show him some respect, instead of looking down on him.[51]

Such experiences deeply affected the young Voelker and influenced his career choices. They awoke in him a desire to become his own boss, which would enable him to live life on his own terms. Voelker believed such independence was his only path to the status and distinction he sought. Convinced that he would ultimately succeed, Voelker accumulated a varied resume of curious odd jobs, such as peddling mops[52] and selling mail-order lingerie door to door.[53] Whatever he attempted, Voelker worked hard and strived to advance, but he seemed to lack the focus and direction he needed to accomplish his objectives.

Through his mother, Voelker was introduced to a mentor and role model who would provide him with the nurturing guidance that he found so wanting in his father. Annie was a devout Presbyterian, while her

20

husband George was nominally Catholic. Annie insisted that "Mary's boys attend St. John's the Evangelist Church and her own boys practiced her beliefs and attended the United Presbyterian Church on Euclid Street in Ishpeming."[54] It was at his mother's Church that John was introduced to Clarence B. Randall, a Sunday school teacher there, who immediately took John under his wing.[55] A young Harvard graduate, Randall was a lawyer in Ishpeming.[56] He impressed upon John the importance of good moral values and broached with him the idea of becoming an attorney. Randall even promised John that he would sign the bank notes necessary to fund Voelker's education should he make it to law school, an offer that Voelker gratefully accepted.

Through it all, Annie continued to push for Voelker's education, leading him to observe years later, "When I saw it was no use for me to expect any help from my father, my mother and I plotted so that I went to college anyway."[57] Voelker said that his "Dad thought higher education was a useless frill . . . But my mother was a teacher and both of us decided a formal education might come in handy."[58]

Nicknamed "Shust" by his classmates, Voelker graduated from Ishpeming High School in 1922. He matriculated to Northern Michigan University in nearby Marquette, then named Northern State Normal School.[59] He took his associates degree there before moving downstate to the University of Michigan, where he received his bachelor's degree.[60] He remained in Ann Arbor and attended the University of Michigan Law School, graduating with a law degree in 1928.[61]

Why Voelker chose to study the law is not entirely clear. Surely his mentor, Clarence Randall, strongly influenced his decision, but Voelker was likely attracted to the law and trial litigation by his sense of justice, devotion to detail, and flair for the dramatic. He may also have sought the esteem and professional status enjoyed by lawyers. Perhaps, like many lawyers, he simply meandered into law school through a lack of direction, or by default. It is sometimes said that law schools are brimming with high achievers who become lightheaded at the sight of blood. What seems clear is that Voelker's decision to pursue the law represented a compromise of sorts between what he longed to do and the demands of practical reality. Reflecting back on his decision to become a lawyer, Voelker said, "I wanted to write but I had to make a living . . . and I wasn't very good at driving nails. The law to this day allows people to do many things."[62] Voelker called the law the last of the romantic professions, which "attracts and harbors dissatisfied dreamers."[63]

While attending law school, Voelker met his future wife, Grace Taylor, of Oak Park, Illinois.[64] Even years later, Voelker would fondly recall their initial encounter, which he described as "one of those fateful,

22

epic meetings."[65] John and Grace were introduced at a dance during Voelker's third and final year of law school. Voelker, then twenty-four years old, served as a member of the school's annual Crease Dance committee. He was therefore obligated, to his displeasure, to rent a tuxedo and participate in the Gala. Also attending was a freshman student named Grace Taylor, then nineteen years old, who arrived at the affair as another's date. Voelker spotted Grace and quickly became enamored, telling friends that he could not take his eyes off her throughout the evening. Voelker later said that he instantly "knew the jig was up for him" and so he followed Grace around "like a Doberman pinscher."[66]

Voelker's enchantment with Grace was interrupted when rival engineering students rushed the Lawyer's Club, "blowing the fuses, and distributing stink bombs."[67] Voelker intervened and soon came to blows with one aspiring engineer, emerging triumphant after the two rolled down the staircase to the lower floor of the law library in a pummeling embrace. During the scuffle, Voelker lost track of Grace. The next day, he saw that the school bulletin board displayed a note instructing him to meet with the Dean of the Law School, Henry M. Bates, without delay. Voelker, who feared disciplinary action and possible expulsion, was more than a little relieved when Dean Bates enthusiastically greeted him and said, "good for getting even."[68] Years later, Voelker dedicated a collection of essays to Dean Bates.[69]

Voelker reconnected with Grace shortly after the Gala and they began dating. They were engaged to be married when Voelker graduated that June.[70] No doubt to Voelker's delight, he learned that Grace came from an affluent family. Her father, Frank Taylor, was a prominent banker, who later used his connections in Chicago to land Voelker a job there. The Taylor family valued education and fostered Grace's intellectual growth. She responded by developing a quick wit and performing well as a student at the University of Michigan. She felt compelled, however, to quit her studies when her mother became pregnant late in life. Grace traveled home to Illinois to help with the birth and care of her younger brother, who was twenty-one years her junior. She settled into a comfortable life in her parent's home, without any expectation that she earn a living. Grace surely reminded John of his own mother: well-educated and refined, with high social standing. Although John and Grace were "from two different worlds,"[71] they maintained an active correspondence of "feverish proportions" during her time in Chicago.[72]

Upon graduating from law school, Voelker promptly returned to the Upper Peninsula, where he worked for a Marquette law firm, Eldredge & Eldredge,[73] and was also employed as an assistant Marquette

County prosecuting attorney.[74] After a two-year separation from Grace, Voelker at last tired of their long-distance relationship,[75] and grudgingly left the Upper Peninsula for Chicago. Soon after his move, he married Grace and practiced banking law at the firm of Mayer, Mayer, Austrian & Platt. Voelker joked that he landed the job in Chicago "due to my vast talents and [Grace's] father being a banker [with connections]."[76] During his brief sojourn in Chicago, he and Grace lived in three different apartments.[77] Despite the higher rent and extended commute, Voelker invariably insisted on a place with a window overlooking trees, because they reminded him of his native Ishpeming.[78]

Voelker had now become, in his words, a "law looker"[79]; "a peasant" banished to "the bullpen ... where the young lawyers stayed, four or five . . . in one big room."[80] In a letter to his mother in 1931, Voelker wrote:

> I will tell you now that I plan on moving from Chicago to a small community. ...I have never liked city life. ...My stay in Chicago has not decreased the intensity of this dislike. The chief reason I came to Chicago was to give it a fair trial and never in future years to succumb to a feeling of thwarted ambition, a common malady, I believe, among small-town attorneys.[81]

In the same letter, Voelker described his commute to work in Chicago as "walk[ing] through the soot" of an "insane city."[82] Another time he said, "I just don't like big cities ... I consider them a

25

temporary aberration upon our civilization. I just don't think they're here to stay."[83] Voelker was convinced that urban living was fundamentally dehumanizing. He once told filmmaker Sue Marx of his belief that "the very anonymity of city life is dangerous to the human animal."[84] On another occasion he said that in Chicago he suffered "terrible loneliness … without solitude."[85]

Voelker illustrated his sentiments about urban living with a story about a dog attempting to cross a busy highway. The dog was hit twice, but no one stopped to help.[86] Voelker concluded that he, like the dog in his story, was unsuited for the pace and isolation of city life, and could not adapt to it.[87] Voelker once explained that while living in Chicago:

> I missed dreadfully the ability to see, to sense, all at once, the limits of the place in which I lived, to view the horizon beyond the place where people dwelt. Why this should have been, I still do not know. I missed the casual society of unhurried people, the opportunity to get to know individuals—the persons I kept passing and jostling in the streets and elevators: a dignified, time-wise old man; a spirited young woman; a wistful child. They were all there, I sensed, not at root any different from the people I had always known, but they were, I sorrowfully saw, afraid, wary, stricken dumb by the huge anonymity of city life. The city's personality was its utter lack of personality.[88]

John and Grace had four children: Robert, Elizabeth ("Honey Bee"), Julie, and Grace (Gracie). The tragic death of their oldest child and only son, Robert, was the final straw that propelled Voelker to leave Chicago and return to Ishpeming. Robert died at seventeen months of age after an operation due to "surgical shock and post ether anesthesia."[89] Voelker was devastated. He later commissioned a painting of his son from Paul Strayer, a noted artist from the Chicago area.[90] The portrait, which he prominently displayed in his bedroom, depicts Robert as a smiling, cherubic toddler wearing a pink nightshirt. He is standing in an idyllic pastoral setting surrounded by pastel flowers. The scene could represent a forest near Ishpeming, or perhaps Eden. Each day Robert's portrait would greet Voelker in the morning, and his gentle countenance would be the last image he would see at night. Close by in his bedroom was a photograph of John Voelker at about the same age as Robert. The two looked nearly identical.[91] One cannot help imagining how the depth of Voelker's grief from the loss of his son was magnified by his own troubled childhood. Voelker's opportunity to distinguish himself from his father, and to give his son everything he had been denied as a boy, was cruelly snatched from him in an instant at an impersonal, big-city hospital. Voelker had lost his chance to create for Robert the idealized childhood that he had always imagined for himself.

In order to marry Grace, the love of his life, Voelker was forced to compromise. He traded the peaceful lifestyle of the Upper Peninsula for Chicago's suffocating urban milieu. Shortly after moving to this urban wasteland to marry, he suffered the crushing death of his only son.

These decisions and events left Voelker demoralized and lost, feeling like a stranger in hostile territory. But through it all he tenaciously clung to his ideals; the overwhelming contradiction between this harsh reality and his unfulfilled dreams animated Voelker's writing and ultimately moved him to return to Ishpeming.

Voelker's youth and early adulthood were indelibly shaped by contradiction and compromise. He was constantly torn between his father's disinterest and abuse and his mother's doting love; the joys of the Upper Peninsula and the urban despair of Chicago; the colorful earthiness of his father's saloon and the intellectual stimulation of his mother's library; his admiration for the common man and his desire to rise above his circumstances and achieve distinction; his longing to be his own boss and his need to support his wife and family; in short, between who he had become and who he aspired to be. These contradictions, and Voelker's struggle to reconcile them, would define him as a husband, father, attorney, and, not least, as a writer.

CHAPTER 3 – NORTHWOODS LAWYER

The pursuit of a dream always comes at a cost. Voelker chose to suffer the congested and dehumanizing conditions of Chicago to marry the love of his life. Throughout his urban exile, however, Voelker's heart and mind never wandered far from his beloved Ishpeming, where, in his own words, "the poplar leaves are as big as squirrel ears."[1] While still in Chicago, Voelker wrote to his mother about his intention to flee the city and "establish a law-office of my own in a smaller town, preferably Ishpeming."[2] But Voelker's return to Ishpeming—his coming "home"[3] as he put it—was motivated by more than a desire to escape his present circumstances and be his own boss.[4]

It is no exaggeration to say that Voelker had a love affair with the Upper Peninsula, which he protected like a fragile mistress. He obsessed about the encroachment of progress and tourists, with their accompanying trash and propensity to spy on him during his backwoods forays for fish and mushrooms.[5] He did, however, manage to find some solace in his belief that "[t]he average tourist drives 500 miles a day and never gets more than 100 yards off the main road."[6]

Voelker was likewise disheartened by indiscriminate logging that threatened his forest refuges. This lasting concern prompted him, in his later years, to work for over a decade to protect a patch of woods near his property from timber interests, observing that two trees in a grove of triple-trunk paper birches had grown together "as if they were lovers." He remarked to a friend that "I'm not much of a lawyer anymore, but I've filed suit, and every month I file a motion. I intend to keep those trees alive as long as I live." And he did, although they were cut down, along with the forest in which they stood, shortly after his death. [7]

Despite the many threats to the Upper Peninsula he saw and opposed, Voelker remained generally optimistic that it would retain its special character. He once observed, "This is rough country, tough country. They've been hacking away at it for a hundred years and haven't hurt it much. And they probably never will."[8]

Voelker reserved his greatest antipathy for the Mackinac Bridge. Opened in 1957, the Mighty Mac is a five-mile-long suspension bridge that connects Michigan's Upper and Lower Peninsulas. After he had become famous, Voelker was invited to be a special guest for the Bridge's inauguration ceremonies. Voelker knew the project would provide easy access to the Upper Peninsula, which had previously required a cumbersome and time-consuming ferry ride. Voelker wired back, "Sorry but I must reveal I've been named chairman of the Bomb the Bridge Committee. However we'll wait until the state has had time to sell the ferries before taking action."[9] He did not attend.[10]

Voelker's extensive private journals[11] reflect a profound connection to the people in and around his hometown. Voelker's appreciation and respect for his fellow Yoopers[12] was a product of his upbringing and experiences. Voelker was not merely in the Upper Peninsula, he was of the Upper Peninsula. His paternal grandparents landed in New York City in the 1850s and pushed west to Sault St. Marie, located at the easternmost point of Lake Superior, in Michigan's Upper Peninsula. Their objective was to find a suitable site to settle down and establish a brewery. Traveling by ox-drawn wagon, the couple continued west, then north, until, at last, they reached Copper Harbor, at the tip of the Upper Peninsula's Keweenaw Peninsula, the northernmost point in the state. There they decided to put down roots as the area had no existing brewery to cater to the needs of the soldiers stationed at nearby Fort Wilkins.[13] Soon after arriving at the post, Voelker's grandmother gave birth to a son they named Jacob. Voelker boasted, "My Uncle Jacob was reported to be the first white boy born in the Upper Peninsula."[14]

Both of Voelker's parents were born in the Upper Peninsula[15] Some claimed that Voelker's father, George, spoke the regional Native American language, Ojibwe, before he learned English.[16] Although this seems doubtful, Voelker did remark that his father "learned to curse in Chippewa Indian before he could swear in English. Not that a late start in the latter ever really cramped his style."[17]

As a boy, Voelker was exposed to a cross-section of the community during his frequent visits to his father's saloon and his mother's library. Regardless of the setting, Voelker became an astute observer of people of all stripes. *Anatomy of a Murder,* like his other works, reflects his profound understanding and respect for Native Americans,[18] as well as for the cultures of the immigrant Finns, Irish, French-Canadians, Germans, Swedes, Italians, and Cornish people who were among the Upper Peninsula's earliest white settlers.

Often a solitary man,[19] Voelker was most deeply connected to the land and the "solitude without loneliness" it offered. As much as possible, he spent his days and years immersed in the splendor and harshness of his northern Michigan environs. In the early spring, he hunted for morels—an elusive honeycombed mushroom delicacy found in the forests near his home.[20] Throughout the spring and summer months, he gathered wild blueberries, serviceberries, and thimbleberries from bushes that carpeted large swaths of the landscape. He regularly picked wildflowers for Grace and collected pine knots for the Franklin stove that warmed his fishing camp's cabin.[21] For a time he prospected for uranium, without success.[22] He was an avid birdwatcher, admired the enterprise of the beavers in the streams he fished, and never hunted the deer and bear that resided in his beloved woods.[23]

Though Voelker could name most of the creatures and plants, and the favorite few edible mushrooms he stalked in their seasons, he connected with the wilderness as an artist—not a naturalist. He once wrote in his journal, "There have been 4 hauntingly lovely days in a row, the earth smoky and fragrant with the yeast of spring, the sky cut by the curling lash of endless flights of honking geese."[24] He whimsically referred to the brightly colored brook trout he stalked so relentlessly as "mermaids."[25] He once recalled sitting by a pond and listening for the mournful sound of a bird he named "lonely bird."[26] When a geologist friend identified the species as a white-throated sparrow, Voelker lamented, "I didn't want to know it's [sic] real name. I just wanted to imagine it as the loneliest bird."[27]

Above all else, Voelker's world revolved around fly fishing. A bait fisherman until his mid-thirties, Voelker came to the avocation relatively late in life.[28] Even as a youth, however, Voelker was an avid fisherman; his high school yearbook photo is captioned: "Like a true fisherman, he has a good line."[29] Once the fly-fishing bug bit, Voelker was as hooked as any trout he ever landed. Voelker confessed, "If you could have showed me a place where trout-fishing was in season all the time, I'm sure I'd never have written a book."[30] Voelker preferred fishing for wild brook trout; he avoided the Upper Peninsula's plentiful rainbow and brown trout and did not deign to fish waters stocked with hatchery trout.[31] Voelker relished the challenge of fly fishing, observing that "[f]ly-fishing for wild trout on quiet waters must be one of the toughest and craziest ways to catch fish ever invented by man, as well as among the most frustrating and humiliating."[32] He called fly fishing "a study in humility."[33]

During some trout seasons, Voelker fished for weeks straight without missing a day.[34] In addition to his regular journal, Voelker kept an extensive log dedicated to fly fishing. For decades, from April 27, 1936, to June 11, 1987,[35] he recorded meticulous and detailed notes in these fishing journals about his activities.[36] He recorded the size and weight of each catch, including notations about the location, weather, water conditions, and time of day. His meticulous records reflect a cumulative *legal* catch for the years 1936-1969 of 5,766 trout.[37]

Beginning with the advent of each trout season, on the last Saturday of April, Voelker would navigate his old "fish car"[38] along fire trails and off-road to reach secret ponds and streams, some so small they had no formal, cartographic name.[39] Voelker's first fish car, a 1928 Ford Model A that he drove from 1935 to 1957,[40] was named "Buckshot." He called his second fish car, a 1957 Jeep Wagoneer,[41] "Bush Car." Voelker expressed an affection for each vehicle more commonly reserved for dear friends and faithful pets. Voelker always kept a broom and rake in the back of his fish cars, which he used to conceal his tracks, to prevent anyone from following him to his favorite fishing holes.[42]

Once Voelker arrived at his secret destination, he would expertly cast handmade flies into cramped openings among grasses and rushes. Voelker did not tie his own flies. He said his hands were too big for it, so he spent his winters writing instead.[43] As Voelker put it, "So far from being able to tie a fly, I am barely able to zip one."[44] One observer said that Voelker "casts for trout as if he was possessed by a private devil exhorting him on."[45] The famous photographer Gjon Mili said Voelker's casting technique was "as beautiful as a ballet."[46] Mili filmed Voelker casting for trout, but Voelker was disappointed, as it depicted the grace of his shadow but did not show his features. Voelker was inducted posthumously into the National Freshwater Fishing Hall of Fame.[47]

Fly fishing emerged as a favorite subject of Voelker's writing, sometimes assuming a leading role, as in *Trout Madness*[48] and *Anatomy of a Fisherman*,[49] and on other occasions providing authentic background texture, as in *Anatomy of a Murder*. Art Flick, a published master fly fisherman, once commented that "[t]he fellow who wrote [*Anatomy of a Murder*] is really a fisherman and doesn't put the stuff in about fishing in the book to fill up space."[50]

For Voelker, fishing was about much more than catching supper or passing time. He wrote in his journal, "I fish because it is one of the best ways I know to [w]ring out the wrinkles in one's soul."[51] As he famously explained in his *Testament to a Fisherman*,

> I fish because I love to; because I love the environs where trout are found, which are invariably beautiful, and hate the environs where crowds of people are found, which are invariably ugly; because of all the television commercials, cocktail parties, and assorted social posturing I thus escape; because, in a world where most men seem to spend their lives doing things they hate, my fishing is at once an endless source of delight and an act of small rebellion; because trout do not lie or cheat and cannot be bought or bribed or impressed by power, but respond only to quietude and humility and endless patience; because I suspect that men are going along this way for the last time, and I for one don't want to waste the trip; because mercifully there are no telephones on trout waters; because only in the woods can I find solitude without loneliness; because bourbon out of an old tin cup always tastes better out there; because maybe I will catch a mermaid; and, finally, not because I regard fishing as being so terribly important but because I suspect that so many of the other concerns of men are equally unimportant—and not nearly so much fun.[52]

Voelker preferred fly fishing in wild backwaters precisely because they were remote and virtually inaccessible, and thus unsullied by modernity and man's imperfections. These sanctuaries provided a refuge for him where virtue was rewarded, compromise was unnecessary, and interruption was unlikely. They were a haven in which his artistic talent and passion could flourish without the noise and falsity of the world. Oftentimes Voelker's desire for fly fishing was a persistent

temptress, luring him away from pen and pad. On other occasions, it was

a connection to the muse that inspired him to write.

For decades Voelker's life seamlessly tracked the rhythm of the

seasons.[53] Beginning in the spring, he fished and obsessed about fishing.

When the season ended, he turned to writing (or motivating himself to

write) and cribbage. One imperative remained constant throughout the

years: his struggle to support himself and his family as a lawyer.

Regarding the tension between his passions and obligations, Voelker

once wrote in his journal:

> The summer, that is the fishing season, whirls to a close, and,
> as in each year, in the past, my sadness is mixed with a
> gladness that soon it will be over, that the <u>compulsion</u> to go
> fishing nearly every day will have ended; that I can put away
> my gear and settle down and read again – always in the
> background being my thought that <u>this</u> fall I will write my
> great novel.[54]

A bit later he ruefully noted, "Tomorrow the damn fishing season

ends, and I can then (but probably won't) give serious attention to

starting a new book."[55]

Over several years Voelker dutifully chronicled in his personal,

"non-fishing" journals a handful of annual events of special

significance: the beginning of the new year (and what he hoped to

accomplish); the "first brave robin" of spring (signaling the approach of fishing season); the opening of fishing season in late April; his successes

or failures during fishing season; his own birthday on June 29

(providing an opportunity to lament being a year older, his lack of

accomplishment, and his continuing poverty); the approach of, and the

end, of fishing season; his progress (or lack of it) in, and his frustrations

with his efforts to write during the winter months; and Christmas.

Voelker initially pursued a career in the law for a variety of

personal and practical reasons. He soon found the demands of the

profession regularly intruded upon his opportunities to write and fish,

not necessarily in that order.[56] In his journal, Voelker described himself

as a "good lawyer who hates his work."[57] He grumbled about being

"constantly interrupted by the DA job,"[58] or being "snarled up in a brief

to write and some estate matter . . . ."[59]

Voelker's legal work was a necessary "distraction,"[60] however, as

he struggled to eke out a living for years, especially upon his return to the

Upper Peninsula during the Great Depression.[61] Voelker frequently

complained about "damn poverty."[62] He once lamented "[i]f I only had

the money to go to a cabin on a mountain lake (with trout) and write this

damn [book]."[63] In 1948, he exclaimed in his journal,

> Here we go again! I walked on my knees into the Negaunee
> bank this morning and increased my mortgage by $1,000 to
> keep the wolf from the door. A fine state of affairs for a 44-
> year-old lawyer. I'm more busted than I was when I began

law practice. No, not more – just about the same. Twenty years of inertia – but twenty years, also, of priceless fun and fishing in an insane world …"[64]

A few months later he vented that he "took in nearly $10,000.00 last year, but am flat broke …"[65] But financial pressures did not dissuade Voelker from indulging his desire for more and better fishing and hunting gear. Voelker admitted in his journal, "The Plaster is falling in the kitchen and bathroom but I just bought a new glass fly rod (Shakespeare Wonder Rod) and a new double-barreled shotgun (Winchester Model 21)."[66]

Although Voelker was sometimes a reluctant or discouraged lawyer, it would be grossly unfair to label him ineffective or inadequate. Quite the contrary, he was a successful prosecutor who lost only one felony case during the last ten years in office.[67] He once described his caseload as a prosecutor as "three grand larcenies, two auto thefts, three burglaries, a brace of bastard cases, one indecent exposure, one assault with intent to murder, two wife desertions, and one dog-tired prosecutor."[68] Likewise, his later work as defense counsel in the Peterson case that inspired *Anatomy of a Murder*, as reflected in his archived trial preparation papers and notes, demonstrates that Voelker was dedicated, knowledgeable, and talented. The trial record shows that he was a well-prepared litigator and quick on his feet. He could dominate a courtroom with his physical stature and charisma. Although there is no evidence that he ever shortchanged his clients,[69] Voelker often resented the demands that his professional responsibilities placed on his time.

Shortly before Voelker attained celebrity status with the publication of *Anatomy of a Murder*, he was appointed to serve as an Associate Justice of the Michigan Supreme Court. His selection was characteristically unconventional. According to Frederick Baker, a close friend of Voelker's, Governor G. Mennen Williams needed to fill a vacancy on the court. He wanted to reestablish the tradition of having at least one seat occupied by a resident of the Upper Peninsula. Like all other candidates, Voelker was interviewed for the position. The last question posed to him was, "Why do you want the job?"[70] The interviewer said Voelker laid his finger beside his nose for a minute to consider the question and then replied, "Because I have spent my life on fiction and fishing, and I need the money."[71] Voelker's candor so delighted Governor Williams that he selected him to fill the vacant "Upper Peninsula seat" on the Court.[72]

Voelker resigned from the Court only one week into his second term. His life and financial circumstances had changed dramatically because of *Anatomy's* success. This new-found affluence liberated Voelker from the drudgery of legal work and freed him to spend his time fishing for trout, writing fiction, and playing cribbage. Out of a sense of obligation and party loyalty, however, Voelker ran for and won re-election before resigning, so that GovernorWilliams could appoint his replacement and keep his seat on the court in Democratic hands.

While serving on the Court, Voelker combined a lawyer's acumen with a writer's flair, seeking to distinguish his opinions from the ordinary. As Voelker put it,

> [T]he average judicial opinion is among the dullest and murkiest writing in the world . . . For every Holmes or Cardozo, who at their best wrote a kind of luminous legal poetry, there are a thousand judges who appear to write with their feet, whose main discernible aim seems to be to impress and project a Socratic image rather than to illuminate.[73]

During Voelker's brief service on the Court from 1957-1960, he authored roughly one hundred opinions.[74] His judicial writing was widely praised and earned him the respect of colleagues.[75] Voelker's experiences and sensibilities as an attorney and jurist informed and shaped his sense of justice, and they affirmed his profound respect for the law, people, and nature. These traits are all prominently reflected in both his judicial opinions and his literary works.

Voelker penned his first story, *Lost All Night in a Swamp with a Bear*, while in the fifth grade.[76] He began writing in earnest while living in the Chicago area. His wife Grace believed that Voelker wrote stories about his early experiences to "escape city life. He really missed his childhood community and the characters he grew up knowing . . . writing was a way to preserve [his] memories."[77]

Voelker's first published piece was a short story entitled *Iron*, which appeared in the February 1934 issue of *American Scene*.[78] It was published under the pen name "Robert Traver."[79] The name "Robert" was taken from his beloved older brother, who served in the United States Navy during World War I and died as a young man in 1920. The surname "Traver" was his mother's maiden name. Voelker claimed he assumed an alias because he, "didn't think the taxpayers would fancy [him] doing [his] scribbling on their time,"[80] but his use of noms de plume was likely motivated as much by a desire to preserve his privacy as by his professed sense of propriety. Years before he became a prosecutor, Voelker had used another pen name, "John Donaldson," for his story "Faithfully Yours."[81] Donaldson was Voelker's middle name.

For several years Voelker received far more rejections than acceptances from publishers. Voelker's first novel, *Troubleshooter*, was published in 1943, but his second, *Danny and the Boys*,[82] was not published until a full eight years later. *Small Town D.A*, the second of what he called his "D.A. books," was published the following year.[83]

Each work was largely biographical and involved legal themes. Collectively, however, they were "small sellers" that did little to ameliorate his financial woes. Voelker quipped, "You could comfortably hold my readers in a telephone booth."[84] On another occasion, expressing exasperation bordering on futility about his struggles as an author, Voelker implored, "Praise me if you can, hurt me if you must, but please dear God, don't ignore me."[85] Voelker's need to write, and his failure to achieve commercial success through his writing, likely helps explain why he kept expansive and wide-ranging personal journals for decades.

Through it all, Voelker "lived life on his own terms."[86] He was an oddly complicated man, seemingly full of contradictions. He was deep, but unpretentious. He had the creative soul of an artist, but chose a profession steeped in forms, norms, and rules. He was kind, but capable of a sharp barb. He was erudite and accustomed to the formal garb of his profession, but frequented bars[87] patronized by "common" men, whose company he savored, and in his leisure time often dressed in tattered clothes.[88] He was sophisticated, but preferred his bourbon from a tin cup and his old fashioneds in a jelly jar.[89] He loved his family, but was often absent by choice.[90] He had cosmopolitan sensibilities, but was, in his wife's words, "provincial," and never considered moving from the humble mining town of Ishpeming, despite his fame and fortune.[91] He

feared nuclear war, but prospected for uranium. He was financially

strapped, but splurged on expensive fishing gear that was beyond his

limited means.

Voelker was thoughtful, contemplative, and imaginative. He

"did not suffer fools," and could "see people as they really are,"

preferring those whom he called "straight shooters."[92] He rejected

organized religion, explaining that he practiced his faith in the woods.[93]

He had an "elegant and lyrical mind."[94] He relished puns,[95] enjoyed

playing with language,[96] and specialized in dialog cast in regional and

ethnic dialects.[97] He had a large collection of records and enjoyed many

genres of music, especially classical and jazz. He would often plunk out

self-taught tunes on the piano, such as his favorite, "As Time Goes By",

from the movie *Casablanca*.[98] Charles Kuralt, the CBS journalist

renowned for his pioneering "On the Road" segments, once called

Voelker "the nearest thing to a great man I've ever known."[99] Joseph

Welch, the famous Boston-area attorney who would later star in

Anatomy of a Murder, went even further, describing Voelker as a "very

great man."[100]

Voelker could be a curmudgeon at times; Grace's gentle, calm

personality was a crucial counterbalance to Voelker's impulsivity, and critical to the family's stability. Family and friends alike consistently identified Grace as the glue that held the marriage together. Grace worked for years to help provide needed financial support for the family,[101] and she was always there to offer emotional support for her husband and the children. Despite the family's often dire financial straits, Grace unfailingly encouraged her husband to write. Their daughter Julie remembers that "Mother made many personal sacrifices, spending the majority of her time raising the girls while Dad was off doing his thing."[102] More than this, Grace could match wits and hold her own with her wise-cracking husband. For example, one time, irritated by John's frequent absences, Grace asked him why he fished all the time. John replied that he needed to fish for relaxation. Grace retorted, "Well, you must be so relaxed by this time you're in a state of coma."[103] It was John's love for Grace that caused him to leave his world behind as a young man and move to Chicago to marry her. Grace so reciprocated that love that she left her parents and the comfort of her wealthy upbringing in Chicago to move to Ishpeming and stay with John. All who knew the couple agree that John and Grace Voelker enjoyed an enduring and loving marriage.

The Voelker children describe their father as kind and sweet. He often left little love notes about the house for Grace and the girls when he left in the morning to fish. His daughters describe their father as bright, with a quick and ready sense of humor. They remember him as non-judgmental and honest. His middle daughter, Julie, recalled three stories that made a lasting impression on the children and are emblematic of the values Voelker instilled in them. The first story recounts her father's considerable investment of time and money to support her interest in studying ballet. In the second, Voelker admonishes his girls that it was an "invasion of privacy" to look through a neighbor's window and watch the couple arguing. The third recalls his threat to cancel a party the sisters were planning to host at the family home unless they invited a classmate they intended to exclude. Julie said that these vignettes underscore that her father was both supportive and considerate, but he insisted that his children be respectful and fair.

Owing in part to the dizzying success of *Anatomy of a Murder*, Voelker achieved a near iconic status in his community. He was considered a minor celebrity by some and a friend by many. Sometimes his notoriety produced unwelcome consequences. To his chagrin, Voelker learned that his likeness, accompanied by excerpts from *Testament of a Fisherman*, appeared on the label of a regional ale sold in Ishpeming and its environs.[104] Voelker had not given permission to the Kalamazoo Brewing Company to appropriate his image, nor did he receive any compensation for its use on the brewer's "Two-Hearted Ale." Voelker

had a lawyer friend write the company to complain. The brewer

responded with an apology, explaining to Voelker that they had been

assured his approval was previously obtained. The company offered

Voelker a share in the royalties in exchange for his permission to

continue using the label—royalties that could have been considerable

given that twelve thousand cases of the brew had already been

distributed.[105] Voelker told his friend,

> If I accept the royalties in this matter, that will mean I'm in
> the beer business, and I have no desire to be in the beer
> business, even though my father was. I take it you'll send
> the appropriate missive in that regard. Just tell them to
> remove my pan and my quote from their damned bottle and
> I'll let it go at that.[106]

Voelker's esteemed status in the community was also manifested

in less formal ways. In his later years, as his eyesight failed, local police

officers would sometimes accompany Voelker in convoy to ensure his

safety as he drove home astride the fog line after an evening of libation

and cribbage.[107] In 2018, many years after Voelker's death, this author

attended a performance of the play *Anatomy of a Murder* in Negaunee, a

small town nestled between Marquette and Ishpeming. While waiting for

the play to begin, I happened to overhear a conversation between two

women seated behind me. One said her father was a drinking buddy of

Voelker's. The other mentioned that Voelker often gave fish to her father. Both spoke of him fondly.

But back in 1934, when he was financially strapped in the depths of the Great Depression, Voelker wanted little more than a steady paycheck. He decided to run for Marquette County Prosecuting Attorney—thus entering what he later reportedly called "the biennial carnival of sentiment"—in no small part due to the allure of its $2,400 annual salary.[108] Voelker mounted a spirited and unorthodox campaign, often attracting attention more out of curiosity than his position on issues. He prevailed on election day, boasting that he was "the first Democrat to win the office since the Civil War," sometimes exaggeratedly claiming, "since the flood."[109]

Despite his successful campaign, Voelker was no politician and abhorred traditional electioneering events, calling them "an invasion of privacy, the final death of democracy."[110] He preferred to meet prospective voters "in bars, the woods and trout streams."[111] Some of his later campaign appearances involved little more than precision casting demonstrations.[112]

When running for office, Voelker routinely distributed campaign cards printed in English and Finnish. On one occasion he put his campaign slogan "Your Support Will be Appreciated" on a blanket draped over a horse. Another time he planned to participate in the

Ishpeming's "Baby" Parade. The annual event did not involve actual babies but rather grown men who dressed the part. Locals would attend the spectacle to see which of their neighbors would don baby costumes. During one such parade, Voelker had arranged to push a carriage and distribute cards and matches bearing his campaign slogan. Voelker paid a man in advance to dress like a baby, but the fellow got drunk and never showed up. Undeterred, Voelker stepped in and played the role himself.[113]

Voelker served a total of fourteen years as a prosecutor. In his book *Troubleshooter*, Voelker wrote,

> There can be no doubt that [a] prosecutor's job will be one of the most fascinating [a lawyer] will ever hold. There is perhaps no form of human endeavor that will bring [a lawyer] into more intimate contact with so large a cross-section of humanity—a humanity usually laboring under the stress of powerful, elemental emotions.[114]

Years later, in his book *Small Town D.A.*, Voelker summarized his life as a prosecutor:

> The D.A. is inevitably in daily collision with life at its most elemental level. His job is somewhat akin to that of a young intern on Saturday ambulance call: he is constantly witnessing the naked emotions of his people—raw, unbuttoned and bleeding. His is a tremendous experience with life itself, and he must leave his job either a better man or a lethargic bum. There is no middle way.[115]

In November 1950, Voelker "left his job" as county prosecutor when he was defeated by his younger Republican rival.[116] He rationalized his loss at the polls thusly: "Sooner or later . . .if you are any good at the [D.A.] job, you will have annoyed enough of your constituents and their friends and relatives that they will combine to throw you out of office. And that's what they did."[117] Reflecting on his failed bid for re-election, Voelker wrote, "Like old Joe Louis I had lingered too long; had fought a hard fight; and had finally got knocked out by a younger man. Oddly enough, once it was done I somehow preferred it that way."[118]

Voelker was now face-to-face with his mid-life crisis. He was approaching fifty and jobless. He had a family to support, but no steady source of income. He flirted with joining the Navy,[119] but instead wisely opted to open a private law practice that served the greater Marquette/Ishpeming area.[120] But business was slow at best, and Voelker often found himself staring at the walls and missing the rush of being a trial litigator.[121] Voelker wrote in his journal that "[a]fter the spotlight thrust and swordplay of the public courtroom, I seemed to have developed an allergy to crouching in an office all day drafting legal documents full of such luminous phrases as 'said party of the first part as aforesaid.'"[122] Moreover, business lagged, forcing Voelker to "face the grim if not bitter fact I can no longer maintain this law office. I'm thinking of moving my diploma to the parlor of our house."[123]

So, motivated as much by professional desire as financial necessity, Voelker evolved into a defense attorney. His first case, in Voelker's words, involved "an aggrieved citizen who, it seemed, had inadvertently sneezed while rounding a highway curve and had been picked up by the cops for drunk driving."[124] He explained how he "soon began popping up in scattered justice courts defending similarly aggrieved citizens" until he "found himself up to [his] ears acting as a defense counsel."[125] Voelker had returned to the crucible of criminal trials for which he was so well-suited, but now he was working for the other side. After several months in this new role, about the only significant omission from his resume as a defense attorney was a high-profile, hotly contested murder case.

On July 31, 1952, Army First Lieutenant Coleman Peterson shot and killed tavern owner Mike Chenoweth in Big Bay, Michigan, a hamlet about an hour's drive northwest of Ishpeming near the Lake Superior coast. Unsurprisingly, Voelker was off fishing somewhere when the news broke.[126] Lieutenant Peterson's wife, Charlotte, whom Chenoweth allegedly had raped, consulted several local attorneys, but none would or could defend her husband. Mrs. Peterson eventually reached Voelker, who ultimately agreed to represent Lieutenant Peterson in what would be Voelker's first murder trial as a defense counsel.

In retrospect, it is as if the fates conspired to place Voelker in precisely the right place at exactly the right time. He possessed the rare combination of aptitude, experience, and motivation to represent Lieutenant Peterson effectively at a murder trial. More to the point, he also was uniquely qualified, and singularly motivated, to create the great American novel that trial inspired.

Before examining that novel, and the film based upon it, let us consider, first, the facts of the actual homicide and the extraordinary murder trial that ensued.

PART II
THE TRIAL

CHAPTER 4 - THE HOMICIDE

During the summer of 1952, the United States Army had been practicing maneuvers near the lighthouse in Big Bay, Michigan, on the Lake Superior coast. Big Bay is an old lumber town founded in 1875 and built by the Brunswick Lumber Company.[1] It is an unincorporated hamlet with a permanent population of less than two-hundred residents. The town is located about twenty-five miles north/northwest of Marquette near the base of the Huron Mountains. It has only a few restaurants, a combination general store and gas station, and two churches. It is bordered by Lake Independence to the east and thick woods in every other direction. The town was named after Big Bay, a half-moon shaped inlet of Lake Superior that lies about a mile north of the town's commercial strip. Mill operations in the town ceased for a time beginning in 1932. Henry Ford reopened the mills in 1942 for use in making panels for "woody" station wagons, but the mills closed again and for good in 1949 after Ford's death.[2] After the mill was shuttered, no industrial or manufacturing activity remained in the area.

The historic Thunder Bay Inn dominates the north side of the town. Originally a warehouse when it was constructed in 1911, the building was converted into a hotel by Henry Ford in the 1940's for the use of his traveling executives. Then named the Big Bay Hotel, it would be remodeled in 1959 for location shooting in the film *Anatomy of a Murder*. Owing to its new-found cinematic fame, the facility was later renamed the Thunder Bay Inn in honor of its fictional namesake. By the early 1950s, with the lumber and milling operations having ceased, the Inn and the local economy struggled, supported now primarily by tourism.

Throughout the Korean War, the Army conducted artillery training in and around the shores of Big Bay. Many of the soldiers assigned there, some with their families, resided at Perkins Trailer Park, located adjacent to the town's commercial strip. The trailer park, which still is in operation today, provides dozens of trailer hook-ups for tourists and transients. It abuts Lake Independence to the east, affording residents a measure of privacy, a splendid view, and fishing for those so inclined. Among the soldiers assigned to Big Bay for training and residing in Perkins Park in July 1952 was Lieutenant Coleman Peterson, accompanied by his wife, Charlotte. Lieutenant and Mrs. Peterson had moved to the trailer park about a week before the events giving rise to the murder trial.[3]

The Petersons were a striking if somewhat unconventional couple. Lieutenant Peterson was a thirty-eight-year-old Army veteran of World War II and the Korean conflict. A doctor's son, he hailed from Illinois.[4] He had a square jaw and a distinctive mustache. Although a juror would later say that Lieutenant Peterson seemed to be a "quiet guy" and not a "hellraiser,"[5] others found him to be aloof and condescending.

Mrs. Peterson was anything but aloof. She was a vivacious Texan with big glasses and bigger hair, and she was four years older than her husband. One juror later commented that Mrs. Peterson "had a body like a brick shithouse."[6] She also had a reputation, both among many townsfolk and within the military community, for loose and "easy" behavior with men. Some even referred to her as a "hussy,"[7] who was reputed to be especially friendly with gentleman admirers when her husband was away for training.

The Lumberjack Tavern, a Big Bay fixture situated just across the town's main road, a few hundred yards north of Perkins Park, was the site of the shooting. It was about the only place for miles that offered an evening of lively entertainment. As the lumberjacks had long since departed after clearing the area of white pines,[8] the tavern catered mostly to vacationers, soldiers, and locals, who gathered there to listen to the juke box, play shuffleboard and pinball, smoke cigarettes, spin yarns, and drink liquor.

On the evening of July 31, 1952, Mrs. Peterson walked from her trailer to the Lumberjack to pick up a six-pack of beer. She went alone while her husband stayed home and rested after a hard day of training. Lieutenant Peterson planned to join his wife later but fell asleep. As one juror recounted, Mrs. Peterson had gone to the tavern "many times before" when her husband was on bivouac, where she "danc[ed] barefooted" and "carr[ied] on."[9] Mrs. Peterson stayed at the Lumberjack for about two and a half hours. While there she drank four shots of whiskey[10] and played shuffleboard[11] with the owner, Maurice "Mike" Chenoweth, to the delight of male patrons. A witness recounted that during her visit to the tavern that evening Mrs. Peterson was not behaving in a "lady-like" manner.[12]

Chenoweth, the owner and proprietor of the Lumberjack, was a disgraced former state trooper[13] who migrated to Big Bay from downstate after being dismissed from the Michigan State Police for misconduct.[14] He was short, but with his squat, athletic build, he cut a wide swath,[15] and the Michigan State Police waived the minimum height requirement to admit him, in part because of his prowess as a Marine Corps marksman.[16] Although well-liked by some residents, many viewed Chenoweth as a "cocky guy" and a "showoff,"[17] a persona he cultivated, perhaps to compensate for his diminutive stature. He once won the county's centennial beard growing contest,[18] but he was better known for his prowess with firearms. At the tavern, Chenoweth regaled patrons with wild tales of his exploits and entertained them with pistol demonstrations. An accomplished marksman,[19] he conspicuously displayed his shooting medals at the Lumberjack.[20] A former juror recalled that Chenoweth used "clothespins on the outside wash line for target practice, picking the tops of the pins off as his wife pinned them onto the wet clothes."[21] Another acquaintance remembers that Chenoweth could keep a can hopping in the air with six shots, and could hit targets using trick shots from under his armpit.[22] It was well known among the Lumberjack's regular patrons that Chenoweth kept an elaborately engraved pistol close at hand on a shelf under the bar he built for that purpose.[23]

Chenoweth also had a reputation as what today would be called a sexual predator.[24] One juror said that Chenoweth was known to "rape a girl now and again and get out of it."[25] It was common knowledge around Big Bay that he had been indicted for raping a teen-aged girl in Munising, a town a little over an hour east of Marquette. It was also believed he raped a second victim, a musician, at a club in Marquette proper.[26] Neither allegation led to a conviction.[27]

As Mrs. Peterson was preparing to leave the Lumberjack on the evening in question, Chenoweth offered to drive her home. Chenoweth told Mrs. Peterson that he suggested this because he was concerned about the intentions of another Army lieutenant who had been eyeing her. Mrs. Peterson initially declined Chenoweth's offer, but finally agreed. According to Mrs. Peterson, on the way back Chenoweth unexpectedly pulled onto a side road near the trailer park,where he threatened to kill her and struck her repeatedly. She said that Chenoweth then violently raped her. During the assault, Mrs. Peterson said she told Chenoweth that her husband would kill him if he found out. She said Chenoweth confidently replied, "He doesn't have the guts. I'm not worried about him—he's just a sissy."[28] Mrs. Peterson claimed Chenoweth tried to rape her a second time after they had driven back to the Park entrance. This time she screamed and managed to escape. Mrs. Peterson reached her home with the aid of her dog George, who held a flashlight in its mouth and led her in the dark through an opening in the trailer park gate.

When Mrs. Peterson arrived at her trailer she was crying and hysterical. Lieutenant Peterson immediately saw that his wife was severely bruised and disheveled, her skirt torn and her panties missing. While Lieutenant Peterson tended to his wife, he observed what appeared to be seminal fluid on her upper thigh, suggesting that sexual intercourse had occurred or been attempted. According to the Petersons, the Lieutenant asked his wife what had happened, and she told him

Chenoweth had raped her. It took more than a half hour for Mrs. Peterson to regain her composure and describe the details of the attack. During this time, Lieutenant Peterson washed his wife's face with ice water and tried to console her. At one point, Lieutenant Peterson had his wife swear to the rape on a rosary, later explaining that he did so "to calm her."

Shortly after he returned to the tavern after driving Mrs. Peterson home, Chenoweth described his encounter with Mrs. Peterson much differently to Adrian Wentzel, his long-time friend and former police partner. Wentzel, who had followed his friend to Big Bay from downstate and became his business partner at the Lumberjack,[29] testified to Chenoweth's version of events at the Army's investigative hearing:

> Buddy that's the finest piece of ass I ever had in my life, that winch [sic] is a Psyco[sic], I'll tell you what happened. When I got to the gate, she was about to get out and said, what do I owe you Mike and I said, you could at least be lady enough to give me a good night kiss and she said, I dare not do that because then I'll want to play for keeps and I told her lady this is not the time nor place to fool and I drove her off to some secluded spot. I told her, lets [sic] do this thing right, take off your clothes, which she did and, "brother, don't fool yourself, those aren't falsies". I said Baby how do you like it and she said, let me get on top. Buddy, when that bitch blew her nuts, I was wet halfway down to my knees.[30]

Whether Wentzel actually believed Chenoweth's rendition of events is not entirely clear. Wentzel testified at the Army hearing that he considered Chenoweth to be "a bragget [sic]," so he assumed that his lurid description of his encounter with Mrs. Peterson was "another of his igotistical [sic] stories and promptly forgot the matter."[31] Yet only days after the fateful encounter, Wentzel repeated this same conversation he had with Chenoweth, as if it were true, to a friend who would later serve as a juror at the Peterson murder trial. Wentzel also told this future juror that Chenoweth had bragged to him that during his tryst with Mrs. Peterson, "she sure rode the boss."[32] Astonishingly, during voir dire, this juror was neither asked about his prior knowledge of the crime nor challenged for cause based on his friendship with Wentzel, who would later testify as an important prosecution witness.

After Lieutenant Peterson finished consoling his wife, he retrieved his loaded 9-mm lüger and hopped into his sedan, spraying gravel as he raced to reach the Lumberjack before closing. Wearing a green Army jacket and without speaking a word, Lieutenant Peterson slipped into the tavern between two customers and saw Chenoweth standing behind the bar. When Chenoweth turned his back to the door to retrieve a six-pack of beer, Lieutenant Peterson made his move. He strode toward the bar and shot Chenoweth twice, with one of the bullets passing through his throat. Chenoweth slumped over and then fell to the floor. Lieutenant Peterson continued moving forward. He stood on the bar rail, leaned over the top of the bar, and shot Chenoweth three more times, emptying his revolver. One of the bullets pierced the right ventricle of Chenoweth's heart.[33]

Witnesses said that the shot sounded like firecrackers.[34] Most patrons scattered,[35] with some men even ducking for cover inside the ladies' restroom.[36] One elderly patron, however, seemed to be more concerned about the destruction of a bottle of top-shelf whiskey than his own safety or Chenoweth's fate. The man reportedly remained seated at table throughout the shooting while others ran for cover. To his dismay, the man observed that one of the shots, probably the first one, had missed or merely grazed Chenoweth before striking and breaking a bottle of liquor and a mirror above the bar. The man exclaimed so loudly that others could hear, "goddamn, he [referring to Lieutenant Peterson] ruined a bottle of top-shelf whiskey."[37] Mrs. Peterson testified at the murder trial that Wentzel had expressed a similar sentiment about the shooting. According to Mrs. Peterson, Wentzel told her husband during a jail visit, "I am sorry, Pete, you had to get in on this, - There is one thing I hold against you, - you ruined one of our good bottles of whiskey and our mirror."[38]

Chenoweth died instantly.[39] Lieutenant Peterson turned and silently exited the tavern. Wentzel, who followed him outside, testified that he confronted Lieutenant Peterson and spoke only one word— "Lieutenant."[40] Wentzel recalled that Lieutenant Peterson turned to face him and "asked me if I wanted one through the head."[41] Wentzel, seeing

Lieutenant Peterson still holding the pistol, replied, "No sir."[42] Lieutenant Peterson then turned back around and left directly for his trailer.

Upon returning home to Perkins Park, Lieutenant Peterson hugged his wife and told her to get dressed because he "shot Mike [Chenoweth] and I am going to tell Sheriff Marsh."[43] They then went to the park's elderly caretaker, who lived on site and was a part-time deputy sheriff. Lieutenant Peterson surrendered his weapon to the caretaker and turned himself in. The caretaker later testified that Lieutenant Peterson said to him, "I have shot a man uptown. I want you to take me into custody."[44] Mrs. Peterson, who was standing next to her husband, asked the caretaker to "[l]ook what Mike [Chenoweth] has done to me." The caretaker observed that Mrs.Peterson "was a mess. Her face was beaten and bruised."[45]

Contemporary reporting and personal interviews about the shooting suggest that the community had strong and opposing views about what had actually happened between Chenoweth and Mrs. Peterson that night. Many locals disbelieved Mrs. Peterson's claim that she was raped. They described her as a lonely and neglected wife, who was bored, restless, sexually promiscuous, and visibly intoxicated and flirtatious with Chenoweth. They believed she fabricated the rape story to avoid a beating at the hands of her possessive husband who, many thought, had actually

inflicted Mrs. Peterson's injuries, enraged because he was convinced her

sex with Chenoweth was consensual. One juror later said that most of his

colleagues believed that Lieutenant Peterson "slugged her" because he

thought his wife enjoyed herself with Chenoweth.[46] Some in the

community had heard or claimed to have witnessed Lieutenant Peterson

strike his wife when he thought she was being too flirtatious with another

officer. Many also believed that Mrs. Peterson did not lose her panties

during a rape, but had simply not worn any undergarments when she left

for the tavern.[47] One juror later said that if Mrs. Peterson had been

wearing panties and Chenoweth removed them, then surely they would

have been discovered during the multiple searches of the area that

followed.[48] Many were convinced that Lieutenant Peterson did not kill

Chenoweth to avenge a rape, but did so because he was a jealous,

cuckolded husband, humiliated by his wife's notorious adultery, who

sought revenge against her lover.

Some disbelieved that Mrs. Peterson was raped simply because,

although Chenoweth was always on the prowl for sex, he would not need

to beat a woman to obtain it. Also, though most would not have put it past

Chenoweth to rape a woman he picked up at a bar, the Petersons and

Chenoweths had partied together at the Lumberjack and at the Peterson's trailer during the week before the alleged rape,[49] and many found it

unlikely that he would he rape a family friend to satisfy his desires.

Indeed, Mrs. Peterson testified at the Army's separate investigation that

when her husband returned to the trailer after the shooting, she said,

"what a fine friend you have in Mike," referring to Chenoweth.[50]

Others were not so sanguine about Chenoweth and believed that

he raped Mrs. Peterson. They heard that Chenoweth had been acting

strangely and drinking more than usual for weeks before the shooting.[51]

They described Chenoweth as an arrogant, violent bully, especially

when he was drunk. They knew the rumored cause of Chenoweth's

dismissal from the State Police and thought he was a serial rapist. They

did not find it difficult to believe that he would exploit a friendship with

the Petersons, and Mrs. Peterson's vulnerability, to isolate and rape her

in his car on a dark and deserted road, especially since campers at the

trailer park said they had heard a woman screaming at about the time of

the alleged rape.[52] They believed it was consistent with his character to

threaten and viciously beat a woman to obtain sex, regardless of whether

she was a friend or acquaintance. Some residents even believed that,

regardless of whether Mrs. Peterson had been raped, Chenoweth got

what he deserved because of his prior crimes, insufferable attitude, and

immoral behavior with another man's wife.[53]

Lieutenant Peterson, for his part, never denied that he shot and killed Chenoweth. He could scarcely demur given the scores of witnesses who knew him, were present in the tavern, and saw the shooting. For all practical purposes, Lieutenant Peterson had performed a public execution. Thus, the limited options available to whoever defended him would be further constrained by several incendiary circumstances:

First, Lieutenant Peterson killed a man who had sex with his wife about an hour earlier. Second, before the encounter, Peterson's wife drank and consorted with the victim, and then, in the presence of witnesses, accepted a ride home from him, unaccompanied and late at night. In addition, though the victim did not enjoy a favorable reputation with many in the community, neither did Mrs. Peterson. Although she had obviously been beaten, some believed it was her husband, rather than the victim, who inflicted her injuries. Then there were the missing panties, and what the inability to find them might signify. Also, why did Lieutenant Peterson have his wife swear on a rosary—to calm her down, or because he doubted her story? And why would he take his gun to the tavern unless he intended to kill Chenoweth? Add to this combustible mix of sex and violence that the defendant was an Army officer and an outsider, Mrs. Peterson was a seductive flirt who hailed from the exotic land of Texas, and the victim was a prominent, if polarizing, member of a small and relatively insular community. Stir these elements together briskly and you have a mixture with all of the ingredients of a sensational, first-rate murder trial or, as Voelker put it, "a fascinating pageant."[54]

CHAPTER 5 – BEFORE THE TRIAL

Lieutenant Peterson's trial for first-degree murder began on September 15, 1952, in Marquette, Michigan, and lasted eight days. At the time, Marquette, the county seat of Marquette County,[1] in which Big Bay is situated, was the largest city in Michigan's Upper Peninsula, with a population of over 18,000. Its enormous iron ore exports made it a major Lake Superior port. Iron mining had long dominated the area economy, and even today the remnants of the iron ore docks extending into Lake Superior survive as an imposing testament to the city's once important role in the growth of American industry.

The trial would be conducted in the county's opulent Beaux-Arts and neo-classical courthouse.[2] Completed in 1904,[3] it consists of a central three-story structure, flanked by two-story wings.[4] Constructed almost entirely of local sandstone over a steel frame,[5] a colossal portico covers an entrance framed by massive Doric columns of Maine granite.[6] A Doric entablature with copper cornice encircles the roofline.[7] A copper dome surmounts the building, illuminating a large, second-floor courtroom, which is finished with mahogany and marble, and overseen by a balcony to the north that leads into an extensive attic library.[8] The courtroom walls are lined with oversized portraits of the judges who have sat in the Marquette circuit, standing sentinel over proceedings in the well and gallery. Mosaic tiles, wool carpeting, and stained glass are found throughout the building.[9] The courthouse is also replete with Masonic symbolism, the most obvious being the thirty-two steps of the Scottish Rite that ascend to its impressive double front doors.[10]

The Peterson case was not the first trial of national significance to be held in the venerable courthouse. In 1913, former President Theodore Roosevelt sued George A. Newett, publisher of the *Ishpeming Agitator*, a local newspaper, for libel. Newett was highly partisan and used the paper to support conservative Republicans and attack political opponents.[11] During a 1912 whistle-stop campaign in Marquette, Roosevelt spoke out against the Republican party, of which he had been a member until he split away to form the Bull Moose Party and challenge Republican incumbent William Howard Taft.[12] Roosevelt also bashed some of the local candidates as "corporate lackeys."[13] Newett responded to Roosevelt's bold campaigning with an editorial entitled, "The Roosevelt Way."[14] The piece accused Roosevelt of getting "drunk . . . and that not infrequently."[15] Roosevelt bristled when he read the article, claiming, truthfully, that he was a teetotaler and thus was defamed by the newspaper.

At first, Newett did not budge. He defended against the suit by noting Roosevelt was a public figure and thus was fair game for the published comments. He also reiterated that the allegations about

Roosevelt's drunkenness were true. A week-long jury trial was held in

the Marquette courthouse to settle the dispute. Witnesses included a

cadre of respected public servants, among them a former cabinet member

and other high-ranking government officials, who testified on

Roosevelt's behalf attesting to his sobriety. At the conclusion of the trial,

Newett dramatically retracted his charges, saying:

> It is fair to the plaintiff to state I have been unable to find in
> any section of the country any individual witness who is
> willing to state that he had personally seen Mr. Roosevelt
> drink to excess . . . I have been profoundly impressed during
> the progress of this trial by the nature and extent of the
> evidence produced by the plaintiff to the effect he did not in
> fact use liquor to excess on any occasion . . . we have
> reached the conclusion that to continue to express or
> implicitly assert that Mr. Roosevelt drank to an excess or
> actually became intoxicated as set forth in the article would
> be to do him an injustice.[16]

Roosevelt responded to Newett's concession by withdrawing his

claim for damages, asking the court to instruct the jury that he wanted

only a nominal sum. The jury accepted his request and awarded

Roosevelt a judgment of six cents.[17] As Roosevelt departed the

courtroom, a reporter asked him what he would do with the token award.

Roosevelt reportedly said that the six cents he received was "about the

price of a good paper."[18] An issue of Newett's *Ishpeming Agitator* cost

three cents.[19] Voelker could not have imagined that the local notoriety and national impact of the Peterson case eventually would eclipse Roosevelt's libel trial.

Of course, Voelker was quite familiar with the Marquette courthouse, having served there for fourteen years as the District Attorney. He was also well acquainted with the new prosecuting attorney, Edmond Thomas, who would oppose him in the Peterson case. It was Thomas who had narrowly defeated Voelker less than two years earlier in the race for DA. Thomas was a lanky, fresh-faced former collegiate basketball player who came across to some as a bit overwhelmed and anxious to please. Others who knew Thomas remarked that he was "too nice to be an attorney," and lacked the necessary aggressiveness for the job.[20] Voelker initially described Thomas in his journal as "a joiner [and] a chap with nice teeth,"[21] who had "never tried a case" when he was elected.[22] A juror in the Peterson case later described Thomas as a "low key" and comparatively unimpressive attorney who appeared to have "hardly had any experience in murder and things like that—this was big time stuff."[23]

Voelker's opinion of Thomas soured after their election race. Voelker was especially offended by Thomas' campaign tactics and the lack of personal honor he believed they reflected. Referring to Thomas, Voelker once wrote in his journal that "constant is my amazement over

72

the lack of honor between individuals, the blithe breaking of solemn word; and frequently in situations where the truth, right action, could not possibly hurt, indeed would be the easier way."[24] Voelker later vented in his journal how

> Ed Thomas and I agree before the election not to use signs (on poles, etc.) or radio or anything but our matches and a few news ads. I tell him I have signs left over from former campaigns, which I had. Then, lo, during my absence Thomas passes handbills all over town; he is (possibly through his party) advertised on the radio, and (clear, barefaced violation) the last weekend he plasters posters all over, without one word of explanation to me.[25]

A subsequent journal entry leaves little doubt about Voelker's estimation of Thomas: "The man has the moral stature of a turd, and I shall treat him that way henceforth. In addition, since he won by but thirty-six votes, it appears likely that his sly, dishonorable stratagems won the election for him. A rather expensive lesson to me, but there it is …."[26] Some believed Voelker ultimately agreed to represent Lieutenant Peterson to spite Thomas.[27] Donna Snider, Voelker's longtime secretary who took the initial call from Mrs. Peterson, said of the case, "It was an important trial. His [Voelker's] one big trial since he was defeated. So he wanted to win it. He was determined to win it."[28]

Ed Thomas confided to a friend that he felt "intimidated" by the prospect of facing Voelker at a high-profile murder trial so early in his tenure as prosecutor.[29] So Thomas reached out to the Office of the

Michigan Attorney General requesting assistance. In response, Irving

Beattie, a slight and balding Assistant Attorney General, was dispatched

from the state capital in Lansing to help in the prosecution. Beattie was

an experienced litigator who hailed from Marine City, Michigan, a small

village located about fifty miles north/northeast of Detroit. Voelker's

contempt for Thomas soon extended to Beattie and the feeling was

mutual. During trial Voelker sometimes referred to Thomas as "Eddie

Thomas from Ishpeming" and Beattie as "the little man from Marine

City."[30] In his notes, Voelker dubbed Beattie "the Marine city mauler"

and "the Marine city mystic."[31]

Voelker took every opportunity to remind the jury that Thomas

and Beattie were ganging up on him, a lone small-town lawyer and one of

their own. During the trial Voelker once complained that he was "willing

to take on two attorneys, but one at a time. I don't want both of them

pitting [sic] spitballs at me."[32] On another occasion, he threatened to

throw Beattie into Lake Superior.[33] Before long Beattie had become

exasperated with Voelker. During Beattie'scross-examination of

Lieutenant Peterson, Beattie blocked Voelker's view of the Lieutenant,

prompting this exchange:

Mr. Voelker: That is the shadiest thing I have seen in years,

Mr. Attorney General.

74

Mr. Beattie: From Lansing.

Mr. Voelker: And Marine City.[34]

By all accounts Voelker stood out as the most impressive litigator at the Peterson trial. He was tall and rugged-looking, and he bore a striking resemblance to the actor John Wayne. Voelker was described as folksy and "engaging,"[35] with a "fishing camp wit."[36] In contrast, observers said that Thomas came across as flat and mechanical, while Beattie seemed to be shrill and humorless. Voelker's small-town background and casual manner may have led Beattie to underestimate him. One former juror said "[t]hat lower Michigan fella [referring to Beattie] thought he'd be playing with a hick."[37] Trial observers agreed that Voelker dominated the courtroom with his commanding presence and dry sense of humor. He was described as the "master of ceremonies" for the trial.[38] A reporter noted that Voelker "consistently made light of the fact that he was 'just a country lawyer,' facing the big odds of a prosecutor and an assistant attorney general. The gallery loved it and the jury was listening."[39] A juror later confirmed that Voelker held the jury's attention far better than the opposing attorneys.[40] Despite Voelker's quick and ready wit, one juror said that he never once cracked a smile throughout the proceedings.[41]

Voelker never said, either publicly or in his journals, that he took the Peterson case to avenge his defeat by Thomas.[42] To the contrary,

Voelker wrote in his journal of his relief that he was no longer DA and

his genuine desire to help Lieutenant Peterson.[43] Still, it is not hard to

imagine that Voelker relished the opportunity to vanquish both his

dishonorable political rival and his big-city comrade.

Apart from any desire for revenge or validation, Voelker was

motivated by his own conclusions about what really happened to Mrs.

Peterson in Chenoweth's car. Voelker interviewed Lieutenant Peterson

and his wife separately for several hours before agreeing to take the case.

He also learned that Mrs. Peterson had previously passed a lie detector

test.[44] Voelker soon came to believe that Mrs. Peterson was telling the

truth about the rape and so he agreed to defend her husband. Voelker

commemorated the decision in his journal as follows: "Last Monday

Honey Bee [his eldest daughter, Elizabeth] began her great nursing

adventure in Chicago and I began the defense of my first big criminal

case for the murder of Mike Chenoweth."[45]

Financial pressures also played a role in Voelker's decision. He

was a strapped ex-DA and a struggling writer with a family and a

mortgage. Sooner than Voelker could have imagined, he would become a

best-selling author, national celebrity, and state supreme court justice.[46]

Later still, after he became financially secure, Voelker would retreat to the woods to write and fish. But in the summer of 1952, Voelker needed a paycheck. As it happened, however, Lieutenant Peterson was even more pressed than Voelker, so Voelker had him sign a $3,000 promissory note in payment for legal services.[47]

Once Voelker committed to the Peterson case, he had to settle on a theory for his defense against the murder charge, but he had few viable options. Alibi and denial were out of the question. Lieutenant Peterson was not threatened, ruling out self-defense, nor could he claim defense of another on behalf of Mrs. Peterson, as the alleged rape was too remote in time and place. Accident and mistake were likewise untenable. By process of elimination, therefore, the only plausible defense theory was excuse, premised on the defendant's insanity, bolstered by a good dose of jury nullification.

Both in his novel, and later in the film, Voelker exquisitely reconstructs the carefully crafted dialogue that presumably occurred between himself and his client, which threaded the ethical needle between properly explaining the law and impermissibly coaching his client and, in the process, possibly even suborning perjury. As a result of this "conversation" between defense counsel and client, which Voelker refers to in *Anatomy* as "the Lecture," Voelker deftly *and ethically* guided Peterson to his assertion of the insanity defense discussed within at greater length.[48] For now, it suffices to say that Voelker had to rely on an

obscure variant of temporary insanity premised on a claim of "irresistible

impulse,"[49] which would require Voelker to solve the practical problems

of retaining a psychiatrist to examine his client despite his near indigency

and confinement in a remote northern Michigan jail. Moreover, an

insanity defense would entail considerable sophisticated and time-

consuming legal work, including comprehensive research, drafting

hypothetical questions for use in examining the defense expert, proposed

instructions delineating the unusual defense for the jury, and preparing to

cross-examine the prosecution's expert witness.

Finally, perhaps the most important participant in the Peterson

case was the trial judge, Charles O. Arch, a balding and bespectacled

jurist who hailed from Hillsdale, near Michigan's southern border.

Judge Arch was assigned to replace Voelker's beloved mentor, Glenn

W. Jackson, the lone circuit judge for all of Marquette County, who

was seriously ill at the time of the trial, and thus unable to preside.

Judge Arch, who taught Criminology as an adjunct professor at

Hillsdale College, had published several articles on the subject and

frequently lectured about it.[50]

The Peterson trial record reflects that all three litigators,

especially Voelker and Beattie, objected outspokenly, often pushing the boundaries of civility. Judge Arch maintained a steady hand throughout the proceedings, consistently ruling thoughtfully on objections, while gently, but firmly, reigning in counsel. Only once did he have to caution spectators, despite the attorneys' antics and the salacious subject matter.[51] One juror later described Judge Arch as a kind of "fixture" at the trial who "did his job."[52]

The jury of eleven men and one woman, with two alternates, was empaneled in less than a day. Voelker barely asked prospective jurors any questions during voir dire and did not exercise a single challenge. The prosecution essentially followed suit. The reasons for Voelker's seeming lack of engagement in the jury-selection process are unclear. It might have been that Voelker was familiar with many of the jurors owing to the small size of the community, his extensive contacts with its citizens in campaigning for and serving seven terms as DA, and his more recent private practice. Voelker once observed, "a county prosecutor's most intimate contacts with the people . . . do not always occur in the dramatic glare of the courtroom. For it is in his office that he gets really to know his people."[53] One former juror acknowledged years later that most of the jurors knew Voelker "well" and some called him "Johnny."[54]

Thomas' apparent passivity during jury selection might be

similarly explained—he was a well-known native son and star local athlete. The whole Ishpeming community took pride in the athletic and academic success he went on to achieve at the University of Michigan, and it was probably on the strength of his high profile in the community that he had recently been elected, defeating another native son, John Voelker. Thomas, like Voelker, may have believed he enjoyed a strong and favorable connection with the prospective jurors, and thus had no need to examine or challenge them.

While the reasons for counsels' passivity during voir dire remain a matter for speculation, the prospective jurors' considerable familiarity with the events and persons involved in the shooting is beyond dispute. Most, if not all, of the jurors had prior knowledge about the killing, and of the parties and witnesses involved in the trial. In addition to newspaper accounts, jurors had been personally exposed to a variety of second-hand conjecture and gossip. Max Muelle, the youngest juror, who later provided an oral history of his service, described in detail the scope of some of this over-the-transom information. Muelle confirmed that many jurors had previous dealings with Voelker, and some may have likewise had prior contacts with Thomas. Several jurors knew, and had strong and often unflattering opinions about, the victim Chenoweth, Lieutenant and Mrs. Peterson, Wentzel, police officers, and others involved in the case.

80

Muelle said some jurors were aware of Chenoweth's alleged criminal past, Mrs. Peterson's reputation for promiscuity, and her husband's jealous outbursts. Muelle harbored a special dislike of Chenoweth, whom he regularly bested in shooting competitions despite Chenoweth's propensity to bend the rules.

Some of the information informally shared with jurors before the trial was surprisingly detailed and well sourced. Muelle said that on the day following the shooting he received "a full report of this thing from one of the trooper friends of mine."[55] Muelle also recounted that on one occasion before the trial, and prior to his selection as a juror, he talked with Wentzel about the events of the fateful evening. Wentzel shared with him Chenoweth's bawdy description of his sexual encounter with Mrs. Peterson. To Muelle's continuing astonishment, he and the other prospective jurors were never asked any questions during voir dire that might have disclosed they possessed disqualifying knowledge, and thus could have been successfully challenged.

On September 15, 1952, Lieutenant Peterson's murder trial at last began. All of the participants were set, and the witnesses were ready. More than this, the entire community and region was fascinated—indeed, transfixed—by the impending spectacle. The prosecutor and defense counsel were local celebrities, and their shared animus was common knowledge. The subject matter of the trial—murder and rape—promised to be provocative, inflammatory, and salacious. The major figures involved in the killing included a notorious local character, a military officer and outsider, and an exotic femme fatale.

Expectations were high, and the trial did not disappoint.

CHAPTER 6 – PEOPLE V. PETERSON

Despite overwhelming and undisputed evidence that Lieutenant Peterson shot and killed Mike Chenoweth in cold blood, Voelker believed he had a fighting chance to win an acquittal at trial. To succeed, he would need to summon a combination of legal precedent, performance art, and hometown advantage. He would be tasked with assuming the dual role of learned advocate and fellow Yooper. He would have to be respectful and deferential to the judge, aggressively out-litigate opposing counsel, and charm and persuade the jury. It was a tall order, but Voelker was more than up to the challenge. He was ready and able to dominate the courtroom and prevail at the trial of his lifetime.

The trial on the merits began with the prosecution's opening statement, which was brief and to the point. Thomas said the evidence would show that Lieutenant Peterson shot and killed Chenoweth with premeditation on July 31, 1952. Accordingly, the jury should convict him of first-degree murder. Even absent proof of premeditation, Thomas said, the evidence would show the defendant was guilty of the lesser included offenses of second-degree murder and manslaughter. Further, he predicted that the evidence would show the defendant was not temporarily insane when he killed his victim. Thomas' opening statement consumed less than one full page of the trial record.[1] Voelker reserved his opening statement.[2]

The prosecution's case-in-chief was straightforward and by the numbers. The testimony of the prosecution's 25 witnesses filled nearly 200 pages of trial record. Witnesses included police officers, the coroner, a photographer, employees, and patrons at the tavern, and, of course, Wentzel. Thomas sought to limit the testimony of Wentzel and the other eyewitnesses to their observations at the tavern at and around the time the defendant shot the victim. In particular, the prosecution sought to minimize—if not prevent—the introduction of evidence related to the alleged rape. Accordingly, Thomas asked each eyewitness he called to testify about the shooting to identify Lieutenant Peterson as the shooter and opine that Lieutenant Peterson appeared to be in complete control of his mental faculties throughout the episode.

During his cross-examination of the prosecution witnesses, Voelker occasionally managed to interject that Lieutenant Peterson was an "insane man" when he shot Chenoweth. For example, when cross-examining Norman Bolden,[3] the village constable in Big Bay who observed the shooting at the tavern, Voelker slipped in,

> Mr. Voelker: "Did you recognize this gun held by this *insane man* as a German Lüger?"
>
> Mr. Bolden: "Yes, sir. I identified it by a knob on the side

of the gun."[4]

Voelker brought out through his cross-examination of another witness that Lieutenant Peterson did not respond when she tried to talk with him at the tavern that evening, "suggesting that [the defendant's] mind had temporarily gone blank."[5] Voelker also established that Lieutenant Peterson and Chenoweth knew each other and were on friendly terms. To this end, Voelker concluded his questioning of Bolden with the following exchange:

> Mr. Voelker: "In other words this whole thing [the shooting] came as a surprise to you?"
>
> Mr. Bolden: "Yes, sir."
>
> Mr. Voelker: "And a shock?"
>
> Mr. Boden: "Yes, sir. Very much so."[6]

Although Voelker scored an occasional rhetorical point during the state's case-in-chief, the prosecution team remained confident when they rested their case that they had presented overwhelming evidence proving beyond a reasonable doubt every element of the principal charge—that Lieutenant Peterson had killed Chenoweth with premeditation and without justification or excuse. Their confidence seemed well-founded. The prosecution had introduced the defendant's confession and called several credible witnesses who saw the shooting and identified Lieutenant Peterson as the gunman. In spite of the prosecution's best efforts to minimize information relating to the alleged rape, this evidence actually seemed to fortify their case because it suggested a powerful motive: that the defendant murdered the victim out of jealously and revenge. The prosecution even produced the proverbial "smoking gun."

Now it was the defense's turn.

Voelker's opening statement, which he literally read to the jury, was more lengthy, descriptive, and evocative than his opponent's.[7] Reading an opening statement, rather than speaking extemporaneously, contradicts the conventional wisdom of trial advocacy experts that counsel should avoid being note dependent and maintain eye contact with the jury. In retrospect, however, it is perhaps not too surprising that Voelker wrote out and then read his remarks. Litigators have also long been instructed to tell a story during their opening statements ("This is a case about …"). Although Voelker was an accomplished trial lawyer, he was first and foremost a consummate storyteller. Voelker may have approached his opening statement as if it were one of the many short essays he had written over the years, and thus he read it to the jury to ensure that he told his story to them exactly as he intended. Also, Voelker may have been a bit nervous and thus wanted to ensure that he did not omit any important points during his introductory remarks.

Voelker began his opening statement by telling the jury that the evidence would show that Chenoweth threatened Mrs. Peterson's life, struck her with his fist, and then raped her. Voelker continued that later, when Mrs. Peterson tried to escape, Chenoweth struck her again with his fist, causing her to fall to the ground, and then kicked her as she lay there. Mrs. Peterson screamed for her life and finally managed to escape from Chenoweth near the entrance of the trailer park. Awakened by his wife's screams, Peterson first saw her when she arrived at their trailer, dazed, sobbing, and hysterical. After a few minutes, she had regained enough composure to tell him what happened. Besides his wife's physical injuries, the defendant saw that her skirt was ripped, and her panties were missing. He spent nearly an hour consoling his wife, while trying to comfort her and minister to her needs.

Further, Voelker said, the evidence would show that the defendant knew Chenoweth was an expert marksman and usually armed. For this reason, the defendant took his pistol from his trailer with him for protection when he left for the tavern to confront Chenoweth. Voelker said that the defendant's purpose for going there was to restrain Chenoweth and hold him for the police, not to kill him. On the way to the tavern the defendant thought he heard repeated shrill screams, but quickly realized these were imagined. The defendant remembers that when he entered the Lumberjack, he saw Chenoweth standing alone behind the bar with one arm hidden. The defendant then walked toward Chenoweth and shot him, emptying all of the rounds in his lüger into Chenoweth's body. Voelker said that to this day the defendant had no conscious recollection of the shooting. The defendant then turned, left the tavern, and drove home to his wife.

Voelker emphasized that with few exceptions, the defendant did not remember anything that occurred after he entered the Lumberjack until he later reentered his trailer. It was only after he returned home, Voelker said, that the defendant noticed by the mechanism of his pistol that all the ammunition was spent, and he told his wife that he had shot Chenoweth. The defendant then notified an unarmed, but deputized, trailer park caretaker of the shooting, who, in turn, called the police. Voelker concluded his opening statement by noting that the defendant had a legal right to go to the tavern and take his loaded lüger with him.

The defense called only five witnesses: Dr. A.L. Sinton, Mrs. Peterson, Dr. Warren Lambert, Lieutenant Peterson, and Dr. Thomas A. Petty, the psychiatric expert assisting thedefense.

Dr. Sinton was called first and his testimony was brief. He said he examined the victim post-mortem and found him to be in excellent physical shape.

      Mrs. Peterson was called next. Her testimony consumed over fifty pages of the record and was generally consistent with her pretrial statements. She said she went to the tavern to pick up a six-pack of beer and to play shuffleboard; she consumed four shots of whiskey and several large glasses of water; she was not intoxicated but was feeling "good"; she did not dance with anyone; she removed her shoes for part of the time she was at the tavern; after a couple of hours, when she was preparing to leave, she accepted Chenoweth's offer to drive her home; Chenoweth drove down a side road and stopped his car; he beat her and then raped her; during the attack Chenoweth ripped her skirt and removed her panties; later she managed to escape and returned to her trailer with the aid of her dog George, who led the way in the dark with a flashlight in his mouth; her husband met her at the door, ministered to her, and departed; he returned to the trailer a short time later and said he had shot Chenoweth; and her husband thereafter immediately surrendered to the deputized park caretaker. Voelker was able to elicit testimony from Mrs. Peterson that Wentzel later told her that he regretted not warning her that Chenoweth was a "wolf."[8] Voelker also received the judge's permission to have George the dog appear in the courtroom holding a flashlight in its mouth to demonstrate the assistance Mrs. Peterson described his having provided.

By this time, Beattie had taken over as lead prosecutor. His cross-examination of Mrs. Peterson focused more on disparaging her character than directly challenging her recollection. In response to Beattie's questioning, Mrs. Peterson disclosed that she was previously married and divorced from another soldier; she "knew" and saw a lot of Lieutenant Peterson for months before the divorce; she married Lieutenant Peterson only two to three weeks after the divorce; she and her first husband were Catholic, and so her divorce rendered her excommunicated from the Church; on a prior occasion, her husband had become jealous of her flirtatious behavior with another officer; and, though she was a lapsed Catholic, Lieutenant Peterson had her swear on a rosary that Chenoweth had raped her.

The defense next called Dr. Lambert. His testimony was relatively brief. He described the bruising and contusions he observed on Mrs. Peterson's eyes, upper cheeks, left shoulder, buttocks, and left hip. He estimated that the injuries were about a week old, consistent with having been inflicted at about the same time as the alleged rape. Finally, he opined that the injuries could have been caused by hard blows and kicks like those Mrs. Peterson had described.[9]

Defendant Peterson was called next. His testimony consumed

90

thirty-five pages and generally tracked the testimony offered by his wife. Lieutenant Peterson said that his wife went to the tavern while he napped; he was later awakened by her screams; his wife was hysterical when she reached the trailer, with her face swollen and her skirt torn; she told him that Chenoweth had raped her; he had her swear on rosary beads to calm her down and make sure she was identifying the correct person; he saw seminal fluid on her legs and wiped it away; he grabbed the loaded lüger he had taken from a German sniper during World War II;[10] and he then looked to see if Chenoweth was still outside the trailer. Observing no one there, he departed for the tavern to confront him. Lieutenant Peterson testified that his only purpose for seeking out Chenoweth was "to grab that individual [Chenoweth], so help me."[11] He continued, "I had no intention of killing or harming him, but if that man made one bad move I would have killed him."[12]

Lieutenant Peterson testified further that he remembered scarcely any details after leaving the trailer for the tavern. He could not recall whether he unlocked the gate to the trailer park. He did not remember driving to the tavern. He did not remember seeing anyone in the tavern except Chenoweth. He did not remember speaking to anyone at the tavern that evening. He did not remember how many shots he fired. And he did not remember encountering Wentzel outside the tavern after the shooting.

Peterson did acknowledge that he recalled exiting from his car upon arriving at the tavern, walking inside, and seeing Chenoweth looking at him in the mirror with his back turned. He testified they were watching each other when Chenoweth whirled around toward him.[13] Lieutenant Peterson said that "from there on it is a jumble. My next recollection is back in the trailer."[14] After returning home he first saw the "empty pistol in [his] hand."[15] He explained he knew all of the rounds had been spent because a gadget "sticks up the top of the magazine when the last round goes off."[16] Soon thereafter he walked to the caretaker's house at the trailer park and turned himself in.

While in the county jail awaiting trial, Lieutenant Peterson said Wentzel visited him twice, bringing him cigarettes and magazines. Mrs. Peterson later testified at trial that on one occasion Wentzel shook her husband's hand and said, "There is one thing I hold against you, – you ruined one of our good bottles of whiskey and our mirror."[17] Lieutenant Peterson concluded his testimony by pledging that he loved his wife before she was raped on July 30, on the day she was raped, and he "still love[d] her today."

Beattie's cross-examination of Lieutenant Peterson was staccato and precise. In response to his questions, Lieutenant Peterson acknowledged that he had been exposed to extensive combat and stress, but never suffered blackouts, except for one occasion involving an explosion-induced concussion. He confirmed that he had never been diagnosed or treated for any psychological disorders or disabilities. He reiterated that he had his wife swear on rosary beads regarding the identity of her attacker, suggesting that he did not believe her about the rape. Beattie next pressed Lieutenant Peterson on whether he was aware before July 30 that the park caretaker was a deputy sheriff. Beattie's purpose was to imply that if Lieutenant Peterson's true intent were to hold Chenoweth for the authorities rather than kill him, he could have enlisted the aid of the deputy sheriff to do this and avoided a fatal confrontation. When Beattie asked about a prior statement Peterson allegedly had made to a police officer that Chenoweth deserved to die, Lieutenant Peterson testified that he did not recall making such a statement.

Near the conclusion of the cross-examination, Voelker and Beattie again crossed swords:

> Mr. Voelker: May the record show that the Prosecutor has deliberately got between on two occasions within the last minute of the defendant and his lawyer, so that his lawyer cannot observe his client and get his testimony.
>
> Mr. Beattie: That would not interfere with anything, would it?
>
> Mr. Voelker: And I object to that statement and the implication – the implication being that I am signaling to my client. I resent it and ask for a ruling of the court. That is the

shadiest thing I have seen in years, Mr. Attorney General.

Mr. Beattie: From Lansing.

Mr. Voelker: And Marine City.[18]

Moments later Judge Arch intoned, "Nothing to rule on. Go ahead."[19]

The final defense witness was Dr. Thomas Petty.[20] He testified that he was an Army Captain presently assigned to Fort Custer Hospital, Fort Custer, Michigan, where he served as the Chief of Neuro-Psychiatric Services. He recounted the extensive education and experience that qualified him as a psychiatric expert. Once accepted as an expert, he described the battery of tests and examinations he performed on Lieutenant Peterson from September 3-5, 1952, while the defendant was an in-patient at Percy Jones Army Hospital in Battle Creek, Michigan. Dr. Petty's testimony provoked much wrangling between opposing counsel regarding hypothetical questions, whether testimony invaded the province of the jury, and other technical legal matters, but, after the dust settled, he was permitted to express the expert opinion he formed after his examination. Distilled to its essence, it was his expert opinion that Lieutenant Peterson (or a hypothetical person under all of the same circumstances) suffered from "psychic shock," which is not uncommon and produced an "almost overwhelming tension;"[21] this mental condition could be classified as a "disassociated reaction," also known as "irresistible impulse;"[22] Lieutenant Peterson and/or this hypothetical man would be "unable to distinguish right from wrong;"[23] a person suffering from irresistible impulse could be in a "trance-like state or spell;"[24] and such a person would be unlikely to go to a caretaker/deputy sheriff and seek help or report the rape.[25] When Dr. Petty concluded his testimony, the defense rested.

On rebuttal the prosecution called Dr. Thomas Thompson, a psychiatrist. He opined that the defendant/hypothetical man could distinguish right from wrong and was not gripped by an irresistible impulse. Dr. Thompson's testimony was brief; it covered only eleven pages of trial record as compared to Dr. Petty's, which totaled thirty-four pages. According to jurors, the greatest weakness in Dr. Thompson's testimony was that the basis for his opinion was limited to his observations of the defendant and witnesses during the trial.[26] On cross-examination, Dr. Thompson admitted that he was "at a disadvantage" in rendering a psychiatric opinion about the defendant's mental state, because he did not personally examine him, as had the defense expert.[27] Dr. Thompson also conceded that it "was not normal psychiatric practice to make a diagnosis without performing a complete examination and compiling a history … of the individual.[28]

Dr. Thompson's limited foundation for his opinion stood in stark contrast to Dr. Petty's extensive in-patient examination of Peterson.

Voelker recognized and anticipated this advantage for the defense, and he

first underscored its significance when he asked Dr. Petty during his

direct examination:

> Mr. Voelker: You may state, Doctor, whether or not you
> would venture or attempt to pass a psychiatric opinion on
> the mental state of either the hypothetical lieutenant or the
> real Lieutenant Peterson on the basis of sitting here during
> the five or six days of this trial.
>
> Dr. Petty: I would consider it impossible to pass my
> professional opinion on the state of this man's mind on or
> about July 30th and immediately thereafter on the basis of
> what I have observed here in the last five days.[29]

Voelker began to ask a follow-up question—could the witness

"state whether or not in your opinion you would consider valid a

psychiatric opinion ..."—but Beattie finally pounced and objected, and

Judge Arch sustained the objection.[30] But by then it was too late.

Voelker had made his point that Dr. Petty offered a more credible

opinion than Dr. Thompson regarding the defendant's psychiatric state

at the time of the shooting given his superior basis for rendering such a

judgment.[31] One juror later remarked that the defense expert was

"brilliant," in stark contrast to the prosecution expert, who was

unconvincing largely because the latter "never examined" the defendant

or even "talked to him."[32]

Voelker prevailed on his request that Judge Arch instruct the jury that it did not matter whether Mrs. Peterson was actually assaulted and raped, only that Lieutenant Peterson believed it to be true when he shot and killed Chenoweth.[33] Judge Arch instructed further,

> The testimony has been offered on behalf of defendant that he was insane at the time the fatal shots were fired and it was a form of insanity sometimes known under the name of irresistible impulse. I charge you that such a form of insanity is recognized as a defense to a crime in the State of Michigan and that it is the law of this State that even if the defendant had been able to comprehend the nature and consequences of his act and know it was wrong that nevertheless if he was forced to its execution by some irresistible impulse which he was powerless to control in consequence of a disease of the mind then he was insane and you should acquit him because of insanity. Even if you should find that defendant knew the difference between right and wrong if at the time of the shooting he had any mental disease or insanity and lost the power to choose between right and wrong, that his free will agency was at the time destroyed and the act was so connected with the mental disease and insanity as to have been the sole cause of it, then defendant would not be responsible and your verdict would be not guilty because of insanity.[34]

After closing arguments,[35] the jury deliberated for a little over four hours.[36] About a quarter of this time was spent "marching [jurors] like a prison gang"[37] to and from the "Coffee Cup restaurant," a nearby "greasy spoon" cafe where they dined. [38] During deliberations, the jury took several straw votes. They initially split eight to four in favor of acquittal.[39] The next vote was eleven jurors in favor of not guilty by reason of insanity and one juror in favor of not guilty without qualification.[40] After the third vote with the same results as the last, the majority tried to persuade the holdout juror that a straight not guilty verdict without an insanity finding would be untenable given there was no dispute that the defendant shot the victim.[41] The holdout juror finally relented, and thus the jury reached a unanimous verdict of "not guilty by reason of temporary insanity."[42] One juror later recalled that Voelker did not smile, even when the verdict was announced.[43]

The Peterson trial was a quintessentially big event in a small town. The courtroom was packed with spectators every day. Many of the regulars were housewives who brought their knitting, though Judge Arch drew the line at bringing in papers, books, or magazines.[44] Children under sixteen years of age were excluded, in part because of the sexual nature of the case and testimony. Voelker once fantasized in his journal,

> The murder trial was crowded for 8 solid days, mostly with panting females. When I began my argument I got up before the jury, slowly looked over the crowded courtroom, and said: 'Wouldn't it have been wonderful to have had a popcorn concession.' Surely no murder argument ever began thus.[45]

Spontaneous applause erupted when the not guilty verdict was read aloud.[46] Mrs. Peterson burst into tears and well-wishers rushed up to shake Lieutenant Peterson's hand.[47] Millie Menze, a local resident[48] who was making sandwiches for the jurors when the verdict was announced, explained that the spectators' favorable reaction signified that "rape would not be tolerated in their community."[49] A juror later said that many residents were "glad we got rid of the son of a bitch," referring to Chenoweth.[50] Others agreed that he "had it coming."[51] When things calmed down, Lieutenant Peterson "went to each juror, looked [the juror] straight in the eyes and shook [the juror's] hand[]."[52] On September 25, Voelker summarized his feelings about the trial in his journal: "Last night at 8:30 he [Lieutenant Peterson] was acquitted on the grounds of temporary insanity after a savage week of trial. I am tired in mind and body."[53]

After trial, Lieutenant Peterson was initially committed to a psychiatric facility to determine his present mental state. He was released two days later, having been declared sane by the same two psychiatrists who had testified at his murder trial.[54] Lieutenant Peterson then rejoined his wife at Perkins Park.[55] He had so far paid Voelker only $150 for his legal services.

The day after his client's release, Voelker went to Perkins Park to meet with the Petersons as they had earlier arranged, so that he could collect the outstanding $2,850 balance of his fee guaranteed by a promissory note.[56] When Voelker arrived there he saw that his client's trailer was gone. The caretaker told Voelker that the Petersons had departed during the dark of the night without a forwarding address.[57] He then handed Voelker a note from his former client explaining that he had been overwhelmed by an "irresistible impulse to leave."[58] Voelker never received another cent from Lieutenant Peterson.

In his journal, Voelker recorded that initially he had "received only $150.00 on case, but I could not desert the man."[59] Years later, Lieutenant Peterson falsely claimed that Voelker had defended him for free because he was indigent. On October 6, 1952, Voelker wrote in his journal, "Lt. Coleman Peterson was freed on a writ of habeas corpus on September 25, 1952. The various veterans' organizations that talked so big about backing him have donated a miserable $55.00. A plague on them."[60] In the end, Voelker's only other compensation for his successful defense of Lieutenant Peterson was the lüger that his client had used to kill Chenoweth and left behind.[61]

The jury verdict is in many ways inscrutable. We will never know how many jurors believed Lieutenant Peterson was acting under an irresistible impulse, how many believed Chenoweth raped and injured Mrs. Peterson, or how many believed that Chenoweth got what he deserved, regardless of whether Lieutenant Peterson was insane, or his wife was raped. Indeed, it will never be known how many believed that Lieutenant Peterson was justified in killing Chenoweth even if he did not rape his wife. Thomas Wilson, a juror at the Peterson trial, said years later,

> I felt the lieutenant was justified in what he did. I was a soldier and a soldier is trained to defend and that's what the lieutenant did—defend his wife. I don't think he was temporarily insane. I felt he had a right to do what he did. Why should he suffer the rest of his life to let a man do that to his wife? [62]

In the end, perhaps only one conclusion about the verdict can be drawn with any certainty: several different, and even conflicting, considerations and attitudes contributed to the jurors' consensus judgment that Lieutenant Peterson should be found not guilty of murder by reason of temporary insanity.

The Peterson trial supplied in abundance all of the material needed for a great lawyer's war story. Voelker had actually lived the experience, and thus he was singularly qualified to put pen to paper and write about it. The Peterson trial furnished all the raw ingredients for a book, but two crucial questions remained to be answered. First, would Voelker summon the commitment and energy needed to tell the story in the form of a novel? And second, even if he did, would anyone ever read it?

CHAPTER 7 - THE NOVEL

Once the trial concluded and trout season ended, Voelker could return to his writing, unburdened by the demands of being a full-time prosecutor or the prospect of an impending murder trial. Soon he "had a sudden impulse . . . to write about a murder trial."[1] Voelker explained, "The courtroom was one arena I knew something about, and by now I'd appeared on both sides in some pretty bang-up murder trials."[2] On December 4, 1952, Voelker first mentioned in his journal the possibility of a writing "a book on the story of the Peterson murder case. … We'll see, We'll see …"[3] He adopted a working title, "*The Trial*."

Even before tentatively committing to the project, Voelker wrote in his journal that he was "taking daily notes on the new book, 'The Trial.' There is no longer any question that I can tell the story: it is a question of whether I can inflame it."[4] Although Voelker would embellish the story for dramatic purposes, he was determined to portray a criminal trial realistically and believably. Voelker explained,

> I wanted to tackle a single courtroom trial [because] I had a small ax of my own to grind. For a long time, I had seen too many movies and read too many books and plays about trials that were almost comically phony and overdone, mostly in their extravagant efforts to overdramatize an already inherently dramatic human situation.[5]

Voelker's guiding principle was to write about "a criminal trial the way it really was."[6]

This was a new type of writing project for Voelker.[7] Two of his early books, *Troubleshooter* and *Small Town D.A.*, were short story collections. The third, *Danny and the Boys*, was episodic, in the picaresque mold. *The Trial*, later renamed *Anatomy of a Murder*, would be Voelker's first full-length novel. In time, his story about the Peterson trial would be credited with launching an innovative and largely original genre of fiction: the realistic criminal trial novel. Many followed the trail Voelker blazed with *Anatomy*, notably Leon Uris (*QB VII*) and the courtroom drama franchises established by Scott Turow (beginning with *Presumed Innocent*) and John Grisham (*A Time to Kill, The Firm, and many others*).[8] Some have suggested that *Anatomy of a Murder* influenced Truman Capote when he devised the entirely new literary genre—New Journalism—with *In Cold Blood*.[9] Certainly the long-running network television drama series *Law and Order*, and its numerous spinoffs and imitators, must be counted among Voelker's heirs. Voelker's DNA can also be detected in true crime documentaries such as those seen on *Dateline* and *48 Hours*, as well as virtually all of the programming on the television network Investigation Discovery. His determination to portray a criminal trial accurately, with technical precision and factual realism, revealed to the literary world that Hitchcock's MacGuffin was not the only device that could drive a plot—realism and actual events could be just as compelling as a coded message or a spare apartment key.

Voelker initially considered writing about the Peterson trial from the perspective of the prosecuting attorney, with flashbacks to events throughout the prosecutor's life.[10] In a September 11, 1953, journal entry, Voelker wrote that the "young prosecutor" would be named Paul Biegler, Voelker's long-time alter ego. He described Biegler as "the youngest son of Oliver and Belle Biegler, and the only one of a large family to go to college."[11] Oliver was a saloon owner. The defense attorney would be named Byron St. Clair, who Voelker described as a "middle-aged divorce [sic], tall, balding and cynical."[12]

After several false starts, on November 25, 1953, Voelker recorded that he had "the main story" of what would become his new novel.[13] While the lead character would still be named Paul Biegler, he would now assume the role of defense counsel. On December 10 of that year, Voelker was "still taking desultory notes for The Trial, which [he] hope[d] to start on writing in earnest after the New Year."[14] The project seemed to stall throughout 1954, but the pace accelerated early the following year. On February 17, 1955, Voelker wrote, "I'm almost afraid to mention it, but I'm just starting the 4th Chapter and I may – I may - be rolling. This is something intensely new and different and exciting."[15] A December 6, 1955, journal entry noted, "I plug along on my book, correcting, adding, making notes, planning, writing a chapter, inching, trying not to think of how long the winter, how locked."[16] On February 16, 1956, he reported, "Have now written 40 chapters, including 5 in the Trial, and I have only now got to the jury sworn & ready for opening statement."[17] Finally, on March 27, 1956, he triumphantly exclaimed, "I just at this moment (4:26 pm) wrote the last line of the last chapter … of the book…It is done, it is done, and if this isn't a good one then I'm hanging up my pen. God, am I weary…."[18]

Voelker kept his draft locked in a safe in his home, not because he was worried it would be stolen, but rather out of fear that a fire might destroy it.[19] This was a legitimate concern in an era before copying machines, electronic documents, and cloud backups. Voelker's massive manuscript was initially handwritten on yellow legal paper and typed by his long-time secretary, Donna Snider.[20] A review of Voelker's archived notes reflects that he was constantly editing and rewriting,[21] with nearly every handwritten and typed page of his drafts adorned with additions, deletions, arrows, and marginal notes.[22] When Voelker later presented a signed copy of *Anatomy of a Murder* to Snider, he added the inscription,

106

"To Donna, who first translated this book into English."[23]

Voelker renamed his book *Anatomy of a Murder*, a title he adapted from *Anatomy of Melancholy*, a work by Robert Burton.[24] Voelker offered that he "read [Burton's] . . . book and liked the sound of the title."[25] Additional reflections about Voelker's title selection are included in Chapter Nine, but for now it is sufficient to observe that, precisely because *Anatomy* would establish a new literary genre, the title probably could not have been more fitting.

Now that Voelker had completed his novel, he needed a publisher. The first draft of the manuscript was massive, totaling eight hundred and forty legal-size pages.[26] At least two publishing houses rejected it initially, in part because of its enormous length. Voelker wrote in his journal that a Dutton publishing representative "allows I write 'well and amusingly' but that I have 'seriously overwritten'... ."[27] A few months later, Little Brown declined the manuscript, but held open the possibility of reconsideration if it was revised.[28] These critiques prompted Voelker to seek help in making the book more publishable, so he approached Sherman Baker, an editor who had worked with him on a previous book,[29] who was employed at the time by St. Martin's Press as a promotion manager.[30] Baker agreed to assist, and he and Voelker corresponded and met in person over several months to rework the novel.

With Baker's help, the manuscript was pared down to 437 pages, and St. Martin's Press thereafter accepted the revised version for publication. Even publishing the work in condensed form was a gamble: because the book was still uncommonly long, it would be priced at $4.95 a copy, a dollar more than standard-length trade editions of the time.[31]

The risk paid off when the novel was chosen as the January Book-of-the-Month Club selection and sales soared.[32] *Anatomy* quickly climbed the best seller list, where it remained for sixty-five weeks, with a record twenty-nine weeks at number one.[33] Dell Publishing paid $100,000 for paperback rights, at that time among the highest amounts ever advanced, in company with *From Here to Eternity*, *The Caine Mutiny*, and *Marjorie Morningstar*.[34] The novel has since been reprinted in at least twenty languages and sold over four million copies.[35]

Grace Voelker said she did not fully appreciate the magnitude of her husband's success until she saw several commuters with the book at a Chicago train station.[36] Voelker wrote a tongue-in-cheek entry in his journal: "Anyone who tries to achieve 'culture' by sticking to the best seller list is burying his head in the sand – with his mouth open, until, of course, *Anatomy* was published."[37] When Voelker was asked about the extraordinary success of *Anatomy of a Murder*, he quipped, "It is a rather heady and unique experience to find myself a rising young novelist in my fifties."[38]

Literary critics were nearly unanimous in their praise for *Anatomy of a Murder*. The *New York Times'* Orville Prescott called the novel "immensely readable and continuously entertaining," noting Traver's "unflagging invention and narrative pace."[39] Bosley Crowther, a long-time critic for *Time Magazine*, wrote:

> Crime does pay, especially when – as in this novel – it is (1) skillfully packaged as fiction, (2) taken by the Book-of the-Month Club, (3) sold to the movies before publication, and (4) optioned by a Broadway producer. The payoff in this case goes to John D. Voelker, 54. Few readers will turn aside until the fate of Lt. Frederic Manion is finally decided.[40]

Clifton Fadiman, who at one time was in charge of *The New Yorker's* book review section and also was the Chief Editor for Simon and Schuster, wrote, "There are many famous trial scenes in fiction; but there are few that, within your reviewer's memory, rival this one for tension, legal chicanery, brilliant cross-examination, high and low comedy, and ability to draw the reader almost bodily into the courtroom."[41]

James M. Cain, the author of *Mildred Pierce*, said in his *New York Times* book review of *Anatomy of a Murder*,

> Rarely have I been so entertained as I have been by this strange novel, and for the life of me I can't tell why. It breaches all canons that fiction knows . . . Nevertheless, however, and yet: It held me as few books have, I couldn't put it down—one must eat, sleep and work. But I was back

at it every minute I had, and at night passed up TV in its favor. On the home stretch, I stayed with it until early morning, as I knew I could never sleep until I had seen how it turned out.[42]

Voelker always publicly insisted that *Anatomy of a Murder* was a fictional work like all of his other projects except *Laughing Whitefish*, which he published several years later and called "his only historical novel."[43] His private papers tell a different story. Voelker once wrote in his journal that *The Trial* "is a working title of a projected novel drafted around a fictional framework of the Peterson murder case which I defended just a year ago."[44] Elsewhere in Voelker's notes, Wentzel's name "from the actual trial appears at the top of rough draft pages for the book."[45] Voelker's insistence that the novel was fiction was prompted, in no small part, by several lawsuits seeking a share of its considerable profits. One lawsuit "revolved around the death of the playwright John Van Druten."[46] Two other suits involved plaintiffs related to the Petersons and the Chenoweths seeking a cut of Voelker's royalties, alleging libel and invasion of privacy.[47] Ultimately, "one case was dismissed and the other was settled out of court."[48] Otto Preminger, who would later produce and direct the movie *Anatomy of a Murder*, helped resolve the suits.[49] Years later, and long after the legal claims had been settled, Voelker acknowledged that *Anatomy of a Murder* is "pretty much the story of the [Peterson] trial."[50]

Many of the differences between the actual trial and the Voelker's

"fictionalized" version are merely superficial. Voelker became Paul

Biegler, his long-time alter ego.[51] Chenoweth became Barney Quill.

Lieutenant and Mrs. Peterson became Lieutenant Frederic and Laura

Manion. Beattie became Claude Dancer. Thomas became Mitch Ludwick.

Judge Arch became Judge Weaver, whose first name is never mentioned

either in the novel or later in the film. Wentzel became Alphonse

Paquette. Dr. Petty became Dr. Matthew Smith. The shooting took place

at the Thunder Bay Inn instead of the Lumberjack Tavern, and the trial

was held in the fictional town of Chippewa rather than Marquette. Mrs.

Manion played pinball rather than shuffleboard. George the dog was

changed from a Labrador mix to a cute little terrier, probably to

emphasize that it could not have defended Mrs. Manion from Quill's

attack. Unlike the actual shooting, in the novel none of the bullets struck

the victim in the throat. In the novel, the sanity hearing was incorporated

into the murder trial for dramatic effect, rather than being held two days

later as a separate proceeding, as actually occurred.[52] These changes

notwithstanding, much of the dialogue in the novel is taken almost

verbatim from the actual court proceedings, including the crackling

examination of witnesses and the verbal jousting by the lawyers.[53]

As Voelker once predicted in his journal, he "inflamed" the

dramatic impact in his novel through additional characters and structural changes. Maida, Biegler's wise-cracking and underpaid secretary, was introduced in the novel. So too was Parnell McCarthy, Biegler's hard-drinking attorney confidant. Many of Voelker's neighbors on West Barnum Street were of Irish descent and included a family with the surname McCarthy.[54] Some of these residents believed, perhaps with good reason, that the McCarthy character was Voelker's fond nod to his bibulous Irish neighbors. Voelker said he created the McCarthy character (and for that matter also probably Maida) to give Biegler someone to talk to and assist the narrative.[55] This makes sense, as McCarthy's exchanges with Biegler freed Voelker, the author, of the need to express ideas and advance his story through an exposition of Biegler's inner thoughts. It also allowed Voelker to voice conflicting opinions and judgments through Biegler's debates with McCarthy, often in a style that mimicked the adversarial character of the murder trial. To his delight, Voelker received fan mail for years asking about how his fictitious friend Parnell McCarthy was doing.[56]

Another change in the novel is that Biegler, unlike Voelker, is a bachelor. The victim, Barney Quill, is a divorced and estranged from his wife (Chenoweth's wife and daughter lived with him in Big Bay). Making Biegler a bachelor and Quill divorced allowed Voelker to introduce an important new character, Mary Pilant.

Pilant was Quill's friend and perhaps his mistress. She worked as a hostess and helped Quill manage the Inn where the shooting occurred. Pilant had apparently fallen in love with a local Army officer, causing Quill to become jealous. As a consequence, Quill drinks too much[57] and perhaps rapes Mrs. Manion to get back at the military. The novel also focuses on Quill's will, which leaves the Inn to Pilant.

Professor Leonard Heldreth explains that by introducing "the Pilant character, Voelker was able to add a subplot which provides a romantic interest for the hero and ended the novel on a positive note with Biegler going off to have dinner with Mary."[58] Pilant's character would later be transformed for the film, where she would assume a pivotal role in the trial's resolution.

Referring again to the novel, Heldreth continues,

> The entire tone of the novel was determined by Voelker's choosing to tell the story through the first-person narration of Paul Biegler, the trial lawyer. Voelker's manuscripts of other works indicate his interest in point of view, for he changes point of view in rough drafts to see what sort of effect such a change would have on the narrative. In Paul Biegler, Voelker creates a knowledgeable, sympathetic character who comments on everything from the architecture of the courthouse to the status of trout fishing in the Upper Peninsula. Telling the story through Biegler's eyes also imposes a unity on the account and a framing device that gives the story depth and detail.[59]

Voelker also introduces a character named Duane "Duke" Miller, a convict who shared a cell with Lieutenant Manion as the latter awaited trial. On rebuttal, the prosecution calls Miller to testify that Lieutenant Manion told him that he fooled his lawyer and would dupe the jury with his insanity defense.[60] Some of the legal and ethical implications of Miller's testimony are discussed later in this book, but the introduction of this character also served to enhance the complexity of both the plot and the moral and ethical questions Biegler was obliged to navigate.

Regardless of the many plot and character changes, Voelker's personal convictions about the actual trial resonate throughout the novel. Above all else, he was angry that the prosecution team fought so hard to prevent the defense from introducing evidence about the alleged rape.[61] Owing to his years as D.A., Voelker believed that a prosecutor's highest duty was to seek justice. This included ensuring that all of the relevant evidence was presented to the jury, even if it might benefit the defense. Voelker made this point clear both as a litigator and a writer, and it, too, is among the ethical questions the novel explores. [62]

CHAPTER 8 - THE FILM

Voelker was sitting on a gold mine, and he knew it. He had

barely scraped by financially for most of his adult life. Now he was a

famous author and national celebrity who traded quips with Johnny

Carson on network television.[1] His novel was a huge commercial

success and sat atop the bestseller list for more than seven months. It

also had obvious potential for adaptation as a movie.[2]

When Voelker sold the publishing rights to *Anatomy of a*

Murder, he took the money up front, was savaged by taxes,[3] and applied

most of the after-tax revenues to outstanding debts. Lesson learned,

Voelker vowed that he would make the best deal possible for the movie

rights, but when producer-director Otto Preminger called and proposed

$300,000, Voelker jumped at the offer, and accepted it on the spot.[4]

Preminger interrupted, "Wait I'm not finished! I am offering you a

percentage of the box office."[5] Without pausing, Voelker repeated, "I'll

take it!"[6] As it turned out, the addition of box-office earnings more than

doubled the money Voelker would make from the movie. *The Detroit*

Free Press reported in 1959 that Voelker's estimated revenues from

book sales and movie rights for *Anatomy of a Murder* had already

totaled $600,000.[7] In all of his negotiations and dealings with

Preminger, Voelker insisted on only one condition: a promise "to keep strictly to the legal procedure."[8]

Voelker had never met Preminger before their phone call, but he was no doubt well awareof the director's reputation and stature in the film industry. Preminger had directed the film noir classics *Laura*[9] and *Fallen Angel*,[10] and he had tackled taboo subjects such as drug addiction in *The Man with the Golden Arm*.[11] He also played a few acting rolls, most notably POW Camp Commandant Oberst von Scherbach in *Stalag 17*.[12] Preminger knew a good story when he read one, and surely, he was intrigued with the possibility of producing and directing a film that frankly addressed another taboo subject—rape.[13]

Preminger, however, was not the first to claim the film rights. John Van Druten's estate asserted that Voelker had previously sold both the stage and screen rights of *Anatomy of a Murder* to Van Druten. Records confirm that Voelker corresponded with Van Druten up until the latter's death. During one exchange, Van Druten even proposed changing the title of the film to "*Anatomy of Murder*," but Voelker disagreed, arguing that the title would be misleading, as each murder is different.[14] According to various *Hollywood Reporter* news items, Voelker made a deal with Van Druten but the contract was never signed. All plans were cancelled after Van Druten died on December 19, 1957.[15] Preminger later stepped in and resolved the estate's claim by paying for an out of court settlement. Preminger said, "I could have kicked myself, for not acting [on the matter of property rights] sooner. I itched to make the movie."[16] Preminger completed purchasing the screen rights in July 1958. Besides the obvious benefits of making a film based on a best-selling book, Preminger also had a soft spot for the subject matter owing to his experiences as a former law student.[17] Foster Hirsh, the author of *Otto Preminger: The Man Who Would Be King*, said that "Preminger was always fascinated by the law," and he resolved to obtain motion picture rights for *Anatomy of a Murder* as soon as he read it.[18]

Voelker did not negotiate any creative control for the movie with Preminger when he sold the film rights of his novel. Voelker mused, "When I sold my novel to the irrepressible producer-director, Otto Preminger, there were no strings attached. For my part Otto could have filmed it in the Himalayas with the Abominable Snowman and Lassie playing the leads."[19]

Preminger chose an unknown scenarist, Wendell Mayes, to write the screenplay, and he retained Voelker as a consultant throughout the filming. Even before shooting began, Voelker reviewed and offered suggestions on Mayes' screenplay. Voelker was impressed with Mayes' efforts, gushing to Preminger,

> I cannot begin to tell you how delighted we are with the splendid job this young man has done. He has caught the

117

flavor and tone of my book and so superbly translated it to this new medium that it has become nothing less than an independent act of creation. It is sheer magic. He has greatly improved parts of it and I am green with envy over some of his crackling dialogue. He has a lovely wry flickering sense of humor. I repeat – we are boundlessly delighted and pleased.[20]

For *Anatomy of a Murder*, Mayes received a New York Film Critics Circle Award for best screenplay in 1959 and an Oscar nomination in 1960.

Voelker was a constant presence during filming, and the case and crew referred to him as"Judgie" or Judge Voelker on the set.[21] Most of Voelker's specific critiques of the draft screenplay involved correcting legal errors, suggesting dramatic choices, and softening descriptions of characters to preserve relationships back in Ishpeming.[22] Once filming began, Voelker corrected legal terminology and instructed actors where and how to stand in the courtroom.[23] He even taught Jimmy Stewart, who played Biegler, the proper way to tie trout files and light a Parodi, the small Italian cigar that Voelker favored and Biegler smoked in the movie. Stewart thought the cigars stunk and could never manage to keep them lit, which added time to the filming and on one occasion caused Stewart to erupt in frustration.[24]

Preminger usually adopted Voelker's recommendations,[25] and the two maintained the friendship they formed during the shooting of the film afterward. Voelker often brought fresh-caught brook trout to the

Mather Inn, where Preminger stayed during filming, for the chef to

prepare for his breakfast.[26] About a year after *Anatomy of a Murder*

wrapped, Preminger treated the Voelkers, Joseph Welch (who played

Judge Weaver), and his new wife, Agnes, to an extended visit in Israel.

Voelker and Preminger continued to correspond and exchanged

Christmas cards for years.

Throughout the filming, Voelker was especially concerned about

the authenticity of the trial scenes. For example, he persuaded Preminger

that the Clerk of Court should pound the gavel to call the court to order,

as at real trials, rather than having the judge do this himself, as he too

often saw in Hollywood depictions.[27] Preminger cast Lloyd LeVasseur,

the longtime clerk in Marquette County, to play the role.[28] Voelker was

especially insistent that "[t]here will be no last-minute witnesses, no

sitting on the lap of those testifying, no finger pointing in the third

degree."[29] Ironically, the film introduced a climactic courtroom scene that

relied upon the explosive testimony of a surprise, last-minute witness,

Mary Pilant.

Pilant's character, who first appeared in the novel, was enlarged

and redefined for the film. She became the illegitimate daughter of

Barney Quill rather than his mistress, and thus she was a more suitable romantic prospect for Biegler. Of greater significance is that as the

defense was about to rest its case, Pilant tells Biegler that she found Laura

Manion's missing and ripped panties below the opening of a clothes chute

at the Thunder Bay Inn. This evidence, of course, supports the defense's

contention that Quill raped Mrs. Manion, as he could have easily disposed

of her torn panties in the chute that was adjacent to his room at the Inn.

When Dancer cross-examines Pilant about the panties, he suggests that

she fabricated her testimony to get back at her lover, Barney Quill,

because her pride was hurt. Pilant says she does not understand the

question, and Biegler comes to her rescue with an objection. The judge

agrees the question is confusing and admonishes the prosecutor. Dancer

presses on, and the skirmishing builds suspense before the dramatic

climax of the movie.

> Mr. Dancer: Miss Pilant, when you found the panties, was
> your first thought that Barney Quill might have raped Mrs.
> Manion or was it that he might have been stepping out with
> Mrs. Manion?
>
> Miss Pilant: What does he mean? I don't know what he means.
>
> Judge Weaver: Mr. Dancer, once again, I must ask you to put
> straight questions to the witness.
>
> Mr. Dancer: Here is a straight question, Your Honor. Miss
> Pilant, were you Barney Quill's mistress?
>
> Miss Pilant: No! No, I was not!
>
> Mr. Dancer: You know it's common knowledge in

Thunder Bay you were living with Quill.

Miss Pilant: That's not true. Barney Quill was …

Mr. Dancer: Was what, Miss Pilant? Barney Quill was what, Miss Pilant?

Miss Pilant: Barney Quill was my father.

Mr. Dancer: [Long pause and a loud reaction from the gallery] "No more questions."[30]

One other change in the movie is worth noting. Professor Heldreth observes, "As with any screenplay adapted from a novel written in the first person, much of the point of view was lost."[31] As a consequence, if the viewer finds himself siding with Biegler rather than the prosecution in the film, his choice will be based on the objective point of view expressed through Preminger's lens, rather than on Biegler's subjective perspective, as revealed in the novel's account of his inner thoughts and feelings. This change in perspective, in turn, diminishes somewhat the autobiographical viewpoint that Voelker conveyed in his book.

During the filming, Preminger obtained a copy of the Peterson trial record from the Marquette courthouse. Some of the testimony from the transcript not included in the book found its way into the movie's script. For example, Lieutenant Peterson having his wife swear upon a rosary was omitted from the novel but reintroduced in the film. Such additions to the screenplay reveal that Preminger, like Voelker, closely based his fictionalized account of the Manion trial on real-world events of the Peterson trial.

Preminger originally intended to shoot the movie in Hollywood with just a few exterior scenes filmed in Marquette. Early in the production process, Production Manager Henry Wineberger and Art Director Boris Levin traveled to the Marquette area to scout potential locations for filming establishing shots. Preminger also visited the area on multiple occasions, spending considerable time with Voelker. Ultimately, Preminger and the others agreed that the film should be shot entirely in Marquette County. This gave *Anatomy of a Murder* the distinction of being "one of the first American movies ever to be shot entirely on location."[32] Preminger also opted to shoot in black and white rather than in color, so as to better convey the lifeless late winter/early spring ambiance of the Upper Peninsula.[33] As Boris Levin put it, "[t]he peculiar provinciality of the area could not be recreated on a studio set."[34] Levin explained further, "It's not only the look of the place that I want to get on the screen. I want the actors to feel it, to absorb a sense of what it is like to live here. To smell it."[35]

Even before filming began on March 23, 1958, Preminger and his crew learned that location shooting in Michigan's Upper Peninsula presented many challenges, especially in the early spring. The opulent

Marquette courtroom was a spectacular setting for the trial, but it was far more cramped than a traditional movie set.[36] Preminger incurred about $100,000 in construction costs, including $4,000 alone for lumber and manpower, to retrofit the courtroom to accommodate the heavy equipment needed to shoot there.[37] To this day, the courthouse's great marble staircase bears chips and scars inflicted by heavy equipment that was used during the filming of the courtroom scenes.[38]

Preminger found that the courthouse library too confining for filming, so the law library scene was actually shot at the same Carnegie Library in Ishpeming where Voelker spent many hours as a voracious reader in his youth.[39] The supposed entrance to the courthouse library in the film was in fact a men's restroom, redesignated by the simple expedient of affixing a "library" sign to the door.[40]

Another $25,000 of the film's budget was spent to construct a one-story addition to the existing Big Bay Hotel (originally constructed by Henry Ford, and later renamed The Thunder Bay Inn, as it was called in the movie), which served as the location for the crucial tavern scene where Quill is shot to death.[41] Construction lasted over four weeks and was performed in near zero-degree weather.[42] Even on an accelerated schedule, work was not completed in time for filming, so the addition still had dirt floors when scenes were shot there.[43] Preminger instructed the

Inn's exterior be painted a gaudy shade of pink, as this would photograph better when filming in black and white.[44] Adrian and Beatrice Wentzel were selected to portray the managers of the Big Bay Inn in the movie.[45] Preminger offered to tear down the addition and restore the Inn to its original condition when filming concluded, but the proprietor declined, because he wanted to keep the new wing as a memento of the picture and to attract tourists.[46]

The harsh conditions also took a toll on the cast and crew, most of whom hailed from sunny California. Arthur O'Connell for one, who played Biegler's friend and associate Parnell McCarthy, was laid up for several days in a local hospital with pneumonia, and many others in the cast and crew suffered colds and similar ailments, including Stewart.[47] The frigid weather subtly affected production in other ways. For example, Preminger decided to shoot the exterior scenes last in sequence, in part as a concession to the lingering cold of late March. He remarked, "Not even Barney Quill's passions were strong enough to lead to an outdoor rape in a Michigan winter."[48] Once, while shooting on Third Street in Ishpeming, Preminger called a halt when he noticed a small tree that had not yet sprouted leaves. He ordered his crew to purchase colored paper at a local dime store, cut out leaves, and paste them to the bare branches to make the tree look lush.[49]

Location shooting took place at several other area sites. The den and living room in Voelker's home on West Barnum Street in Ishpeming served as Biegler's office in the movie.[50] Several scenes were shot inside the Lumberjack Tavern, which was the first time that a fictional murder was filmed at the actual crime scene on which the story was based. Although in the movie the site of the fatal shooting was changed to the Thunder Bay Inn, true to the facts of the Peterson case, the murder scene is referred to as a "tavern." The dance hall scene, in which Stewart plays piano with Duke Ellington and whisks Laura Manion away, was filmed at the Mount Shasta Lodge, located in the small town of Michigamme, a few miles west of Marquette.[51] Among the extras dancing in the background was Voelker's youngest daughter Gracie.[52] The railroad station scene was filmed at the now long-closed Ishpeming train station,[53] and the car crash involving Parnell McCarthy was shot at night in Big Bay, using stunt doubles.[54] The final scene of the movie, where Biegler and McCarthy visit the Manion's abandoned campsite, was filmed near the same spot where the Petersons once lived in Perkins Park.

Preminger's first choice to play Biegler was James Stewart.[55] He was adamant about signing Stewart, despite the actor's busy schedule.[56] Stewart had won a best-actor Oscar for his performance in *Philadelphia Story*,[57] and he was a popular movie star, owing in large part to his many collaborations with directors Frank Capra,[58] Alfred Hitchcock[59] and Anthony Mann.[60] Preminger believed that Stewart's stature, combined with his consummate ability to portray a flamboyant and folksy trial litigator, would "assure box-office and Oscar clout."[61] His calculation proved to be correct: Stewart received his fifth and final Best Actor nomination for his work in *Anatomy*.[62]

Before Preminger came on the scene, Voelker had once suggested Henry Fonda for the role of Paul Biegler.[63] But Voelker's first choice for the part was always John Wayne.[64] Voelker and Wayne looked so much alike that they both could have been selected to fill out a police lineup, and it delighted Voelker whenever someone commented to him about the resemblance, which was striking, especially in Voelker's middle years.[65] Stewart, who was well acquainted with Wayne, was the first cast member to note the physical similarity between Voelker and the Duke, which included not only their physiognomies, but their height and impressive physical stature. Even Grace thought her husband "looked like John Wayne!"[66] Beyond their similar physical traits, Wayne had cultivated the on-screen persona of a rugged individual who struggled on the frontier, guided by an unwavering moral compass. Though, understandably, Voelker saw the Duke as the actor who would best embody his own dauntless character, he was pleased with Stewart's

126

performance, his initial preference for Wayne notwithstanding.[67]

Stewart later said that he considered Paul Biegler his most challenging role since George Bailey, in *It's A Wonderful Life*.[68] Stewart once commented, "It was worth all the extra effort. I spent a lot of time memorizing my lines for that movie. The picture demanded an awful lot of time and thought. As the defense attorney I knew I had to be glibber than usual. Trial lawyers are neither shy nor inarticulate. I read my script each night until I fell asleep."[69]

Paul Biegler was also Stewart's most controversial role. In an interview years after the movie's release, Stewart recalled, "I got an Oscar nomination for [*Anatomy of a Murder*], but boy, did I hear from my fan base. They thought it was very, very risqué and asked me not to do that kind of material anymore. And I didn't. Maybe I made a mistake."[70] Even Stewart's father was so offended by the sexual content of the film that he took out an ad in his local newspaper telling people not to see it.[71]

Despite the controversy it stirred, critics praised Stewart's portrayal of Paul Biegler. Bosley Crowther, film critic for *The New York Times*, wrote that "[s]lowly and subtly [Stewart] presents us [with] a warm, clever, adroit and complex man—and, most particularly, a portrait of a trial lawyer in action that will be difficult for anyone to surpass."[72]

Besides his Academy Award nomination, Stewart was named Best Actor at the Venice Film Festival, and the New York Film Critics voted him best actor over Charlton Heston for *Ben-Hur*.[73]

Preminger's first choice to play Laura Manion was Lana Turner, but the two clashed when the actress insisted on wearing designer gowns that Preminger believed would look "ridiculous" on an Army wife who lived in a trailer park.[74] Preminger told Turner's agent that if she would not comply with his wardrobe choices she could turn down the role; within half a day the offer was withdrawn.[75] Some claimed that Turner balked, in particular, at wearing the tight slacks favored by Laura Manion.[76] Turner denied all of this, saying "I would not walk out of a picture for anything as trivial as a costume. It was simply impossible to deal with Mr. Preminger's unpredictable temper."[77]

With Turner out of the running, Preminger next turned to Lee Remick, who had made her film debut just a year earlier in *A Face in the Crowd*.[78] Preminger was so impressed with Remick's performance in that film that he arranged to meet with her months before negotiations with Turner had collapsed. When Remick was introduced to Preminger she was eight-months pregnant.[79] Preminger told Remick that he had hired Turner for the role of Mrs. Manion and offered her the second lead, Mary Pilant.[80] Remick declined.[81] When Turner ultimately pulled out,

Preminger offered Remick the lead role and she accepted immediately.[82]

Remick's performance, so critical to the movie's success, was brilliant and nuanced. In her portrayal of Laura Manion, Remick possessed "an aura of old-fashioned femininity and submissiveness. She likes men and is flirtatious with them."[83] She is also vulnerable and damaged. Upon first meeting Mrs. Manion, Biegler's secretary Maida describes her as, "Soft. Easy. The type men can take advantage of and do."[84] Given all of the conflicting evidence about the alleged rape and the nuanced ambiguity of Remick's performance, the viewer cannot be sure what actually happened in Quill's car that fateful night. This is what jurors must have been thinking at the Peterson trial, and it is exactly the reaction that Preminger hoped to achieve in his film. Remick received a Golden Globe nomination for her portrayal of Laura Manion.[85]

The most surprising casting choice was Joseph Welch for the role of Judge Weaver. Reportedly, Spencer Tracy and Burl Ives were first considered, but Preminger ultimately settled on the real-life Boston attorney to preside over the trial. Welch had recently garnered fame through his prominent role at the Army-McCarthy hearings. In particular, he is remembered for his 1954 confrontation with Senator Joseph McCarthy, during which he famously chastised the Senator,

"Have you no sense of decency, sir, at long last? Have you left no sense of decency?"[86] This rebuke is widely seen as the beginning of the end of McCarthyism.

Welch joked that he took the role as Judge Weaver because "it looked like that was the only way I'd ever get to be a judge."[87] But he had other incentives. Besides being the highest paid actor in the film, Preminger acceded to Welch's demand that his new bride Agnes, whom he had married just three weeks earlier,[88] be cast as a juror.[89] Mrs. Welch can be seen in the film seated in the front row at the far right of the jury box, wearing a polka dot dress.

Preminger could have selected any number of experienced character actors to play Judge Weaver, but casting Welch had its special advantages. The addition of Welch

> offered, in a single stroke, the opportunity to coalesce the two warring natures of a producer: the artist and the businessman. [Preminger] felt that Welch would give exactly the right freshness to the film and add great reality to the trial sequences. He was equally aware that he was on the verge of the publicity coup of the year.[90]

It is difficult today to appreciate fully the notoriety and esteem that Welch enjoyed when he was cast for the movie. He was a national celebrity and a hero to many, and he had appeared on the cover of *Life Magazine*.[91] He brought a quirky charm and sense of authenticity to the role, while his gravitas, as the man who felled McCarthy at the height of his power by looking him in the eye as he rebuked him, enabled him to portray convincingly the role of the trial judge who controls the antics of the fierce litigators portrayed by Stewart (Biegler) and George C. Scott (Dancer). When Welch died on October 6, 1960, barely fifteen months after *Anatomy's* release, a local newspaper called him "perhaps the country's most famous lawyer."[92]

The production and filming of *Anatomy of a Murder* were a boon for Marquette County. The City Manager of Marquette called it "a godsend."[93] The area had suffered greatly the previous year when hundreds of miners were laid off.[94] With unemployment compensation about to run out for many, the movie promised to inject thousands of needed dollars into the community. All told, about one-quarter of the film's budget was spent on location.[95] The local newspaper reported that the production poured over a half-million dollars into area coffers.[96] Hotels, construction workers, drivers, food service employees, and a myriad of other local residents benefited, as did the film's many extras, who were paid $10 a day.[97] To his credit, Preminger insisted that the extras be paid at the same daily rate as those in Hollywood, even though he could have filled all the roles on location for much less.[98]

Casting and production of the film took only five months.[99] Shooting concluded on May 15, 1959, after only 46 days.[100] Preminger streamlined production by editing the movie as it was being filmed.[101] This was made possible through an arrangement with the Nordic Theater in Marquette, which enabled Preminger to view the rushes as they were being cut.[102] Preminger expressed his gratitude by hosting fund-raising premieres of the movie in Marquette and Ishpeming before the grand opening in Detroit.[103]

Preminger's film, like Voelker's manuscript, was much too long for commercial success in its original form. Preminger once estimated that the movie's running length would have been in excess of four hours had he not radically cut scenes and limited dialog.[104] Still, the final version of the film released to the public was unusually long, with a running time of two hours and forty minutes.[105]

The film's impact in the community extended beyond its financial benefits. When the train bringing the cast and crew arrived in Ishpeming from Wisconsin in near zero-degree temperatures, the *Mining News* reported that the "more than 200 persons gathered there to greet them were gripped with giddy excitement."[106] Michigan Governor G. Mennen Williams flew to Ishpeming to extend an official welcome to the cast and crew.[107] The arrival was telecast on the *Ed Sullivan Show*, and the production was covered by the national magazines *Life*, *Look*, *Newsweek,* and *Family Circle.*[108] In recognition of its enormous impact,

Anatomy of a Murder was named Michigan's Product of the Year for 1959.[109]

The cast and crew became a visible and positive presence in and around Marquette, and the area's social life revolved around the filming. The celebrity visitors regularly signed autographs and mingled with the locals, and they were "swamped with requests to officiate at anything from a hockey game to a hat-making contest."[110] Stewart danced with a local girl and took jeep rides in Big Bay with soldiers and children, including extras.[111] Duke Ellington, who scored the film and appeared in an uncredited role as Pie Eye, played his signature piece, "Take the 'A' Train," at a sorority dance.[112] Preminger visited an area hospital and supported local charities. Arthur O'Connell bought $4,000 of new carpeting for the rectory of a church in Ishpeming where he often practiced his lines.[113] Cast and crew members dined at area restaurants and tried pasties, a Cornish meat-pie staple in the Upper Peninsula. The first time Stewart was presented with a pasty, he eyed it cautiously and then asked the waitress, "How do I attack this?"[114] The cast and crew also took in a ski tournament at Suicide Hill,[115] and braved the cold to visit local beaches. A few Hollywood visitors even managed to go fishing with Voelker, who on one occasion gladly shared an excursion into the woods with Remick where they drank bourbon from tin cups.[116]

Several vignettes revolved around the Mather Inn, where the principal cast and crew stayed during filming. Even with two dinner seatings each evening, reservations were needed as scores of curiosity seekers traveled by train from all over Michigan's Upper Peninsula and northern Wisconsin for a chance to dine in the same room as Hollywood stars.[117] Celebrities would sometimes attract attention while performing mundane chores, such as when a curious group of onlookers gathered to watch Katherine Grant, who played Mary Pilant, wash clothes in a sink.[118] Eve Arden, who played Biegler's secretary Maida, signed the cast on the arm of a thirteen-year-old girl who was smuggled inside to see her.[119] Several high school boys were disciplined for trying to sneak into the Mather Inn one evening to steal a glimpse of Lee Remick;[120] one group chanted her name, scattering only after police were summoned.[121]

Julie Voelker Cohen, Voelker's middle daughter, shared a charming story about her father and Duke Ellington that occurred during the filming of the movie. Voelker, who by then had become good friends with Ellington, hosted the composer and a few guests one evening at his West Barnham Street home. After dinner, Ellington offered to play requests on Voelker's piano. Voelker asked if Ellington would mind if he recorded the performance on his prized new tape recorder. After initially hesitating because of contractual obligations, Ellington relented and permitted Voelker to tape the session if he promised not to share the recording with others. Time after time, Ellington began playing a piece only to be interrupted by Voelker, who signaled that the recorder was not operating correctly. Finally, Voelker announced that the machine was working, and Ellington played several songs. Actually, Voelker never was able to figure out how to operate the contraption that evening, but pretended that he had, fearing that Ellington and the other guests were growing impatient and annoyed.[122]

When *Anatomy* was released, on July 1, 1959, it was well received by the film industry, general public, and legal community. Although it won no Oscars, it garnered seven Academy Award nominations,[123] four Golden Globe nominations,[124] and three Grammy Awards.[125] It grossed nearly $12 million at the box office,[126] a considerable box office at that time, and it earned an estimated $5.5 million in rentals in the U.S. and Canada during its first year of release.[127] The film was listed as No. 6 of the 25 "Greatest Legal Movies" by the American Bar Association,[128] and it has been used as a teaching tool in several law schools.[129]

Movie critics, then and later, were overwhelmingly effusive. The *Los Angeles Times* raved that *Anatomy of a Murder* was "[o]ne of the most extraordinary films ever made."[130] Adrian Turner, of *Radio Times* wrote, "This is probably the greatest courtroom drama ever made and it features James Stewart's finest screen performance."[131] Johnathan Rosenbaum, of the *Chicago Reader,* called it "spellbinding all the way, infused by an ambiguity about human personality and motivation that is Preminger's trademark, and the location shooting is superb."[132] Bosley Crowther, film critic for *The New York Times*, wrote,

> After watching an endless succession of courtroom melodramas that have more or less transgressed the bounds of human reason and the rules of advocacy, it is cheering and fascinating to see one that hews magnificently to a line of dramatic but reasonable behavior and proper procedure in a court. Such a one is *Anatomy of a Murder* . . . It is the best courtroom melodrama this old judge has ever seen . . . Outside of the fact that this drama gets a little tiring in spots—in its two hours and forty minutes, most of which is spent in court—it is well-nigh flawless as a picture of an American court at work, of small-town American characters and of the average sordidness of crime.[133]

And *Anatomy's* appeal has endured: in June 2008, after polling over 1,500 people from the creative community, the American Film Institute published its 10 Top 10 (the best 10 films in 10 "classic" American film genres). *Anatomy of a Murder* was selected as the seventh best film in the courtroom drama, even after 50 years of competition from films in the genre that *Anatomy* virtually created.[134]

Not all reaction to the film was so positive. By today's standards, the movie seems relatively tame, and retroactively received a "PG" rating. But when it was released, in the late 1950s, the film was controversial and the target of protests. It was even briefly banned in Chicago because of its explicit dialog and sexual themes.[135] While most of the correspondence Voelker received about the movie was positive, a few letters were critical of the movie's subject matter and language. One concerned viewer wrote to Voelker that:

> Things fit only to discuss in a Dr.'s office or a bedroom are freely mentioned in the story. Also using God's name in vain and profanity never helps any situation-real or imaginary. We expect decency of a judge. You obviously are trying to follow the trend today and go all out in an effort to be nasty. Wake up![136]

Similarly, although most local residents reacted favorably to the film and the economic benefits it generated, some objected to it because of its suggestive content. This antipathy is illustrated by the saga of cement impressions made by the film's cast. These handprints and footprints were to be placed near an entrance to the Marquette courthouse once filming had concluded. Because some residents protested about the movie's racy content, the impressions were never installed.[137] Instead, they were secreted for years in a farmer's barn, and only much later displayed in front of an area theater.[138]

Owing to their extended separation from family and friends during the production of the movie, cast and crew often socialized together in the evenings. A favorite spot for cast members to gather was the basement lounge of the Roosevelt Night Club. The Roosevelt was within a short walk of the Mather Inn, where cast members resided.[139]

Voelker jokingly referred to the Roosevelt as the local "Club 21."[140] At

both the Roosevelt and the Mather, Duke Ellington would regularly

entertain on the piano while cast and crew sang along and danced.[141]

Murray Hamilton, who portrayed Paquette, would sometimes accompany

Ellington on the guitar.[142] Hamilton and Orson Bean, who portrayed the

defense psychiatrist Dr. Smith, occasionally performed impromptu

plays.[143] Joseph Welch organized marathon gin rummy tournaments

during breaks in filming and after hours.[144]

　　　After filming the dance club scene at the Mount Shasta Lodge, at

about 2:00 a.m., the principal cast and crew returned to the Roosevelt in

search of food and drink. They pounded on the door until Gigs Gagliardi,

the owner, awoke and greeted them. Half asleep, Gigs said he was not

going to fix breakfast for the group, but he would allow them access to

the downstairs kitchen so they could prepare it for themselves. For the

next several hours, Hollywood A-listers took turns frying bacon and eggs

and mixing Bloody Marys.[145]

　　　As filming drew to a close, Eve Arden, who played Biegler's

secretary Maida, suggested that cast members and principals indelibly

autograph a long side wall in the Roosevelt's basement lounge.[146] The

wall, which is about seven feet high and twenty-three feet long, bears thirty-eight signatures, each first written in pencil and then painted over a cream background in vivid black and red paint, the same colors used in Saul Bass's logo for the film. In addition to the autographs, Bass himself painted the iconic black corpse figure from the logo in the center of the wall.

The wall famously bears the signatures of Voelker, Preminger, Stewart, Remick, Welch, and all of the other principal cast and crew. Two of the writings on the wall are more obscure. On the left side, the inscription "BLOODY FRANKIE – Sign or you don't get it," was written by the film's production paymaster, known to all as Bloody Frankie. It was in fact a cryptic instruction that the cast and crew must sign the wall if they wanted to be paid. On the right side, an American Airlines logo with a signature beneath it reflects that even the pilot of the chartered cast transport craft had to sign the wall to receive his pay.[147]

With iron mining on the wane and the local economy suffering, the Roosevelt shuttered its doors decades ago. Globe Publishing, which produces a variety of silk-screened and printed materials, bought the building, and has preserved "the wall." An observant viewer of *Anatomy ofa Murder* might note that a calendar in the Sheriff's office prominently bears the name "Globe Printing Company."[148] On occasion, visitors are allowed downstairs to view the wall, which is usually draped with blankets to prevent it from being damaged by the solvents and ink used in the silk-screening process. When the covers are removed, the wall is revealed: large red and black signatures, some nearly a yard long, are randomly intermingled on a dry-wall surface covered with a protective coating that has yellowed over the years. The wall evokes an *avant garde* rendering of the bottom portion of the Declaration of Independence. With the passage of time, it has been transformed from a whimsical artifact into nothing less than a fascinating and historically significant work of art. It bears witness to a magical moment in time when the sleepy little town of Ishpeming hosted Hollywood royalty.

Images

Many images courtesy of Central Upper Peninsula
and NMU Archives

John Voelker's father and mother, George Voelker (left) and Annie (nee Traver) Volker (right) (Images courtesy of Central Upper Peninsula and NMU Archives).

John Volker's childhood home, Ishpeming,
Michigan, which was the site of Paul
Biegler's home and office in the movie
(Photo by author).

John Voelker as a child (left), and the painting commissioned by John Voelker of his late son, Robert (right) (Image on the left courtesy of Central Upper Peninsula and NMU Archives) (Photo on the right by author, with permission by Ernest "Woody" Woods).

Purportedly George Voelker's saloon, Ishpeming, Michigan (above), and the Carnegie Library, Ishpeming, Michigan (below) (Image above courtesy of Central Upper Peninsula and NMU Archives) (Photo below by author).

From left to right, Lieutenant Coleman Peterson, the defendant, Charlotte Peterson with her dog George, and John Voelker (Image courtesy of Central Upper Peninsula and NMU Archives).

Mike Chenoweth, the victim (Image above courtesy of Central Upper Peninsula and NMU Archives).

Lumberjack Tavern, Big Bay, Michigan, circa 1958 (above) and today (below) (Image above courtesy of Central Upper Peninsula and NMU Archives) (Photo below by author).

Silhouette depicting the location of the victim's body (top left), shattered glass in the mirror over the bar (bottom left), and the victim after the shooting (right), all in the Lumberjack Tavern (Images at the bottom left and right courtesy of Central Upper Peninsula and NMU Archives) (Photo at top left by author).

Mike Chenoweth's autographed pistol, which he never drew before being shot and killed (Photo by author).

The Petersons' trailer (top left), entry sign (top right), and the wooden flagpole (bottom left), all at Perkins Park, Big Bay, Michigan. The flagpole is seen in the movie (Image top left courtesy of Central Upper Peninsula and NMU Archives) (Photos top right and bottom left by author).

Marquette County Courthouse, Marquette, Michigan, circa 1958 (left) and today (right), featuring its thirty-two steps to the main entrance (Image on left courtesy of Central Upper Peninsula and NMU Archives) (Photo on right by author).

Interior of the Courthouse circa1958 (top left), interior of the Courthouse today (top right), and Voelker's portrait in the Courthouse near the men's room door, which was relabeled and served as the entrance to the law library in the film (Image on top left courtesy of Central Upper Peninsula and NMU Archives) (Photos at top right and bottom left by author).

153

The Prosecution Team: Irving Beattie (left) and
Edmond Thomas (right) (Image courtesy of Central
Upper Peninsula and NMU Archives).

Jurors in the Peterson case. Max Muelle, the youngest juror, is seen in the top row, second from the left (Image courtesy of Central Upper Peninsula and NMU Archives).

Big Bay Inn, later renamed Thunder Bay Inn, Big Bay, Michigan. The new addition constructed for the movie is in the left foreground. The Inn was painted pink so that it would film better in black and white (Photo by author).

Mount Shasta Inn, Michigamme, Michigan, the site of the dancehall scene featuring Duke Ellington (Photo by author).

Cast and crew of Anatomy of a Murder, with John Voelker in the foreground, flanked immediately behind, from left to right, by George C. Scott, who played Claude Dancer, the prosecutor from Lansing, Brooks West, who played Mitch Ludwick, the local prosecutor, Jimmy Stewart, who played Paul Biegler, the defense counsel, and Lee Remick, who played Laura Manion, the defendant's wife (Image courtesy of Central Upper Peninsula and NMU Archives).

John Voelker (fourth from the left) with cast and crew, including Jimmy Stewart (second from the left) and Otto Preminger (third from the left). Voelker's resemblance to John Wayne is striking (Image courtesy of Central Upper Peninsula and NMU Archives).

John Voelker (left) teaching Jimmy Stewart (right), who played Paul Biegler in the movie, how to light a Parodi, the small Italian cigar that Voelker favored (Image on left courtesy of Central Upper Peninsula and NMU Archives).

John Voelker (left) teaching Katherine Crosby (right), who played Mary Pilant in the movie, how to tie a fishing line (Image on left courtesy of Central Upper Peninsula and NMU Archives).

Left side of the autograph wall in the basement of Globe Printing, Inc., Ishpeming, Michigan (Photo by author, with the permission of Globe Printing, Inc.).

Right side of the autograph wall in the basement of Globe Printing, Inc., Ishpeming, Michigan (Photo by author, with the permission of Globe Printing, Inc.).

John Voelker, Associate Justice of the
Michigan Supreme Court (Image courtesy of
Central Upper Peninsula and NMU
Archives).

Frenchman's Pond (Photo by author, with permission by Ernest "Woody" Woods).

"Uncle Tom's Cabin," with the author in the foreground (Photo by Ernest "Woody" Woods, and with the permission of Mr. Woods).

Interior of "Uncle Tom's Cabin."

It looks as it did in Voelker's time (Photos by author, with the permission of Ernest "Woody" Woods).

Voelker and his first "fish car," a 1928 Ford Model A named "Buckshot" (Image courtesy of Central Upper Peninsula and NMU Archives).

Voelker at "Uncle Tom's Cabin" in his later years (Image courtesy of Central Upper Peninsula and NMU Archives).

Voelker and his wife, Grace (Image
courtesy of Central Upper Peninsula
and NMU Archives).

Voelker in his element, fly fishing at
Frenchman's Pond (Image courtesy
of Frederick Baker, Jr.).

PART III

COMMENTARY AND REFLECTIONS

CHAPTER 9 – THE TITLE

Both novel and film are rich with details worthy of deeper consideration and analysis. Voelker precisely invites this; he intends, through the authentic portrayal of the criminal justice process, to reflect the ambiguity and complexity of real life with its many gray areas. Voelker knows that both legal counsel and juries must sometimes grapple with complicated and morally ambiguous situations, forcing them to decide and choose from among conflicting and sometimes unsatisfying resolutions. In *Anatomy*, Voelker masterfully uses the story of a murder trial to expose and explore a variety of ethical and moral issues, carefully refraining from attempting to dictate how they should be properly resolved. He also raises the more fundamental question of whether any human institution can consistently and appropriately resolve the question of guilt or innocence, what one might refer to as "true justice." Voelker leaves it to his readers to act as literary "jurors," allowing them to evaluate for themselves the choices and behavior of his characters, especially the attorneys. When the reader renders its verdict on Paul Biegler's defense of Lieutenant Manion, he also, by proxy, passes judgment on John Voelker's defense of Lieutenant Peterson. The thoughtful reader who passes a considered judgment on the actions and choices of the prosecution and the defense is also obliged, perhaps uncomfortably, to acknowledge and come to terms with his or her own values and ethics.

The title Voelker selected for his novel provides one touchstone for reflecting on the issues Voelker raises in his novel. As Shakespeare asked, "What's in a name? / That which we call a rose / By any other name would smell as sweet."[1] His idea, of course, was that the substantive quality of a thing remains the same regardless of what one calls it. However true that may be, it is also often true that what we choose to call a thing can be freighted with a meaning that no other words could convey, which may not only describe but also impart the nature and content of the thing. Never is this more so than for the title the author chooses for a novel. Just as Lake Superior, the largest freshwater body in the world, could never be dubbed, "Lake Inferior" or "Lake Mediocre," expectant parents, marketing experts, and novelists alike all understand the power and import of a name. The "name" given to a novel—that is, its title—is typically selected to convey ideas and promote sales. When the title of a novel refers to legal terminology, the particular words that are used can take on additional significance and call for special precision. This is surely true for Voelker's great work, *Anatomy of a Murder*.

The original working title of Voelker's novel about the Peterson trial was simply and fittingly *The Trial*. After toiling on his draft manuscript for several months, Voelker said that he was moved to change its title to *Anatomy of a Murder*. The source of his inspiration was Robert Burton's famous text, *Anatomy of Melancholy*.[2] Voelker claimed that he opted for the now-iconic new title simply because he preferred the sound of it. Although this is likely true enough, it is surely only part of the reason for the change. A closer examination of the facts and law demonstrates that Voelker's decision was not as frivolous as he pretended; he selected his new title, at least in part, because it conveyed a particular meaning critical to his novel's underlying theme.

The revised title prominently includes the word "murder." This same legal term is immediately invoked in the very first sentence of the book's introduction, which reads: "This is the story of a murder, of a murder trial, and of some of the people who engaged or became enmeshed in the proceedings."[3] "Murder"[4] has a venerable and well-established legal definition—it is a homicide[5] committed with malice aforethought[6] without legal justification[7] or legal excuse.[8] Voelker, a student of the law, surely knew the meaning of the word "murder," so his choice to include that word in his new title certainly was informed by and consistent with its meaning under the law. He could have chosen another term—"homicide" or "killing"— that conveyed the victim's death without implying the defendant's guilt—but he chose "murder. "This choice was conscious, purposeful, and imbued with significance.

Also consider that "insanity," the criminal defense successfully asserted by Lieutenant Manion in the novel and Lieutenant Peterson in real life, is likewise a legal term of art with a well-settled definition. Under Michigan law at the time of the Peterson trial through the present day, insanity is an affirmative defense that excuses a defendant from criminal responsibility due to a lack of cognition, lack of volition, or both.[9] A defendant may be legally insane because of a cognitive deficiency, i.e., an inability to distinguish right from wrong, or because of a volitional deficiency, i.e., an inability to conform his conduct to the law. And, of course, a defendant might be deemed insane based on both cognitive and volitional grounds.

A defendant who is determined to be insane, for whatever reason, cannot be convicted of a crime under the traditional criminal law, including the Michigan murder statute. To hold such a defendant criminally responsible for any offense, let alone murder, would be inconsistent with both the retributive and utilitarian theories of culpability and punishment. It would offend the principles of retributive justice, because one who lacks the requisite culpable state of mind does not deserve to, and indeed, cannot be found criminally responsible. It would likewise conflict with utilitarian-based theories of guilt because an insane person cannot be deterred by criminal punishment, and any legitimate rehabilitation and incapacitation objectives can be better and more fittingly accomplished through civil commitment.

It follows from the very definition of the crime of murder that if one charged with murder is found not guilty by reason of insanity, no murder has been committed by the person so acquitted.[10] Consider, then, that if Lieutenant Manion were actually insane when he killed Quill, the title of Voelker's novel would be seriously misleading if not outright mendacious: his novel would not be "the story of a murder," as the title proclaims and the introduction asserts. Put simply, if Lieutenant Manion murdered Quill he was not insane; conversely, if Lieutenant Manion was insane he did not "murder" Quill, even if he killed him. Mere homicide is not murder if the perpetrator is not culpable.

As a seasoned criminal attorney, Voelker was surely aware of the meanings of these basic legal terms, as well as their precise import in the context of the tale he told.[11] Further, as a writer who meticulously crafted and revised every word and page of his novel, it seems clear that Voelker chose his words carefully, especially when employing legal terminology. Voelker insisted on preserving his title when a screenwriter suggested an alternative that omitted the words "of a," observing that "each *murder* is

different."[12] Voelker's scrupulous concern for legal accuracy is further

confirmed by the many technical corrections he recommended to the

screenplay and during the shooting of the film. Even after his novel was

completed and published, Voelker contacted St. Martins to correct

printing errors and offer suggestions for improving the text in future

editions.[13] Taken together, all of these facts and inferences lead to the

unmistakable conclusion that Voelker's decision to substitute "Murder"

for "Trial" in his title was far more deliberate and purposeful than simply

reflecting a preference for how it sounded.

If we accept that Voelker's choice of "Murder" for his title was

calculated and meaningful, then the only reasonable explanation is that

the title was intended to inform the reader at the outset that the

defendant, Lieutenant Manion, was factually and legally guilty of that

crime. As a lawyer, Voelker opted to convey Lieutenant Manion's guilt

organically, by using a legal term of art. Yet, by writing in the first

person, rather than relying on an omniscient narrator to tell the reader

what to think, or on gimmicky flashbacks or other inauthentic literary

devices, Voelker forces the reader to do the work and conclude—based

on all of the facts, a deft explanation of the law, and the title itself—that

Lieutenant Manion is legally guilty of murder. There is no other plausible conclusion.

Had Voelker simply been enamored with the words "Anatomy" and "Murder," and insisted upon including them in his title only for this superficial reason, he would have been obliged by his deep allegiance to accuracy of language, to instead call his novel "*Anatomy of a Murder Trial,*" to avoid the title's unmistakable implication that Lieutenant Manion was, in fact, a murderer. The first eleven words *of Anatomy's* introduction, "This is the story of a murder [and] of a murder trial …,"[14] leave no doubt that Voelker was aware of his title's import.

To conclude otherwise—that Voelker's choice of "murder" was based solely on superficial reasons such as phonetics—requires several leaps of faith. First, it would entail discarding the maxim "*in arte non adveniunt aliqua accidentia*" ("in art there are no accidents'). Second, it would require us to accept at face value Voelker's sly explanation that his choice of "murder" was merely aesthetic, despite his full appreciation of the precise meaning of the legal term he chose, debasing Voelker both as an author and as a lawyer. Even putting all of this aside, any fair reading of *Anatomy's* first few chapters reveals unmistakably that Lieutenant Manion is actually guilty of murder. Further, because Biegler's role as an advocate exempts him from forming that judgment, he proceeds to defend Manion with the zeal that the presumption of innocence requires.

This is precisely what Voelker intended the reader to understand, and it is what a perceptive and honest reader must acknowledge at the outset, however conspiratorially. Only once one grants both that Lieutenant Manion is factually and legally guilty of murder, and that Biegler is certain of his guilt, can the reader fully appreciate the moral and ethical dimensions of Biegler's aggressive defense of his client. The percipient reader must confront the uncomfortable fact that Biegler is not on the side of the angels in his defense of Lieutenant Manion. Biegler is not a heroic figure tilting against stacked odds to prevent the wrongful conviction of an innocent man, nor is he even just dutifully putting the prosecution's evidence to the test in a case in which guilt is genuinely in doubt. Rather, Biegler is unapologetically striving to undermine the letter of the criminal law and get his guilty client off on a murder charge. For Biegler, it is enough that the awesome power of the State, and all of the resources at its command, are arrayed against his client. As one presumed innocent, Manion is entitled to a defense.

In the end, Voelker presents the Manion trial as a contest between dueling combatants, and he offers three possible choices for the reader's rooting interest: the prosecution team, Lieutenant Manion, and Biegler. The reader, of course, will not root for the prosecutors to prevail, for a variety of obvious reasons. Similarly, the reader will recoil at rooting for an arrogant wife-beater such as Lieutenant Manion. Inevitably, therefore, the reader is cleverly induced either to view the trial dispassionately, which is all but impossible given Voelker's skill as a storyteller, or to choose the only remaining option and root for Biegler, though his resourceful and relentless efforts are devoted to absolving a murderer. *Anatomy* skillfully involves the reader as a participant in the ethical and moral issues it poses by seducing the reader to root for Biegler. And when the reader roots for Biegler, he must acknowledge that he prefers jury nullification over the law's strict application, at least in this case.

Readers who consider themselves to be law-abiding and of good moral character may find this an unsettling experience. Beginning with its title, then, *Anatomy* is a crucible in which the reader explores not only the characters and moral compasses of those involved in the murder trial, but his or her own, as well. And keep in mind, Voelker is only getting started.

CHAPTER 10 – THE "LECTURE"

The most famous, or perhaps infamous, ethical question presented by *Anatomy of a Murder* is Biegler's conduct during what Voelker refers to as "the Lecture." An understanding of the applicable law and rules of professional conduct brings the problem it poses into stark relief.

As defense counsel, Biegler of course had a duty to represent his client zealously, without regard to his client's guilt, within the bounds of the law and ethics.[1] The legal and policy reasons for imposing this duty extend beyond the rights of any individual client; this rule benefits society, and the legal system, as a whole. The theory on which our adversary system of justice rests is founded on the belief that a zealous defense at a criminal trial forces the prosecution to prove every element of the offense charged beyond a reasonable doubt, as required by the most fundamental precept of our system: the presumption of innocence. This provides some assurance that prosecutors will bring to trial only those cases in which they believe the defendant is guilty and they can prove it to a jury. The clash of opposing forces in our adversary system of justice is traditionally accepted as the best way to ferret out the truth and protect the innocent.[2] This adversary dialectic, coupled with the heavy burden of proof allocated to the prosecution by the presumption of innocence and the requirement of proof beyond a reasonable doubt, provide the highest possible degree of confidence that those convicted of a crime are truly guilty.[3]

Most reasonable people approve and accept defense counsel's role in achieving these desirable ends, even if we sometimes recoil from a particularly repugnant defendant, or object to the time, effort, and cost required to convict an obviously guilty defendant. We deem defense counsel's actions legitimate, even if we consider his client guilty, because they serve a higher objective.

But when Biegler outlines the possible defenses to a charge of premeditated murder to Manion in his cell, he seems to be doing something quite different. In "the Lecture," Biegler consciously enables, and thereby tacitly encourages, a murderer to fabricate a defense where one does not exist to create a possible path to an acquittal. Voelker makes it crystal clear to the reader that Biegler recognizes that insanity is his client's only plausible defense. Further, to succeed as a defense, the "insanity" must be temporary, because Manion plainly was in full control of his faculties both shortly before and soon after the shooting. Voelker makes it clear that the temporary insanity defense is neither based on Biegler's independent evaluation of the facts and application of the law, nor the organic conclusion to be drawn from his client's authentic reconstruction of events. Rather, Biegler's "Lecture" artfully and disingenuously implants the defense in Manion by equipping him to embrace a version of events that can lead to jury nullification. Voelker ensures that the reader understands all of this through Biegler's first-person ruminations, his conversations with Parnell McCarthy, and his detailed descriptions of Biegler's interactions with his client and others.

Put simply, there would be no insanity defense were it not for Biegler's machinations. When Biegler first meets with Lieutenant Manion, it quickly becomes clear to him that his future client has never even considered the possibility of claiming insanity, presumably because Manion knows he was in full control of faculties when he killed Quill. At first, Lieutenant Manion tries to defend the killing as a conscious decision justified by the "unwritten law,"[4] but Biegler quickly disabuses him of the notion that this would constitute a legal defense.[5] Biegler realizes that he desperately needs the insanity defense to win at trial, but he is also fully aware that the ethical rules of his profession forbid him to overtly suggest the defense to Lieutenant Manion. The current version of this rule, Model Rule of Professional Conduct 3.4(b), Fairness to Opposing Party and Counsel, provides that a lawyer may not "counsel or assist a witness to testify falsely."[6] So this is Biegler's dilemma: he can prevail at trial only if he can assert the insanity defense to provide a "legal peg"[7] for jury nullification, but the *idea* that Lieutenant Manion was insane must originate with the defendant (who believes he was sane), not his lawyer (who also believes he was sane).

Biegler navigates this razor's edge with a rhetorical ploy familiar to defense lawyers, which he disingenuously refers to as, "the Lecture." Speaking through Biegler, Voelker writes:

> The Lecture is an ancient device that lawyers use to coach their clients so that the client won't quite know he has been coached and his lawyer can still preserve the face-saving illusion that he hasn't done any coaching. For coaching clients, like robbing them, is not only frowned upon, it is downright unethical and bad, very bad. Hence the Lecture, an artful device as old as the law itself, and one used constantly by some of the nicest and most ethical lawyers in the land. 'Who, me? I didn't tell him what to say,' the lawyer can later comfort himself. 'I merely explained the law, see.' It is a good practice to scowl and shrug here and add virtuously: 'That's my duty, isn't it?' Verily, the question, like expert lecturing, is unchallengeable. I was ready to do my duty by my client and he sat regarding me quietly, watchfully, as I lit a new cigar.[8]

Now that Biegler has explicitly described his intent and purpose, "the Lecture" may commence. Over the next several pages, Biegler deftly shepherds Lieutenant Manion on a journey of self-discovery that leads to his epiphany: he must have been insane when he shot Quill. This revelation is based not on Manion's sudden recollection of his actual mental state at the time of the shooting, but rather, upon his belated realization that no other defense strategy can lead to his acquittal.[9] Biegler has achieved his objective: his client now has a viable defense.

The initial question is whether Biegler has secured the ability to assert this defense in a manner consistent with the rules of professional conduct. Commenting on "the Lecture," Professors Michael Asimov and Shannon Mader correctly explain:

> There is a fine line between advising a client about what the applicable law provides (which is proper) and suborning perjury by helping the client concoct a false version of the facts (which is improper). . . . Obviously, this rule is difficult to enforce because conversations between lawyers and clients or witnesses that might violate the rule occur in the privacy of the lawyer's office. Besides, the rule is vague and many possible violations, like Biegler's lecture, fall into a gray area between proper and improper conduct.[10]

A major impediment to the enforcement of this prohibition in actual practice—the veil of the attorney-client privilege and the resulting absolute secrecy of their discussions—has been lifted in *Anatomy*; the reader knows precisely what each has said to the other and why they have said it. The reader is even told what the parties are thinking. With no need to speculate about the parties' dialogue and motives, the legal and moral issues "the Lecture" raises are clearly visible to the reader.

Professor Timothy Holt expresses the legal implications of "the Lecture" as follows:

> Manion poses a major problem of professional responsibility for Biegler because of his reluctance to tell his side of the story unless Biegler first tells him the law. That puts Biegler in an ethical quandary familiar to anyone who has practiced law. Telling the client the law in advance of hearing the facts will allow the client to shape his story to fit

the law, and may subject the lawyer to a charge of suborning perjury. Rules of professional conduct provide that a lawyer should not assist a witness to testify falsely. On the other hand, some experts in the field of professional ethics argue that a lawyer is entitled to act as if he did not know that his client might perjure himself. These experts maintain that the lawyer's primary task is advocacy and that the judicial system will be best protected against fraud and perjury by the effective working of the adversary system. Biegler tells Manion just enough to help his client and probably only enough to avoid a charge of unethical conduct.[11]

Judged by letter of the law, Biegler's conduct most probably complies with formal standards of professional responsibility. But though his actions are ethically defensible,[12] the broader question Voelker invites, indeed, forces the thoughtful reader to consider, is whether Biegler's conduct is *morally* justified, especially when he employs "the Lecture" to assist a guilty murderer to avoid a conviction.

Additional circumstances not relevant under the rules of professional ethics may influence the conclusion a lay person reaches in this case. First, consider the victim, Quill. He is a despicable human being, and perhaps a violent rapist, who engenders little sympathy. Next, consider Lieutenant Manion. Despite his many serious faults, he is a more sympathetic character than Quill. Although Lieutenant Manion is unlikeable and perhaps struck and injured his wife in a jealous rage, he is also a decorated military officer and a combat veteran who has experienced the stress of battle. Regardless of whether his wife was

190

initially receptive to Quill's advances, or even consented to them, Manion is understandably enraged by Quill's brutish conduct.

Finally, consider Biegler. He is portrayed neither as a heroic figure, like Atticus Finch in *To Kill a Mockingbird*, nor as a villainous archetype, like attorney Ed Concannon in *The Verdict*. Rather, Biegler is a real person: decent, talented, and flawed. In the movie, Biegler could be describing himself when he tells Mary Pilant, "As a lawyer, I've had to learn that people aren't just good or bad, but people are many things."[13] He is likeable, and we connect with him as we are told the story through his first-person narrative. More than this, he has zealously fulfilled his legal and ethical duties to his ungrateful client and the system, even as he naively trusts his inherently untrustworthy client.

On the other hand, Biegler seems to be motivated, at least in part, by personal animosity towards his successor. He also may be tempted to cut the odd ethical corner out of personal financial considerations, as he is unlikely to collect his unpaid fee if his client is convicted and imprisoned. In addition, Biegler is hyper-competitive, even to the point of being perhaps a bit narcissistic, which impels him to avoid defeat at a high-profile public trial out of considerations purely personal to himself.[14] That Voelker includes this ingredient in the complex mix of Biegler's motivations bespeaks his own honesty and self-awareness.

Although the reader "irresistibly" roots for Biegler to prevail, one is left to contemplate the considerable moral baggage that accompanies this sentiment. Is it simply that the reader prefers Lieutenant Manion to Quill, or Biegler to his opponents? Is the reader charmed, even seduced, by Biegler's considerable courtroom skill and flair, regardless of the merits of his client's cause, as one might be impressed with a gifted surgeon who deftly operates on a loathsome patient unworthy of such skill.[15] Or is it, more viscerally, that the reader believes that Quill got what he deserved and Lieutenant Manion was justified in killing him? Put another way, has Voelker achieved "reader nullification," just as he achieved juror nullification in the Peterson trial?[16]

It is tempting to imagine that Voelker's portrayal of "the Lecture" might also be an exercise in personal introspection. Voelker did not live an unexamined life. Throughout his published works and personal journals, Voelker wages an unrelenting campaign for truth and against injustice. An early journal entry reads, "There is no substitute for personal integrity..."[17] Another journal entry fairly rails against the injustice of the price his integrity exacts: "With a mortgage on the house and loans at three banks the irony of the situation is superb ... The penalty for not being a grabber and a cheat is poverty. This is the age when those on the 'make' inherit the earth."[18] On the other hand, Voelker was a durable, battle-tested candidate for public office, experienced in the rough and tumble of political campaigns. There is little doubt that over the years he had to navigate the murky waters of influence peddling and backroom deals. And like Biegler, Voelker was a result-oriented and highly competitive veteran of trial litigation.

With all of this as background, consider whether Voelker compromises his core values when he administers "the Lecture," and where, if ever, he seems willing to draw a firm line regarding counsel's ethical responsibilities. On the one hand, even acknowledging that perhaps we confuse the author with a fictional protagonist, Voelker (Biegler) enthusiastically asserts an unmeritorious defense (temporary insanity) to seek the acquittal of a guilty murderer. On the other hand, he feels compelled to comply with applicable ethical prohibition against suborning perjury (via "the Lecture") when endeavoring to do so. Further, Voelker (Biegler) is more than willing throughout the trial to ask improper questions, or even to suggest the existence of inadmissible evidence, if it will help his cause, yet he strenuously (and perhaps a bit hypocritically) objects when the prosecution seeks to do likewise. The distinctions Voelker draws might seem indefensible, even unprincipled, unless viewed in the larger context of the adversarial character of the American criminal justice system. Perhaps Voelker is positing that a litigator is duty-bound to obey all applicable rules outside the courtroom (such as when meeting privately with a client) precisely because these activities are largely self-regulated, and thus depend upon each counsel's good-faith adherence to ethical standards. But once the trial begins, the same imperative does not apply, because opposing counsel and the judge are present to invoke and enforce the rules and restrain counsels' excesses. Applying this interpretation, the adversary system relieves litigators of an absolute duty to self-regulate their conduct when they enter the crucible of the courtroom, as each counsel's behavior can be policed by the judge and his opponent.

Through his alter ego Biegler, Voelker confronts the question whether he acted with integrity in defending Lieutenant Peterson. We can only speculate whether Voelker believes he crossed a moral or ethical line by elevating form over substance when he deployed "the Lecture" in the Peterson case. We cannot be sure whether or how he reconciled the artful machinations he used to present a winning insanity defense with his core principles of justice and fair play. But the conclusion is inescapable that Voelker critically examined the legitimacy of his own actions, just as he invites the reader to examine Biegler's conduct.

CHAPTER 11 – ETHICAL ISSUES AND THE PROSECUTOR

Prosecutors and defense counsel have complementary but distinct and often adversarial functions and ethical responsibilities. Defense counsel, like Voelker and Biegler, are obliged to be laser-focused on achieving the best results possible for their clients (usually an acquittal, if avoiding a trial is not possible) within the bounds of the law. The American Bar Association Standards for the Defense Function, Standard 4-1.2(b), provides:

> Defense counsel have the difficult task of serving both as officers of the court and as loyal and zealous advocates for their clients. The primary duties that defense counsel owe to their clients, to the administration of justice, and as officers of the court, are to serve as their clients' counselor and advocate with courage and devotion; to ensure that constitutional and other legal rights of their clients are protected; and to render effective, high-quality legal representation with integrity.[1]

In contrast, a prosecutor's fundamental obligation is to serve justice and not simply obtain convictions. The American Bar Association Standards for the Prosecution Function, Standard 3-1.2(b), instructs that:

> The primary duty of the prosecutor is to seek justice within the bounds of the law, not merely to convict. The prosecutor serves the public interest and should act with integrity and balanced judgment to increase public safety both by pursuing appropriate criminal charges of appropriate severity, and by exercising discretion to not pursue criminal charges in appropriate circumstances. The prosecutor should

seek to protect the innocent and convict the guilty, consider the interests of victims and witnesses, and respect the constitutional and legal rights of all persons, including suspects and defendants.[2]

As a long-time D.A., Voelker recognized a prosecutor's imperative to seek justice when he wrote that a person entrusted with this office has "the duty of carefully investigating the facts of each case brought on for trial; that he [owes] a duty to the defendant, as much as to the complainant and the public, not only to know his case, but at all times to be fair to all concerned."[3] Voelker explained that as a prosecutor he rarely asked the jury to convict, as he believed this would "reduce the People's case to the competitive level of wrangling civil litigants."[4] Further, he cautioned that a prosecutor's duty to justice instructs that he "cannot operate in a legal vacuum . . . [nor is] the 'just' way to handle his cases always to be found lurking in thick books."[5]

Conventional wisdom holds that the adversary system operates at its best only when the often-conflicting imperatives of the prosecution and the defense vigorously clash within the context of a criminal trial. Given the prosecution's overriding obligation with respect to justice and fair play, however, it is clear that defense attorney Paul Biegler is not the only litigator in *Anatomy of a Murder* whose conduct raises legal and ethical concerns. The behavior—or better stated, the misbehavior—of the prosecuting attorneys in the Manion trial, in service of their quest to

196

obtain a conviction at all costs, likewise invites careful scrutiny.

First, consider the prosecution's dogged efforts to prevent the introduction of evidence relating to Mrs. Manion's alleged rape by the victim. The fact of her rape, or at least the defendant's actual belief that this occurred, is obviously relevant to the issue of whether the defendant was temporarily insane. The prosecution knows this, but it is also aware that Biegler seeks to introduce such evidence as much to achieve jury nullification as to establish temporary insanity.[6] The prosecution fights hard to keep the evidence out for no other reason than that it will hurt its case, both because the jury may conclude the defendant was insane and also because it may cause them to acquit regardless of the defendant's legal guilt. Although courts and commentators often disapprove of jury nullification, it remains an accepted basis for acquittal.[7] In its efforts to exclude evidence of rape, the prosecutors seem just as blatantly result-oriented as defense counsel Biegler.

More broadly, Voelker is troubled by the prosecution's use of a criminal trial as a means to resolve and impose accountability in response to legally irrelevant but popularly held attitudes and pressures. Voelker summarizes this concern in his book *Small Town D.A.*, observing, "There are some prosecutions that the D.A. is occasionally forced to bring where the natural equities are so far with the defendant that the D.A. could never win, however brilliant; others so revolting to the public conscience that the D.A. could never lose, however stupid."[8]

Voelker was especially attuned to the impact of public pressure on high-profile cases involving sex offenses. He once lamented "how helpless the machinery of the law is to cure, even remotely, the situation [presented by a 'sex case']".[9] In a journal entry years before the Peterson trial, Voelker recalls a rape trial in which he was the prosecutor. The victim was a thirteen-year-old girl who was pulled off of her bike by three youths, dragged into the bushes, and raped. Voelker describes the crime and trial as "[a] sorry and pitiful case, in all of its aspects. We – the law – come in when the pustule bursts, wax indignant, and sent three boys away. Yet I would probably want to strangle the little bastards if they did it to one of our daughters. What to do?"[10]

Granting that the Peterson and Manion cases involve adults rather than youths, Voelker's concerns remain well placed. Is the blunt instrument of a criminal trial, with all of its elaborate procedures and limited range of possible outcomes, sometimes an insufficiently nuanced venue in which to achieve substantive justice, especially in some cases involving alleged sexual assaults? Are informal and more flexible procedures for resolving such matters sometimes preferable? Are prosecutors often obliged to exercise their discretion too harshly because of community expectations and pressures,[11] what Voelker derisively refers to in *Anatomy of a Murder* as "saving face?"[12] Should the prosecution team, and for that matter, Biegler, have been more open to a compromise resolution of the Manion case?

Voelker directly confronts a prosecutor's duty to seek compromise resolutions in *Small Town D.A.* There he recalls a case in which he was the prosecutor and a woman claimed to be raped. Following a thorough investigation, Voelker concluded that "whatever the degree of assault of which [the defendant] might have been guilty, it was certainly not rape."[13] Voelker also noted the forces that pressured him to prosecute the suspect for rape and thereby avoid political fallout notwithstanding his legal conclusion that such a charge would lack merit. Here Voelker draws a firm line and would not compromise his professional ethics, explaining:

> I felt that no man—prosecutor, senator or peasant—had any right to play politics with the destinies of his fellow men. It also seemed to me that a defendant was just as much entitled to receive the benefit of the doubt before an investigating prosecutor as he was later before a jury; and that when such a reasonable doubt plainly existed, it was the D.A.'s duty to "acquit" the man across his battered desk rather than force him through the useless expense and turmoil of a public trial. That was not only honorable; it also happened to be sound law.[14]

Another questionable action taken by the prosecutor, framed

especially well in the film, involves the irresistible impulse prong of the insanity defense. In the movie, Biegler and McCarthy discover a seemingly long-forgotten case precedent recognizing irresistible impulse during a weekend morning cramming session in the courthouse's law library. Later during the trial, the defense psychiatrist testifies that Lieutenant Manion was under the influence of an irresistible impulse when he shot and killed Quill. The expert also opines that Lieutenant Manion may have been capable of distinguishing right from wrong when the shooting occurred. The ability to distinguish right from wrong, the so-called cognitive approach to insanity, is universally recognized as an excuse defense in American jurisdictions. Exculpation via irresistible impulse, the so-called volitional approach to insanity, is comparatively rare. The relative obscurity of the irresistible impulse variant of the insanity defense provides a plausible explanation for why two small-town attorneys, such as Biegler and McCarthy, might be unaware that it was recognized under Michigan law.

After the defense psychiatrist had concluded his testimony, Claude Dancer, an Assistant Attorney General dispatched from the state capital to shore up the prosecution, asks to meet with Biegler and Judge Weaver in chambers. Once there, Dancer suggests that Biegler may want to change Lieutenant Manion's plea to guilty because even the defense expert conceded that Lieutenant Manion could have known right from wrong when he killed Quill. One might confidently assume that Dancer, an Assistant Attorney General and experienced prosecutor, would have been well aware that irresistible impulse was a recognized variant of the insanity defense under Michigan law. Indeed, Dancer admits as much in the movie later during this same in-chambers conference with the judge and defense counsel. Because Dancer was aware of the unfavorable case precedent relating to irresistible impulse, he had an obligation to "make timely disclosure to the defense of all evidence or information known to the prosecutor that tends to negate the guilt of the accused or mitigates the offense…"[15] Dancer makes no such disclosure to Biegler or the judge. More than this, he deceptively tries to leverage a guilty plea from the defendant based on its presumed ignorance of the law, which also violates his professional responsibilities.[16] Biegler, of course, has already uncovered the favorable precedent, and thus, his client is not prejudiced by Dancer's ploy.

If pressed about whether he violated his ethical duties, Dancer might argue that the irresistible impulse claim was a bogus defense for Lieutenant Manion, and thus he had no duty to broach the matter with the judge or defense counsel. Even assuming if Dancer's assessment of the strength of the defense position is supportable, however, this would not excuse him from his ethical obligation to reveal the unfavorable precedent

and then argue to the judge or jury that irresistible impulse was a sham in

that case. Dancer might also assert that he did not violate his ethical duties

as he never formally moved for a directed verdict. This response,

although factually accurate, would most likely be insufficient to excuse

Dancer's silence. A prosecutor has an overriding obligation to seek

justice, which includes a duty to prevent an injustice. This duty extends

beyond affirmative acts and includes preventing an injustice that would be

facilitated by a prosecutor's omission or silence in the face of unfavorable

precedent.

Voelker introduces another morally questionable decision by the

prosecution, this time relating to its conduct on rebuttal. Recall that after

the defense has rested, Dancer calls Duane Miller, a convict who shared a

cell with Lieutenant Manion while the latter awaited trial.[17] Miller's

testimony, which is embellished through Voelker's ear for dialects and

idioms, is that he

> heard the Lootenant chucklin' to himself durin' this noon
> hour an' I says, 'Things lookin' up, Lootenant?' and he
> chuckles some more an' says, 'You damned tootin', Buster,'
> or words to that affect, and I says, 'Buck up, Lootenant—
> I'll bet you my tonight's coffee ration you won't get more'n
> manslaughter outa this rap,' an' then he laffed out loud an'
> says, 'You got yourself a bet, Buster. I've already fooled my
> lawyer an' my psy—' I can't say it but he meant his brain
> doctor—'an' I'll bet you my pet lüger against this awful swill
> they call coffee here that I'll fool that bumpkin jury too an'

beat this rap all the way.'' The witness paused. 'That's all him and me said.'[18]

Biegler's cross-examination of Miller exposes that his testimony is likely fabricated and possibly the product of the prosecution's deployment of its own version of "the Lecture." Miller is not a very credible witness on his best day. Under the circumstances of his testimony at Manion's trial, he is virtually unbelievable. Biegler suggests to the jury through cross-examination that the prosecutors have deliberately facilitated the presentation of false testimony, i.e., they advised Miller that if he could recall and testify about an incriminating statement made by the defendant, this would be favorably considered with regard to his outstanding legal troubles. Despite Miller's compromised credibility, his testimony hurts the defense and Dancer knows that it will. Did Dancer successfully traverse the same legal tightrope as Biegler? Do two presumed reciprocal moral wrongs (Biegler's and Dancer's) balance the scales? Should the prosecutor be held to a higher standard that the defense in this regard? Is all of the dubious "witness preparation" and cross-examination that is undertaken by both sides in *Anatomy of a Murder* not only merely condoned, but perhaps even expected if not endorsed, by the adversary system's faith in confining the search for the truth to a fierce battle of opposing parties that presumptively achieves the desired objective?

Further, both Dancer and Biegler knowingly ask improper questions of several witnesses throughout the trial. They repeatedly do this, not out of inadvertence or ignorance, but rather to make a point and influence the jury. On one occasion, for example, after an objection to an improper question posed by Biegler is sustained by the judge, Lieutenant Manion asks Biegler, in whispered tones, how can the jury forget a question and the answer to it simply because the judge has instructed them to do so. Biegler responds that the jury cannot forget. This exchange exposes that Biegler, like the prosecutors, has knowingly posed objectionable questions to backdoor information to the jury that could not otherwise be introduced. Whenever either a prosecutor or defense counsel intentionally ask improper questions, they violate their ethical duties.[19]

One other matter involving ethical conduct, this time involving only defense counsel Biegler, should be mentioned. Mrs. Manion passed a polygraph examination regarding the question of whether she was raped. Although polygraphs are used for a variety of investigatory purposes, they are not admissible at trial as substantive evidence or to assess the credibility of witnesses.[20] The reasons for the exclusion include the uncertainty about their accuracy and the risk they will be accorded undue weight by juries.[21] Biegler is an experienced attorney and is well aware of this prohibition. He nonetheless deftly conveys to the jury, in part through the use of objectionable questions, that Mrs. Manion has passed the exam. Biegler may rationalize this as a necessary countermeasure to the prosecution's unjust efforts to exclude evidence of the alleged rape, which is clearly relevant and admissible. Still, an ethical attorney can hardly justify the use of improper questioning on the basis of his opponent's unethical behavior. In any event, Biegler's reference to the favorable polygraph results probably did not matter, either at the actual trial or during the fictionalized case, as jurors seemed well aware of those results before the trial began through media coverage and by word of mouth.

Voelker's depiction of prosecutorial misconduct serves several purposes. First, it gives the reader another reason to root for Biegler. Remember that Voelker has already dissected Biegler's moral compass via his exposition of "the Lecture." Dancer's misconduct casts Biegler's ethics in a more favorable light, making his actions seem less concerning for the reader or viewer. Second, the prosecutor's misconduct enflames the duel between the trial combatants and exposes their personal animosity. This makes for a more compelling story. Finally, the prosecutor's misconduct underscores the ethical tension that is often confronted by a defense counsel. A defense attorney, especially in a murder case, must zealously represent his client within the bounds of the law. When the prosecutor repeatedly violates his ethical duties, this raises the specter of how far the defense counsel ought to depart from the straight and narrow and instead fight fire with fire. If prosecutorial misconduct would deny the defendant a fair trial, his counsel must come to grips with what he is willing to do to balance the scales and seek substantive justice for his client.

CHAPTER 12 – THE JURY

The preceding observations about counsels' duties and ethical obligations highlight the critical role of the jury in the American legal system. Juries have an important but rather straightforward function: to find the facts and reach a verdict. The jury's fact-finding authority often includes resolving conflicting evidence and making credibility judgments about witnesses. The judge, on the other hand, is the sole source of the law, and the jury has no authority with regard to purely legal matters. Rather, the jury is required to accept the law as the judge instructs them and then apply it to the facts as they determine them to be. Once this is accomplished, the jury is tasked with reaching a verdict, which is essentially a straightforward and mechanical exercise with no apparent allowance for a juror to exercise extra-judicial discretion or personal sentiments. Jurors are told that if the evidence proves every element of a charge beyond a reasonable doubt, they must vote to convict. On the other hand, if one or more elements are not proven up to this standard, they must vote to acquit. In reaching a verdict, the jury is deliberately not informed that it has the authority to depart from the law as given to it by the judge, or to render a verdict that is inconsistent with that law.

In the film, Parnell McCarthy pays tribute to the institutional responsibilities of juries with this soliloquy:

Twelve people go off into a room: twelve different minds, twelve different hearts, from twelve different walks of life; twelve sets of eyes, ears, shapes, and sizes. And these twelve people are asked to judge another human being as different from them as they are from each other. And in their judgment, they must become of one mind - unanimous. It's one of the miracles of Man's disorganized soul that they can do it, and in most instances, do it right well. God bless juries.[1]

Under our system, it is for a jury to decide a defendant is guilty on behalf of the community. This responsibility is not left to a judge to determine as a legal proposition or a blue-ribbon panel to resolve through its special expertise. Nor is the task assigned to a computer to decipher by applying complex algorithms and equations.[2] Rather, it is a lay jury, comprised of the defendant's peers drawn from the community, that is entrusted with passing judgment on a defendant's guilt.

Some have suggested that a better alternative than lay jurors would be a panel of legal experts, perhaps composed of three judges. These critics argue that such a learned body would be less susceptible to emotion and prejudice. They also claim that experienced legal experts would be better equipped than untrained lay jurors to identify perjury and ignore the theatrics of counsel.

In his book *Troubleshooter*, Voelker responds to this criticism:

[N]one of the many suggested jury reforms is itself free from the weaknesses which seem to be inherent in any system devised to reconcile the conflict of interests and personalities present in every trial. It appears that the human

208

factor can be quite as much a problem to three learned judges as it can be to twelve illiterate ditch diggers. Susceptibility to flattery, considerations of self-interest, favoritism and prejudice, are human frailties which are the exclusive attributes of the poor.[3]

Because jurors are legal novices and susceptible to unfair influences and passions, an elaborate system of trial rules and procedures has been instituted to help ensure fairness. Speaking again through McCarthy, Voelker recognized the purpose and function of the law's processes and procedures in this regard: "The very slowness of the law, its massive impersonality, its insistence upon proceeding according to settled and ancient rules – all this tends to cool and bank the fires of passion and violence and replace them with order and reason."[4]

Important among a trial's governing rules is the presumptive exclusion of potential jurors who have been exposed to unduly prejudicial hearsay evidence[5] and evidence of prior bad acts.[6] In the Peterson trial (and to a somewhat lesser extent in the fictionalized Manion trial), these restrictions were often honored in the breach. For example, before the Peterson trial began, many if not all jurors knew about the defendant's jealous outbursts and that he was suspected by some of having previously inflicted the injuries on his wife. They also knew about Chenoweth's lecherous character and alleged prior sexual assaults. Further, they knew about Mrs. Peterson's reputation for promiscuity and Chenoweth's explicit description of his consensual encounter with her.

It appears that neither the prosecution nor the defense was troubled enough about any of this extra-judicial knowledge to conduct a vigorous voir dire and exercise many, if any, challenges against prospective jurors. Perhaps counsel reasoned that everyone in the small community knew about this inflammatory evidence and a change in venue would be impractical. Perhaps Voelker and the prosecutors all believed they were the superior trial advocates and thus this prior knowledge possessed by the jury could be leveraged to their advantage. Perhaps Voelker thought that the best way for the community to express its collective conscience, which included the possibility of nullification, was through presenting to the jury a relatively unfiltered version of all the surrounding circumstances that were already known to them as members of thecommunity.[7] Or perhaps it was simply that Voelker (and perhaps Thomas) did not challenge prospective jurors who had been exposed to facts that might influence their verdict because he was on friendly terms with many of them. Regardless of the reasons for counsels' passivity, legitimate concerns about the impact of inadmissible evidence upon a jury in Marquette County in the late 1950s resonate even more powerfully today, given the ubiquity of social media, fake news, and the incessant repetition of "breaking news" by 24-7 news providers.

While we will never be certain why counsel engaged in so little voir dire and exercised so few challenges, we do know that Voelker expressed conflicting attitudes about juries and their capacity to render a just verdict. In another of his published works, Voelker writes,

> I would still preserve the jury, of course, as the ultimate judges of guilt or innocence. But the present star system of trial, these thrilling courtroom battles of gifted professional pleasers seeking to build or enhance a reputation, to extend a record of conviction or acquittals, to gain some political notoriety or advantage - all this may tend to make an exciting show for the bystanders and sensational newspapers and TV but has damn little to do with the business at hand: the quest for Truth and Justice.[8]

We also know, from reading Voelker's journals, that he believed sex crimes were especially endemic and challenging in places like the Upper Peninsula. Years before the Peterson case, Voelker wrote in his journal about his "theory … [that] the North … is more likely to have the worst crimes of unbridled sexual passion … the long, lonely, frigid winter; the slow unlocking of the earth; spring, the emotion – churning smell of damp earth – the rape."[9] Add to these environmental influences the troubling reality that alleged sex crimes are sometimes more difficult to resolve because they go unreported, lack corroboration, or involve little more than a credibility contest between the prosecutrix and the defendant. Perhaps Voelker concluded that jurors drawn from the local area are better suited to cope with the institutional and practical inadequacies of a criminal trial, and thus they were more capable of satisfactorily addressing alleged sex offenses that occur there.

Voelker's faith in the Peterson jury may reside in his confidence in the good judgment of his fellow Yoopers. The Peterson case occurred in the 1950s in a socially conservative area. The mores of that time and place would seem to be incompatible with the enlightened idea that a woman such as Mrs. Peterson could be a rape victim rather than an adulteress. Mrs. Peterson had a reputation for promiscuity. She was drinking and consorting "barefooted" with her alleged rapist just before the attack while her husband was absent. She accepted a ride from her alleged rapist to her home, which was within easy walking distance of the tavern, alone and late at night. Her panties were missing and perhaps she did not wear any. The novel and film explore whether a woman in these circumstances could have actually been raped and, if she were, whether anyone would believe her.

This was bold subject matter for that time, but for Voelker at the Peterson trial it was more than a mere fictional device or an opportunity for social commentary. Voelker counted on the jury being open to the possibility that Mrs. Peterson was raped as the premise for his defense strategy. Perhaps, given the hand he was dealt, Voelker, like Biegler, had no choice but to embrace the idea that a rape occurred. The fact remains, however, that the defense argued that the victim raped the defendant's wife and, ultimately, this strategy achieved an acquittal. The film, and especially the novel, do not draw a firm conclusion about whether Mrs. Manion was raped. It is left to the reader and the viewer to make a judgment about whether a rape actually occurred, and whether this even matters in determining whether Lieutenant Manion should be convicted of murder.

Throughout Voelker's works, he recognizes that the criminal justice system's central purpose is to resolve issues about guilt and punishment through reason based on principle, rather than brute force relying on power.[10] The justice system tamps down emotion, replacing passion with order and sound judgment. Fundamental to this understanding of the law and how it operates is the idea that when a jury determines guilt and a judge imposes a sentence, retribution replaces revenge as the legitimate objective of punishment.

Retribution is a venerable and well-accepted basis for criminal sanctions. A retributivist would contend that a guilty murderer justly deserves to be punished,[11] and that it is morally fitting that an offender should suffer in proportion to his culpable wrongdoing.[12] Accordingly, retribution is inflicted by a legitimate public authority, restores the common good and the individual, and protects against over-reaching by

213

the state. Revenge, in contrast, is inflicted by private persons, motivated by a desire to humiliate the offender, and aggrandize the punisher, and facilitates over-reaching by a person acting on this impulse. One could question whether the jury acquitted Lieutenant Manion/Lieutenant Peterson based on passion and emotion rather than reason and the law. If the former is what actually happened, the jury abdicated its assigned and proper role by exacting revenge on the victim rather than imposing retribution on the victim's killer.

Another matter relating to the jury verdict should be briefly mentioned. For a host of reasons discussed earlier, most readers are likely to root for Biegler and thus welcome the jury's decision to nullify. But consider that the most powerful source of this sentiment is probably that the reader, like the jury, dislikes the victim and what he did far more than it dislikes the defendant and what he did. This greater antipathy toward the victim is bolstered by the favorable relationship that the defense counsel has established with the jury and the prosecution team has failed to achieve. These pro-defense sentiments are further magnified for the reader in the book because the story of the trial is told from Biegler's subjective perspective. While this favorable attitude toward the defense might seem benign with regard to the prosecution of Lieutenant Manion, a thoughtful reader might be less sanguine about how different kinds of irrelevant, superficial, or objectionable considerations or attitudes could influence jurors in other cases. What if the jury's decision to nullify was instead predicated on the defendant's or the victim's race or ethnicity? Suppose it rested based on a party's religious persuasion, gender, or political affiliation? Imagine the intensity of a reader's outrage if prejudice or racism led to the conviction of an innocent person.

Years ago, during a trip abroad, Director Otto Preminger screened *Anatomy of a Murder* at the Russian Academy of Film. Preminger was taken aback by the audience's outrage over the jury's decision to acquit the defendant. Many in attendance told Preminger it was inconceivable that such an obviously guilty person like Lieutenant Manion could be found not guilty and set free, or that this outcome could be considered acceptable or just. Preminger responded that the jury's verdict was attributable to the presumption of innocence accorded to Lieutenant Manion and every other defendant in American courts. The audience was left unsatisfied by this explanation.[13]

The Russian viewers' steadfast disapproval of the Manion verdict is understandable given that the justification for it offered by Preminger badly misses the point and does not address their objections. Of course, Lieutenant Manion, like any criminal defendant in an American criminal court, is entitled to the presumption of innocence. This principle means that the defendant will be found guilty only if the initial presumption of innocence he is to be accorded is rebutted and overcome by proof of guilt beyond a reasonable doubt. Thus, understood correctly, Manion's acquittal cannot be attributed to or explained by the presumption of innocence. Indeed, one really has nothing to do with the other. Rather, the jury's verdict of not guilty by reason of insanity expresses its collective judgment that Lieutenant Manion should be acquitted notwithstanding the overwhelming evidence of his guilt that superseded his presumptive innocence.

The idea of jury nullification was seemingly foreign to Russian sensibilities. Perhaps this should not be too surprising, as there appears to be something distinctively American about the public's receptivity of jury nullification. It is fundamentally reassuring to most citizens of a nation born of a desire for self-governance, individual liberty, and free expression, that a jury composed of one's peers has the capacity to nullify and thus say "no" to the government. Jury nullification protects against political and prosecutorial overreaching, and it leaves important judgments about standards of behavior to be determined by community sensibilities rather than political elites or legal experts. But these benefits come with potential costs. Jury nullification can foster lawlessness and make the law less certain and predictable. It can facilitate our most evil inclinations. It can undermine the very system of justice established by the community through its laws and rules and assigned to juries to apply and enforce.

In *Anatomy of a Murder*, Voelker invites the reader to consider which legally irrelevant sentiments and prejudices should be allowed as a basis for jury nullification, and which should be prohibited. And, just like individual jurors at a criminal trial, each reader must confront these questions from a uniquely personal perspective. What forms of prejudice and bias should be permitted? What role should situational ethics play? Which values are absolute, and which are relative? These troubling questions may leave the perceptive reader feeling uncertain and uncomfortable, which seems to be exactly what Voelker intended.

These conflicting impulses help explain why jury nullification exists in a sort of legal limbo in the American criminal justice system. Jury nullification is not prohibited by the law, and yet judges rarely charge juries that they possess such power even when the defense requests that they be so instructed. Defense counsel can directly appeal to the jury in closing argument that it should nullify, but judges have the authority to limit such entreaties. Voelker recognizes that in most successful cases of jury nullification, the defense must present a passible even if ultimately unconvincing legal peg, such as insanity, to achieve an acquittal. This approach facilitates jury nullification by subterfuge, insofar as the jury nullifies based on an extraneous rationale that is inconsistent with the judge's instructions to it. While presenting the issue of jury nullification in all its glory in *Anatomy of a Murder*, Voelker also exposes its many lurking dangers. Characteristically, Voelker presents both sides but leaves it to the reader to reach his own conclusions.

Although Voelker supports and occasionally champions the advantages of an adversarial trial played out before a jury, at other times he expressed grave reservations:

> [I have an] uneasy suspicion, growing into a conviction, that our present system of determining criminal guilt or innocence is in many respects imperfect ... [i]t is remarkable and also disheartening to realize how much depends upon the lawyers in the trial of a criminal case; upon the D.A. and his legal opponent, their relative competence or incompetence, whether they are on the ball or not. Too often, I feel, the result in the trial of a given case depends entirely too much upon this theoretically irrelevant factor. I have a companion grievance. Most big criminal trials in our day have become nothing more or less than a talent show, a forensic duel between two glittering legal personalities— however thrilling the duel or compelling the personalities— with the judge reduced to a master of ceremonies and the bewildered jury frequently awarding the prize to the side which puts on the better show. This would all be very well and even amusing if it did not happen to involve vital interests of the public as well as the fate of an anxious defendant. As it is we happen to be dealing with a clash between two of the most pressing concerns of our lives: the public welfare and the freedom and liberty of an individual human being.[14]

Voelker's novel and Preminger's film identify these concerns without offering a firm judgment about the efficacy of juries. The novel and movie, each in their own way, are authentically descriptive portrayals of the criminal justice system, which afford the layman an intimate peek behind the curtain. The reader and viewer observe lawyers with varying degrees of competence performing critical tasks and pushing the envelope in service of a desired verdict. They see the judge preside over the trial with no investment in the outcome, focusing solely instead on ensuring that the proper procedures are followed. It is likely that readers identify most closely with the jurors, who are legal novices thrust into a pivotal role at a criminal trial. Often a confused and bamboozled lot, jurors are called upon to decide important matters they seem ill-equipped to address, especially after being entertained and perhaps misled by the opposing counsels' theatrics and histrionics.

In *Anatomy of a Murder*, Voelker and Preminger lay bare the many deficiencies of the American jury system without prescribing or even advocating for a preferable alternative. Indeed, the lesson may be that the present system, despite its many flaws and frailties, may be the best we can ever hope to create. To paraphrase Winston Churchill, a jury trial is the worst forum for deciding guilt except for all those other forums that have been tried from time to time.[15] Or, as Voelker puts it in his book *Troubleshooter*, "Conceding the many weaknesses of the present jury system . . . I still rather lean to the tentative conclusion that there has not yet been found a better or more democratic way for men to determine legally their clashes with each other and with society."[16]

CHAPTER 13 – WAS JUSTICE SERVED?

The most compelling and complicated question Voelker poses in *Anatomy of a Murder* is whether Lieutenant Manion was justly acquitted even though he was legally guilty.[1] The answer may turn on one's definition of "justice." *Black's Law Dictionary* defines justice as the "fair and proper administration of laws."[2] This definition presumably encompasses both processes and outcomes, and is achieved by "[p]rotecting rights and punishing wrongs using fairness."[3] As Voelker puts it, a criminal trial is about "big things like truth and justice and fair play."[4] *Anatomy of a Murder* reveals that specifying and achieving substantive justice is often a far more difficult proposition than merely ensuring procedural compliance.

Professors Asimov and Mader have observed:

Many lawyers are uncomfortable with notions of substantive justice because they understand how difficult it is ever to find out the truth, especially about events that occurred in the past. Who is telling the truth, who is lying? What did happen, for example, between Barney Quill and Laura Manion or between Laura and Lt. Manion? What was Lt. Manion's state of mind when he gunned down Quill? We, the audience, never find out, because the movie lacks the customary flashbacks to the bloody events. Neither do Biegler, Dancer, Judge Weaver, or the jurors. Lawyers are also uneasy discussing substantive justice because, in the real world, human behavior defies easy representation; there are at least two sides to every question worth talking about. Even when we claim to be certain about what happened, it can still be hard to know for sure what would be a "correct," "just," or a "moral" response.[5]

Evaluated in terms of process and outcomes, the Manion trial is at once an unqualified success and an abject failure. Clearly Lieutenant Manion was provided all of his procedural rights, and then some, at his trial. Biegler and the judge made sure that the defendant received every protection afforded by the rules of evidence and trial practice. Lieutenant Manion clearly had a competent counsel who zealously represented him. Had Lieutenant Manion been convicted of murder, he would have no apparent basis for reversal. The goal of procedural justice was thus fully satisfied, and this seems to be a comparatively straightforward objective to assess and accomplish.

The trial utterly fails to achieve substantial justice, however, insofar as the defendant was not held criminally accountable for his homicidal conduct. Regardless of Lieutenant Manion's precise motivations for killing Quill, we know that he was not legally insane. Accordingly, at best he was guilty of the lesser-included offense of voluntary manslaughter,[6] and at worst of premeditated murder.[7] Given that Lieutenant Manion was legally guilty of a felony homicide, but was acquitted, he was neither held responsible for his crime under the law nor was he proportionally and retributively punished for it. A reader or viewer is left to resolve why he has rooted so hard for Biegler to prevail despite his client's obvious guilt and the resulting failure of the system to achieve substantive justice.

Both Voelker in his novel and Preminger in his film conspicuously elevate procedural compliance above substantive justice. The point is made especially clear in the final courtroom scene in the movie when the jury's verdict is announced. The camera is positioned behind the bench and views the courtroom from the perspective of the trial judge. When the jurors enter, they are called to stand shoulder to shoulder before the bench and face the camera. Thus, when the jury foreman announces the verdict, he is addressing the viewer and the judge, who is the final arbiter of procedure but is not invested in the result. Lieutenant Manion and Biegler are seen behind the jury and in the background, almost blending into the first row of the gallery. Mrs. Manion is not even in the courtroom; instead, she waits outside in a car, once again clad in her preferred attire of tight slacks, high heels, and no girdle. After the verdict is announced in court, the camera stays with a static long shot from behind the judge. There is no jump cut to a close-up that captures the reaction of the defendant or Biegler. And the camera does not linger; the scene ends shortly after the verdict is announced. The effect is that at the climax of the trial, the defendant, his wife, and his counsel are portrayed as afterthoughts. The content of the verdict, and its

223

impact on the parties, is assigned less importance than the stylized combat that preceded it and the manner in which it is announced. Preminger accepts—he even embraces— the irreducible ambiguity of objective reality, and he focuses instead on how the legal system processes this. In Preminger's film, as in Voelker's novel, substance is subordinate to procedure.

Indeed, the preeminence of proper procedure over substantive justice resonates throughout the novel and the film. Biegler's introspective reflections about his maneuvers involving "the Lecture," for example, are confined to ensuring procedural compliance and do not concern substantive truth or guilt. The same preeminence of procedure is emphasized in the many other adversarial machinations by counsel involving witness examination and objections thereto. The judge, for his part, presides over the trial and rules on objections like a good umpire; he does not care who wins but rather is focused on ensuring that the rules of the game are properly applied and enforced. The priority of process over substance is an attitude that is widely shared within the legal the community. It is also denigrated by many in the public as "loophole chasing" that can subvert justice. The scrupulous adherence to process at the expense of substance, as reflected in *Anatomy of a Murder*, has several important implications. It reveals and informs society's values and preferences. It shapes who we are and what we deem important. It helps explain why the reader and viewer are not disappointed, let alone outraged, by the defendant's acquittal, as were the Russian viewers who considered this result to be a miscarriage of justice. And it influences public attitudes about lawyers and the justice system. Procedural justice reigns supreme, and this objective was fully served at Lieutenant Manion's trial.

While jury nullification may seem as being at odds with a preference for process over substance, it is in fact wholly consistent with this. Jury nullification is allowed under the rules of the American justice system. If nullification were procedurally prohibited, the trial rules would insist that the judge have the power to substitute a guilty verdict for an acquittal where the evidence clearly proves the defendant's guilt beyond a reasonable doubt. But in both the Peterson and Manion trials, the judge is helpless to intervene and find the defendant guilty even if he felt compelled to do so in the interests of justice. Likewise, the prosecutor has no authority to contest an acquittal, even in cases when the jury obviously nullifies. A not guilty verdict based on jury nullification is accepted by all because it comports with proper procedure, and not because it achieves substantive justice.

Next, consider whether Lieutenant Manion's acquittal served

justice in a broader sense of the term, i.e., when the idea of justice is removed from a strictly legal construct. The great philosopher St. Thomas Aquinas wrote that "justice" is a virtue, a good habit, whereby a person has a constant and ready will to give each his due.[8] Voelker puts it this way in *Troubleshooter*:

> [B]y and large, it has been my observation that the twelve-man jury somehow tends, in the majority of cases, to achieve a fair average of a sort of rough justice. One does not use calipers when daring to talk about Justice. And, too, what strikes one as a just or an unjust verdict depends a lot on one's point of view.[9]

With regard to this idea of substantive and rough justice, a few admittedly superficial observations are now offered about the abstract question of whether each of the major players received "his or her due," or what here will be referred to as true or poetic justice.

First, consider whether Chenoweth/Quill received what was due to him. We suspect that he is a serial rapist, but he was never convicted. We know that once he was dispatched, he could never rape again. With regard to his encounter with Mrs. Peterson/Mrs. Manion, we believe that he is either a violent sexual predator or an incorrigible and indiscreet adulterer. In either case, he seriously transgressed the community's mores and sensibilities. He was killed by someone who ostensibly defended his wife's honor and was indirectly victimized. In a final and ironic twist, he consistently boasted about his prowess with firearms, but he is shot to

226

death with his pistol within reach. The actual jurors, as well as readers and viewers, are left to ponder whether, all things considered, the victim got what he deserved. The answer may be uncomfortably visceral and difficult to reconcile with a properly formed conscience.

Second, consider whether Lieutenant Peterson/Lieutenant Manion received what was due to him. Knowing that the defendant was not insane, the question then becomes whether he should have been acquitted via jury nullification despite his legal guilt? This is not a case of a jury disapproving of an unjust law, suspecting prosecutorial misconduct, or believing that the defendant has already been sufficiently punished.[10] Rather, the decision here to nullify involves an exercise of each juror's individual judgment, expressed collectively, and informed by community standards, relating to equities and moral privileges. In other words, the jury tasked itself with deciding whether the defendant has the right (or more properly, should have the right) to defend his wife's honor and kill her alleged rapist? A related question is whether the jury, as the representatives of the community, should have the leeway to apply their sensibilities about a just result in an ad hoc fashion when deciding whether the defendant should be convicted of murder or be excused for acting on this impulse? Further, was the blunt instrument of a criminal jury trial an efficacious means for dispensing justice under all of the circumstances? Voelker does not answer these questions, but he compels the thoughtful reader to confront them by weaving these issues, unconcealed and seamlessly, throughout the story he tells. These kinds of questions remain as relevant today as they were when Lieutenant Peterson was tried.

Third, consider whether Voelker received what was due to him. He zealously represented his ungrateful, deadbeat client. His conduct most probably comported with the letter of the law. He vanquished his dishonorable political rival. He became wealthy and was celebrated. He was able to support his family and live well. His writings were widely read. But all of these laudable ends and his good fortune were derived from his successful defense of a guilty murderer. Assuming Voelker administered "the Lecture" to Lieutenant Peterson, as Biegler did to Lieutenant Manion, his deliberate actions intentionally resulted in the fabrication and presentation of a successful but fictious claim of insanity. Voelker challenges the reader to question whether his alter ego Biegler served justice in his defense of Lieutenant Manion. One cannot help but imagine that Voelker, in moments of quiet self-reflection, may have asked himself the same question.[11]

During the film's final scene, Biegler and McCarthy arrive at the trailer park to execute a promissory note to guarantee payment by

Lieutenant Manion of the substantial remaining balance of Biegler's legal fees. As we recall, the Manions, having been possessed by an irresistible impulse, have fled the area. Upon learning this, Biegler informs McCarthy, now his law partner, that they need to meet with their newest client, Mary Pilant. Biegler and McCarthy have been retained by Pilant to be the executors of her late father's estate, whose assets include the Inn in which he was shot to death by their erstwhile client. McCarthy, expressing a combination of thoughtful consideration and understated bemusement, remarks to Biegler that this is "poetic justice for everybody."

McCarthy's pronouncement about poetic justice is hardly an off-hand comment. "Poetic justice" is a common expression that is synonymous with certain aspects of the natural law. Professor John Barton has explained,

> [Old Testament P]rophets who use the notion of poetic justice are implicitly appealing to a human consensus about what sort of acts are just and unjust, which is not logically derived from the revelation of moral norms by God, but rests on ideas about ethics formed by reason—which one might conveniently refer to as natural law. For the moral principles which rational men can recognize are not other than the principles on which God himself works when judging the actions of men.[12]

Human consensus about what is just and unjust suggests that each of the major players in the novel and film were punished in accordance with the natural law, i.e., poetic justice. Proverbially speaking, Mrs. Manion received sexual attention, albeit more than she bargained for—"what goes around comes around." The sexually violent, gunslinging tavern owner, Barney Quill, got paid in his own coin—"he who lives by the sword dies by the sword." The smarty-pants prosecutor, Dancer, proves to be too smart for his britches and sets himself up for humiliation at the end of the trial—"pride goeth before the fall." The defendant, Lieutenant Manion, was set free only to run away with his flirtatious wife who will torment him with a jealous rage all the days of his life, and so he will live miserably ever after—"Better a small corner in the attic than a whole house with a quarrelsome wife." And Mary Pilant, the quiet and hardworking illegitimate daughter of the victim, who turns over the crucial piece of evidence against her violent father based on principle, is bequeathed his estate—"and the meek shall inherit the earth."

Even the minor players in Biegler's circle received their due. McCarthy stayed on the wagon and uncovered crucial legal precedent and evidence while serving as Biegler's associate on the Manion case. He was thereby redeemed and reclaims his dignity, and he can again practice the profession he loves. Maida, Biegler's chronically underpaid secretary, continued to work diligently for Biegler motivated by loyalty and the faint hope that Lieutenant Manion would someday pay his legal fees. After the trial, Mary Pilant hired Biegler and McCarthy as executors of Quill's estate, thus assuring that Maida will at last be financially compensated for her faithful service.

Each of the above-mentioned characters received what McCarthy would call poetic justice. But what about Biegler? He is by far the most difficult character to pin down. We can surely agree he performed the honorable role of a defense counsel with acumen and skill. But his efforts resulted, as he intended, in the acquittal of a guilty murderer. As a consequence of his defense of Lieutenant Manion, Biegler was ultimately retained by an honorable, paying client—Mary Pilant. Could this amount to poetic justice for Biegler? Perhaps it is enough to say that all things considered, Biegler got what he deserved: a respectable and honorable client whose interests he could honorably assert and defend.

Upon reflection, perhaps Biegler was mistaken when he admonished Lieutenant Manion during their first meeting that the unwritten law is a "myth." It might instead be that the unwritten law, or poetic justice as McCarthy puts it, is an omnipresent subtext that ultimately will win out. In this regard, *Anatomy of a Murder* is not unlike Dostoevsky's great novel *Crime and Punishment*. There, a guilty murderer eludes human justice only to be pursued by the furies of his conscience executing the unwritten law. Among the secondary precepts of the unwritten law is thou shall not murder, thou shall not commit adultery, thou shall not steal, and thou shall not bear false witness under oath. Lieutenant and Mrs. Manion have collectively violated all of these tenets. In the end, they received the poetic justice they deserved in accord with the unwritten law.

In the preface of his movie *The Ten Commandments*, Cecil B. DeMille said, "This is a story about those who try to break the laws of God but find they are broken, instead, by them."[13] Poetic justice, what others may call irony or karma, is a real concept. It strikes sure and true in *Anatomy of a Murder*, even when human justice waivers. Indeed, extra-juridical poetic justice—the so-called unwritten law—ultimately triumphs in *Anatomy of a Murder*. It prevails even against the court's dogged attempt to adhere to the law's formal rules and procedures, which at the Manion trial seem to be designed to frustrate poetic justice.

Return again to the film's final scene at the trailer park, where Biegler and McCarthy learn that their client and his wife have skipped town without paying their legal bills. Biegler looks down at the mess they left behind and picks up a broken high-heel shoe. He examines it briefly and then hooks it over the rim of a large trash barrel. McCarthy offers his remarks about poetic justice and they both leave. The camera remains fixed on the trash barrel and the shoe.

This is the film's final, lasting image.

Perhaps this is a stretch, but the image of the broken shoe perched on the trash barrel seems imbued with symbolism. It evokes a broken sole (soul) that is banished from the idyllic environs of Big Bay (heaven, or perhaps paradise) and destined for eternal damnation in a garbage dump (hell). This sole is relegated to the trash heap because, in its ruined condition, it is where it deserves to be. Even if all the supernatural allusions are eliminated, the natural law recognizes that all things are finite—"ashes to ashes and dust to dust." For Mrs. Manion's shoe, its unceremonious banishment to a landfill is a fitting end to its sordid, earthly existence. The shoe, and what it symbolizes, receives the poetic justice that it deserves.

McCarthy's pronouncement about poetic justice suggests that this concept is not bounded by the four walls of a courtroom and the jury's official verdict. True justice, in other words, cannot be fully attained under man's law. Rather, it is found beyond the written law, and at times in spite of it. It is incapable of being fully realized solely through the formal rules of procedure and counsel's faithful adherence to them. And it encompasses much more than a slavish and narrow insistence on right and wrong, as often times these concepts are difficult to discern with clarity and are infused with subjectivity. Voelker, through McCarthy, might be suggesting that we, as mere mortals, lack the capacity to comprehend, let alone administer, true justice with all of its complexities and imponderables. For us, as for the participants at the Peterson trial and the characters in *Anatomy of a Murder*, perhaps it is simply that justice is what actually happens, and in the end, everyone gets at least as much of it as they deserve.

CHAPTER 14 – FINAL THOUGHTS

After basking in his new-found fame for a while, Voelker settled down again to Ishpeming—this time for good. At first, he and Grace returned to his childhood home on West Barnum Street where they had raised three daughters and struggled to make ends meet. John once told Grace he hoped that the revenue from *Anatomy of a Murder* might pay for a remodeled kitchen.[1] This projection proved to be far too modest, and the Voelkers were able to build a beautiful, rambling home north of town. Voelker sometimes referred to his new country home as the house that *Anatomy* built.[2] It featured a fitting office for his writing, complete with a spacious closet roomy enough to accommodate all of his gear and "fishing uniforms."[3] At long last, Voelker's need to confront contradiction and contemplate compromise had evaporated.

Besides building their dream house, Voelker spent a portion of his royalties purchasing a fishing cabin (Yoopers refer to these as a "camp") that would later become famously known as "Uncle Tom's," or "Uncle's," for short. The cabin rested next to a peaceful and idyllic fishing hole that Voelker dubbed Frenchman's Pond. The name Frenchman's Pond does not appear on any official map. Voelker choose this sobriquet, at least in part, to preserve its secrecy.

Virtually every day for many years during fishing season, Voelker would maneuver his trusty "fish car" along uneven back roads known as "two tracks" until he reached his camp's guarded location. The route could be a bit precarious. One time, a visitor lost a muffler to a pothole while driving to the cabin. Voelker left it along the side of the trail to discourage others from venturing any further. Only close and trusted friends were told of Uncle's location. In late April each year, Voelker would host a gathering of this select few at his camp to celebrate the opening of fishing season.

Voelker returned home from his cabin almost every night to be with his family. His wife, Grace, did not care much for the cabin and rarely accompanied her husband there. But once a year, Grace dutifully trekked to Uncle's for a large gathering with friends. While at the cabin, she retrieved china and silverware that her husband neglected to bring back home during the preceding months.

Voelker continued writing for several years after returning to the Upper Peninsula. He published *Laughing Whitefish* in 1965, a historical novel based on a trilogy of actual Michigan Supreme Court cases from the 1880s. The final case in the series, *Kobogum v. Jackson Iron Co.*,[4] established in Michigan the general rule that state courts must defer to tribal law in cases involving the internal, domestic relations of American Indians residing within their own territory. Although the novel was favorably reviewed,[5] it, like all of his other writings, never approached the commercial success of *Anatomy of a Murder*. Voelker published his final novel, *People v. Kirk*, in 1981. He was then seventy-eight years old.

Voelker still ventured into the wilderness, although less frequently, through the 1970s and early 1980s. Although he was quite familiar with the environs, his journal entries often reflect a sense of wonder and enthusiasm about his surroundings that might be expected of a novice. In a 1981 journal entry, for example, Voelker wrote, "I saw and counted 72 deer on this fabled afternoon driving on a back road through the cedar swamps where they winter, most of them grazing out in the open and rarely running, so starved were they for something other than their long winter diet of cedar."[6] Later that spring he wrote that he and a friend "saw a butterfly and a flock of bees and picked a huge batch of pregnant pussy willows on a run in the Karen road area."[7]

Voelker's health began to decline later in life. He may have never fully recovered from his bout with pneumonia during his time in college, and he seemed to suffer lingering colds every winter.[8] Voelker had cataract surgery to address his failing eyesight, and he was later admitted to hospital for tests of his weakened heart.[9] During this stay, Monsignor Spelgatti, a priest assigned to the hospital, tried to visit with Voelker several times to see if he wanted any spiritual comfort but he declined. Although Voelker was raised Catholic, he had not been observant for decades. But the priest was persistent, so at last Voelker relented. "Oh, all right," he told a nurse, "if it will make him feel better." When the priest was admitted to his room, Voelker asked what he was doing there. The priest responded that he was "fishing, John, just fishing." Voelker and the Monsignor went on to have a pleasant conversation.[10]

Grace said that eventually her husband lost his desire to write.[11] In 1985, about five years before his death, Voelker reflected,

> I've chased trout and wild mushrooms for still another twenty-five years, also managing to write seven more books during our long winters. During that time I haven't practiced law or even owned a law book, and it comes as a shock to realize that it's almost sixty years since I won my law diploma down in old Ann Arbor town.[12]

In his final years, and as a concession to his age and failing health, Voelker ventured to the cabin less frequently, preferring instead to remain in Ishpeming proper. His daily routine included a stop at the post office to send correspondence and retrieve his mail. He would also visit the Wonder Bar on Pearl Street, just off Main,[13] or Polly's Rainbow Bar on Canda Street, and play cribbage for hours.[14] It is possible that Paul Biegler's nickname, Polly, is an homage to one of Voelker's favorite cribbage hangouts. On occasion, Voelker would visit the Crow's

238

Nest restaurant on the top floor of the Landmark Inn in Marquette, where he entertained diners by playing jazz piano.[15]

On March 18, 1991, the date of his passing, Voelker followed his usual routine. He visited the post office and played cribbage at the Rainbow Bar. He then traveled to Marquette, where he checked out books from the Northern Michigan University Library. On the way back he stopped at a deli to purchase some candy and then continued home. It was then that Voelker suffered a massive heart attack. He somehow managed to ease his car gently into a snowbank. He was later pronounced dead at a local hospital. Voelker was eighty-seven years old. He was laid to rest in his native soil in the Ishpeming Cemetery.

When Voelker's good friends Frederick Baker and Richard Vander Veen learned of his passing, they went home to pack a few things before meeting to drive up North together with their friend Norris McDowell for his funeral. Before leaving, they found letters from Voelker, in his familiar felt pen scrawl, postmarked Ishpeming on the date of his death. It stunned each to think that one of the last things Voelker did on earth was to mail letters to them.

On their way to the Upper Peninsula, the three hatched a small scheme: they bought a deck of cards and extracted from it the makings of a perfect cribbage hand, which they slipped into Voelker's coffin to play in his first game on the other side.

Baker related a poignant vignette about their trip that captures the

essence of Voelker and his environs. Baker recalls:

> It may sound strange, but John's funeral was at once the
> most moving and the happiest I ever attended. There was no
> eulogy, and certainly no religious component. It consisted
> simply of John's family and friends milling about in hushed
> conversation until we were asked to be seated and invited to
> take turns sharing a remembrance or a brief tribute to John.
> When my turn came, I said simply: "John did not suffer fools
> gladly, but he was always very kind to me."
>
> After the funeral, Rich, Norris McDowell, and I decided to
> offer a libation to John at Frenchman's Pond. Unfortunately,
> I overestimated the capabilities of my new Jeep, which I had
> looked forward to giving John a ride in on our next visit; it
> bellied out in the snow where the plowing ended, and the
> two-track to John's camp was impassable. A couple of UP
> Power Company linemen, who had knocked off a little early
> and parked their truck at the end of the plowed segment to
> drink a beer, watched with what I imagine was some
> amusement as I tried to bull my way through the snow then
> backed out with some difficulty after almost getting stuck.
> As we were putting on the warmest gear we had and
> preparing to strike out on foot for Voelker's camp, which
> was almost two miles in from that point, they ambled over.
> One of them said, "What was ya tryin' to do?" We explained
> that we were going to have a drink in John's honor at his
> pond. He said, "Oh, yeah, we knew Johnny, everybody did."
>
> After a pause he said, "We was rootin' for ya, eh?" Then the
> two of them walked back to finish their beers in the warmth
> of their truck. I honestly don't know how we made it all the
> way back there, let alone there and back – Norris had just
> undergone chemotherapy for cancer, and was weak as a
> kitten. By the time we got to the pond, we were half frozen
> and soaked to the bone. But we built a fire and our pants and
> socks and shoes steamed on the stove while we shared more
> than one glass in John's memory. Then we donned our still

240

damp clothes and, using the trail we had broken on the way in, made for the Jeep, reaching it just as night fell. It was a crazy thing to do, but we have always been glad that we did it, not least because it added an expression to our private language as friends: now when we want to offer each other encouragement, we say, "I'm rootin' for you, eh?" [16]

The many obituaries of Voelker's passing noted his accomplishments as a writer and his appointment to the Michigan Supreme Court. Most mentioned his love of fly fishing and listed his next of kin. What the obituaries could not begin to capture was Voelker's passion for the Upper Peninsula, and for its land and its people. Nor could they express his fierce commitment to the criminal justice system despite its many flaws that he encountered as a litigator and chronicled in his writing. And they could not begin to do justice to the wide-ranging and profound repercussions of his life and of his masterpiece, *Anatomy of a Murder*.

Several years after her husband's death, Grace Voelker wrote a short note that was meant to encapsulate the John Voelker that she knew so well. The note read in part:

> He became the writer Robert Traver, the fisherman, the lawyer, and the Michigan State Supreme Court Justice. He gave us Anatomy of a Murder and Hollywood, served [it] up proper.
>
> John was a gracious man. In a tattered old hat and old boots he was gracious. In a jacket with proper tie, he was gracious. Notice how carefully he listened and looked? He had the knack of storing things away in his head for future

241

use. Besides – he looked like John Wayne![17]

The American Dream has been described as:

> the belief that anyone, regardless of where they were born
> or what class they were born or born into, can attain their
> own version of success in a society where upward mobility
> is possible for everyone. The American Dream is achieved
> through sacrifice, risk-taking, and hard work, rather than by
> chance.[18]

And "chance," as Louis Pasteur recognized, "favours only the prepared mind."[19]

These thoughts and ideas about the American Dream and chance epitomize John Voelker's remarkable life. The son of a backwoods saloon keeper, he rose above his circumstances to achieve his personal vision of the American Dream through uncommon perseverance and fortitude, and a dogged unwillingness to compromise about the most important things. He worked hard for decades but always in the context of a balanced life. He sacrificed and took risks without abandoning his core responsibilities. And when opportunity finally knocked on Voelker's door when he was well into his fifties, he was exceptionally well prepared and motivated to respond. He fulfilled his destiny by summoning his passion for writing and thinking, his gift for understanding people, and his informed insight about the criminal justice system. John Voelker was an idiosyncratic combination of John Wayne, Clarence Darrow, Harper Lee, and your sweet uncle who liked to fish. He is an American treasure.

Leonardo da Vinci instructed, "Learn how to see. Realize that everything connects to everything else."[20] In contemplating the interdependence of all things in the context of Voelker's experiences, one cannot help but grasp that each life's journey seems to be defined as much by happenstance and coincidence as by decisions and destiny. Who are our parents? Where are we born? What paths have been taken and forsaken? Who have we come to know and love or by chance have we never met? The pivotal events and near misses. The inevitability of contradiction and the possibility of compromise. The educated guesses and lost opportunities. The unintended consequences. All that is seen and unseen. The many lives that each life affects. The countless intertwining threads that comprise the grand tapestry of everything.

The story of John Voelker's life, the Peterson trial, and *Anatomy of a Murder* vividly illustrate the ripple effects of a million random variables. One might speculate what would have happened if Voelker had never met his mentor at Sunday school in Ishpeming, or his wife Grace at a law school dance in Ann Arbor. One might also wonder what would have unfolded if Voelker remained in Chicago, or if he had defeated Thomas and won re-election as prosecuting attorney.

More to the point, one might contemplate what would have happened if Charlotte Peterson had hired another lawyer to represent her husband while Voelker was away fishing. Chances are that Lieutenant Peterson would have been convicted, or pled to some lesser offense, as Voelker possessed a unique combination of professional aptitude and personal motivation to obtain an acquittal. It seems unlikely that an indigent defendant in that remote location could have retained another lawyer capable of besting the prosecution team that had been arrayed against him.

Regardless of Lieutenant Peterson's fate, Voelker's life and legacy would have been dramatically different but for the Peterson case. One suspects Voelker would have left the Michigan Supreme Court sooner than later, fleeing the big city and coming back full-time to Ishpeming as he had decades earlier. He surely would have found the 300-plus-mile commute to Lansing too draining[21] and the allure of Frenchman's Pond too powerful to remain away from home for extended periods. Voelker once said, "If I hadn't made a cent on the books . . . I would be back [in Ishpeming] working on $10 wills and simple divorces. I have to be here."[22]

After Voelker had returned to the Upper Peninsula for good, he likely would have spent his days performing effective but generally mundane legal work, playing cribbage, and drinking bourbon with his friends. He would have loved his family, fly-fished religiously, and communed with nature in the exercise of his other religion. He would

have continued writing well, but without much commercial success. He

would have lived a rich and meaningful, but largely anonymous, life.

Months before Voelker first met Lieutenant Peterson, he wrote the

following passage in his journal with uncommon insight and prescience:

> Every man – every person leaves the seeds of an absorbing
> biography. Things that would attract no notice whatsoever,
> if the subject remained obscure [,] take on a vast significance
> if he achieves some sort of special fame. Scholars will dig
> and vie to find them. This is my journal. Many obscure souls
> write journals or what not. When they die it is ordinarily
> used to start a fire, but if he becomes famous or notorious
> the poor scribbling will be saved and preserved and quoted
> and misquoted and terrible is the significance that will be
> allowed to the most insane device. I've a notion to become
> famous just to prove the point. But even if I could [,] I should
> hesitate to forsake the joys of anonymity and solid animal
> comfort of obscurity. Must do an essay on that someday.[23]

Had Voelker not served as defense counsel at the Peterson trial,

he would have been incapable of writing *Anatomy of a Murder*. Had he

not written his great novel, Preminger could not have made his great

film. Had the novel and film never been written and produced, this would

have been a true injustice.

EPILOGUE

After completing the first draft of a law review article that would later evolve into this book, I presented my research to colleagues as part of a faculty development series at our law school. Before the presentation, I circulated copies of the draft article to them. One colleague e-mailed me suggesting that at the presentation I address how and why I became first interested in John Voelker and *Anatomy of a Murder*. I was reluctant to share my account about this because it revolves around one of my own war stories. While I have told more than a few such tales over the years, they were usually shared in an informal setting and reciprocated by friends. Sometimes the repartee was lubricated by an adult beverage. Telling my *Anatomy of a Murder* war story at a semi-official gathering of fellow professors would be altogether different. Surprisingly, the thought of it made me a bit uncomfortable. Ultimately, I relented and told mystory.

During my presentation and in feedback I received afterwards, my colleagues expressed two common reactions and recommendations. First, they suggested that my draft law review article be expanded and published in a book format. Second, they urged me to include my war story about *Anatomy of a Murder* in an epilogue to the book. And so, again with more than a little trepidation, I will now retell the tale here.

247

Remember, it has no doubt evolved through the years and likely has been embellished by me for self-serving reasons. It is, after all, a war story.

Years ago, I believe it was while I was in high school, I first saw the movie *Anatomy of a Murder*. It was nothing short of a revelation. I later purchased the novel, which I devoured from cover to cover with few breaks. Part of the attraction was my sense that the novel and film were unusually authentic portrayals of a criminal trial, which afforded a largely unjaded glimpse behind the curtain. They seemed real and raw, and I was intrigued by the planning and execution, and the gift for theatrics, required of a skilled litigator. I found myself unabashedly drawn to the competitiveness and pageantry of it all.

At the same time, I struggled with the ethical and moral questions that the novel and the film presented but did not resolve. I imagined how I might have addressed these matters had I been a prosecutor or defense attorney in the Manion case. More broadly, and in admittedly a nascent and tentative manner, I questioned the efficacy of the criminal justice system and whether it generally achieved true justice or even sought it. While all of my musings were blissfully uninformed by experience or the requirements of the law, this fact did not diminish the impact that the novel and film had upon me. They challenged me to ponder important issues and question assumptions while being wildly entertaining.

I cannot say I became a lawyer because of *Anatomy of a Murder*. It was, however, one of the dozen or so influences rattling around my brain that ultimately led me to law school and then a legal career. Upon graduating from the University of Michigan Law School, which happens to be Voelker's alma mater, I joined the Army Judge Advocate General's Corps for a host of reasons. Crucial among them was my desire for trial-litigation experience, and I concluded Army JAG was the best way for me to obtain this immediately.

To my surprise, my first assignment was to an appellate division in the Washington D.C. area. It was good work, and I learned a great deal, but I still longed to be a trial litigator. With this in mind, I requested that my second assignment be as a defense counsel in Korea. This was an attractive posting to me for several reasons, including the opportunity for extensive trial litigation experience. As few JAGs sought an assignment to Korea in those days, the brass happily approved my request. I was assigned to Camp Humphreys, Korea, which at that time was a relatively small and isolated post with a single prosecutor and defense attorney. Upon my arrival in the country in May 1983, I became the installation's sole defense counsel.

As it turned out, my assignment to Korea was the best thing that ever happened to me. I met Dianna there, who would become my loving wife of thirty-eight years and counting. Ironically, she was an expatriate from the same environs that Voelker so gladly fled, Chicagoland. While in the Far East, I was also exposed to a fascinating culture and my horizons were forever broadened.

Professionally, I was thrown into the deep end without much in the way of flotation. When I first stepped into my Quonset-hut office, my attention was directed to a formidable stack of files that had been conspicuously piled upon my Army-issue metal desk. Each file contained the preliminary discovery materials and allied papers for a pending court-martial. As I recall, every case in this first group involved drug offenses, a longtime staple for military courts. As I began reviewing the individual files, I was disappointed to find that without exception each one contained an airtight confession signed by the defendant and accompanied by a properly executed rights/waiver certificate. There was little I could do for these clients at a contested court-martial, and so this first group of cases were ultimately resolved through guilty plea agreements. I nevertheless gained invaluable experience in interviewing and examining witnesses, and I developed solid relationships with judges, lawyers, and law enforcement personnel. And, of course, I looked forward to my first contested trial.

About one month into my tour, I received my first court-martial file that did not involve drug distribution. It was a serious case. The charge was aggravated assault, but my initial review of the evidence suggested that a more aggressive prosecutor could have comfortably charged attempted murder.

The basic facts of the case were as follows: the defendant (my client), a young soldier, struck another young soldier in the head several times with a large wooden object, fracturing his skull and inflicting other injures. The weapon the defendant used was referred to by several witnesses as a "beating stick." A photo of the stick was included in the file. I saw, to my chagrin, that the stick was actually a large and hefty tree limb that had been stripped of its bark. It was four to five feet in length and weighed several pounds. Some of its surface had been tempered and blackened by fire. A few nails were embedded in it, their heads protruding and facing outward. Most of its surface was carved with obscenities. The beating stick's appearance was as formidable as its moniker.

As I continued leafing through papers, I came to a document that made my heart sink. Like all of my other clients before him, this defendant had confessed to police. A proper rights warning/waiver certificate, signed by my client and properly witnessed, dutifully accompanied the confession. I was crestfallen and quickly became resigned to the idea that this case, like all the others, would probably be resolved by yet another guilty plea.

The next day I met with my client for the first time. He struck me as a squared away soldier and a good-looking young man. Before meeting him, I thankfully noted that he had no prior brushes with the law. As we began talking, I could tell he was well spoken and respectful, and he looked me in the eyes when he talked. My initial thought was at least he would make a good impression on the jury, or what the military refers to as the court members, and that this could help in obtaining a break on sentencing.

After guiding my client through the ordinary preliminary matters, I turned to a discussion of the particulars of his case. My client confirmed to me that he had freely confessed after a proper rights advisement. He also admitted that the confession accurately described what had happened, i.e., he had taken the beating stick with him and sought out and confronted the victim. During his encounter with the victim, my client said he grasped the stick like a baseball bat and savagely beat him about the head and shoulders with it. My client confirmed that he struck the first blows and the victim appeared to be unarmed. The police report confirmed that no weapons were discovered on the victim's person or in the vicinity of the confrontation. My client did not suffer any notable injuries.

I explained to my client that in light of these circumstances I would, among other tasks, begin exploring the possibility of negotiating a favorable pretrial agreement that limited his punishment in exchange for a guilty plea. My client immediately interrupted. "Sir," he said, "I cannot plead guilty." I explained that such a decision would be his and would not be made today, but rather this possibility would be evaluated much later in the process when we were in a better position to assess the strength of the government's case and consider all options. My client insisted, "Sir, you don't understand. My father is a retired command sergeant major. He does not know I've been arrested. I can't plead guilty and he can't know about the trial." I suggested that with my client's permission, I could arrange for a joint phone call with the two of us and my client's father. This would afford my client the opportunity, with my participation and support, to break the news to his father and answer all of his questions. My client remained adamant—he would not plead guilty under any circumstances and his father could never be told about his troubles. My client never wavered from this position throughout my representation of him.

For the next several days, I was consumed by the case and the poor prospects for a favorable result. It seemed each night I would lie restlessly in bed and struggle with how I should proceed. A conviction seemed all but certain. Moreover, given the serious injuries suffered by the victim and the inflammatory appearance of the beating stick, I feared that my client would be punished with a dishonorable discharge and a substantial term of confinement. And I grew resigned to the idea that there was little I could do on the merits and my principal objective would be to manage damage control on sentencing.

One evening while lying in bed, as I was contemplating the seeming hopelessness of pending court-martial, my mind wandered to a distant memory—*Anatomy of Murder*. Smiling, I asked myself what would Paul Biegler do? After all, my circumstances were not so different from his. Here I was, a lone defense counsel in an isolated peninsular location. My client's factual guilt seemed unassailable. Yet, this would be a contested trial and I would need to discover a path towards a possible acquittal.

Like Biegler, I reasoned my only hope for success seemed to be via jury nullification, as the confession could not be suppressed, and the evidence of factual guilt was overwhelming. Also, like Biegler, I needed to identify a legal peg upon which the jury could rest its decision to nullify. Unlike Biegler, however, insanity was not an option in my case for a host of reasons. Thus, by process of elimination, it seemed my only hope for an acquittal was to fashion a self-defense claim as window dressing for jury nullification.

The following morning when I met with my client, I quickly engaged him in my version of "the Lecture." Navigating the same ethical tightrope as Biegler, I succeeded in having my client present to me the rudiments of a self-defense claim. He told me, among other things, that he heard that the victim had been violent in the past and threatened future harm to him and his friends. Some of these threats, my client said, related to the sale of illegal drugs. Because the victim was a drug dealer, my client said that he feared the victim would likely be armed and dangerous when he went to confront him. My client said that because of these fears, he took the beating stick with him for protection. My client said that when he met with the victim and verbally confronted him, the victim responded by threatening his life while moving toward him. My client said that he protected himself by preemptively striking the victim with the stick. I now had my legal peg for jury nullification—self-defense. Like Biegler, I was aware that I had guided my client down this path towards a plausible defense but was confident that I did so consistent with the rules.

In *Anatomy of a Murder*, Biegler recognized that to obtain an acquittal he had to put the victim on trial. I concluded I had to do the same in my case. Through pretrial witness interviews, I established that the victim was a known drug dealer who frequently made threats and was reputedly involved in a few physical altercations. I also learned from a police source that the victim was under investigation by local authorities for drug dealing. In addition, the agent who took my client's confession told me that he had a low opinion of the victim's character and veracity. I now had some ammunition with which to prosecute the victim at the trial.

I also had to deal with the "beating stick." I learned through interviews with my client and his friends that they belonged to an informal social group that sometimes used the stick for certain ceremonial purposes. At trial I referred to this group as a "social club"; the prosecutor, over my objection, called it a "gang." While somehow managing to keep a straight face, I referred to the stick as the "ceremonial staff"; the prosecutor, over my objection via a motion in limine, was allowed to call it a "beating stick," a term she repeatedly invoked with great relish throughout the trial. Anticipating that she would do this, I sought to minimize the damage by proactively embracing the staff, literally. During voir dire and opening statement, and with the judge's permission, I held the stick and displayed it to the court members. While doing this, I explained to the court members that the evidence would show that my client acted reasonably by taking the stick with him for protection when confronting a dangerous drug dealer who was likely armed.

Most troubling of all for the defense case was my client's confession. Like Biegler in *Anatomy of a Murder*, I could not get it suppressed. And so, like Biegler, I decided to embrace my client's rendition of events. Throughout witness preparation and mock cross-examination, my client concentrated on testifying without variance from his confession. Then, in my opening statement, I told the court members that after all the evidence was presented, they would conclude the defendant would be the only witness to appear at this trial who consistently told the truth throughout this entire episode, including on the witness stand before you. I said that when the defendant was questioned by police, he freely and accurately told them what he had done despite being advised he had a right to remain silent and consult with an attorney. And I said that the defendant would likewise testify truthfully in court and submit himself to cross-examination by the prosecutor, even though the judge has advised him that he has an absolute right not to testify. Through it all, I said my client would never waiver in his testimony because he was being truthful and candid.

I then turned to the victim's (of course I did not refer to him in this manner) lack of veracity and propensity to lie. I predicted that the law enforcement agent who took the defendant's statement will testify he believed what the defendant said to him, and that this agent found the defendant to be credible. I said this same agent would also testify that the victim had been dealing drugs and was not being completely truthful when he questioned him.

At trial, the prosecution called the victim as its first witness. Unlike Biegler, I had a living, breathing victim I could "prosecute." On direct examination, the victim recounted the defendant's attack and the injuries he suffered. His demeanor was poor, and he seemed evasive. During his testimony on cross-examination, the victim admitted to lying to police on past occasions and was inconsistent about several matters. Further, the victim denied ever dealing drugs and making threats; the testimony of several other witnesses, including some of the prosecution witnesses, contradicted these claims. Taken all together, the victim's credibility and character were substantially damaged. From a defense standpoint, the victim's testimony went as well as could have been hoped.

Later, the prosecutor called the agent who took the defendant's statement. His testimony was needed by the government to lay the foundation for admitting the defendant's confession. On cross-examination, the agent opined that the defendant was truthful throughout his interrogation of him. The agent also said that while obtaining the confession, he (the agent) was absolutely truthful with the defendant and did not try to deceive him. Later during the cross, the agent reluctantly acknowledged that he told the defendant that the victim was a bad person and that many people could understand why he had beaten him. The witness then confirmed that he was being truthful when he made these disparaging remarks about the victim to the defendant.

The prosecution objected to this line of questioning, but the judge allowed it for the limited purpose of assessing whether the confession was voluntary. The judge cautioned the court members that whether the agent lied to the defendant in obtaining the statement was relevant only for this limited purpose. From the defense standpoint, the judge's instruction was meaningless. My actual motivation for this line of questioning was unrelated to voluntariness. Rather, my purpose was to have the court members hear from the lead agent that the defendant was truthful, the victim was a lying drug dealer, and reasonable people, including law enforcement personnel, could genuinely appreciate why the defendant had beaten the victim.

I also asked the agent if the victim was the subject of an on-going criminal investigation involving drug distribution, which I had a good faith basis to believe. The agent said, as I was well aware and expected, that regulations prohibited him from either confirming or denying whether this was true. His inability to confirm the substance of the question was meaningless. The court members understood from our exchange that the victim was a drug dealer, but the agent was prohibited from confirming it.

After the prosecution had rested, the defendant testified during the defense case-in-chief. He was careful to avoid any contradictions between his trial testimony and his pretrial confession. Indeed, the defendant expressly confirmed that his statement to police was all true and that he stood by it. The defendant then addressed several additional matters not included in the confession, such as his knowledge about the victim's past violence and threats, and his concern that he might be harmed by the violent victim who was usually armed. As we anticipated, the prosecutor asked the defendant on cross-examination why he did not mention any of this additional information in his earlier statement to the police. The defendant replied, consistent with our pretrial preparation, that he would have done so had the police asked him about it at the time. The defendant explained he was fully cooperative and responsive to the police, but the agents seemed interested only about the circumstances immediately surrounding the confrontation and were unconcerned about the reasons that led up to it.

After both sides had rested and during the conference on charging the court members, the prosecution objected to the judge instructing on self-defense, claiming that the defense was not reasonably raised by the evidence. In support of its position, the prosecution argued that the defendant was the aggressor, there was no imminent threat of force by the victim, the use of deadly force by the defendant was disproportional and unjustified, and the defendant could have safely retreated. These were all reasonable arguments, and they were likely ones I would have made if the roles were reversed. I countered that all of the prosecutor's contentions were questions of fact and witness credibility that she was free to argue to the jury. That said, I submitted that the defendant was entitled to defend against the charge on the basis of self-defense, with the benefit of an appropriate instruction, and to have the jury resolve any contested questions of fact. I urged that to deny a self-defense instruction was tantamount to preventing my client from presenting a defense. The judge agreed with the defense and instructed on self-defense. After a relatively short deliberation, the court members found the defendant not guilty.

I am convinced that the major reason why the court members voted to acquit is that they liked my client and despised the victim, and thus they concluded it would be unfair and unjust to convict in this case. I suspect some of the members imagined their son or brother when they looked at the defendant. Even granting all of this, it still seems remarkable to me that a group of commissioned and senior noncommissioned officers, who live their lives following and enforcing rules, would decide to nullify in seeming contradiction to their oath and the judge's instructions. Such an outcome would not compute for the Russian observers described by Preminger. The members' verdict in my case speaks to the pervasiveness of the unwritten law and the natural inclination towards poetic justice.

This was my first acquittal. For this reason alone, it will always hold a special place in my memory. Looking back decades later, I doubt whether I could have achieved the same outcome without the assistance of John Voelker and his alter ego, Paul Biegler. I lost track of my client soon after the trial. I choose to think he was scared straight by the experience and lived a good and productive life. Regardless of the path he later followed, my client's acquittal represents another distant ripple that can be traced back to *Anatomy of a Murder*. As Leonardo da Vinci said, "Everything is connected to everything else."[1]

I am not, however, blinded by the favorable outcome of the trial. I understand that by the letter of the law, the defendant was guilty. That said, I cannot help but believe that justice was served by his acquittal. I have also examined my own conduct and concluded I acted ethically. That said, I know that I straddled the line between advising a client and suborning perjury. I am also quite aware that I was personally and professionally motivated to obtain an acquittal. Writing this book has caused me to relive the trial and think about my actions, now with greater perspective and more experience. And although I might entertain a slight residue of doubt about some of my conduct, I am certain I would do the same thing again if confronted with a similar situation.

Despite all troubling implications of Voelker's actual trial and my own case, I believe in the end they help affirm the efficacy of the American criminal justice system and the professionalism of those who toil in it. Voelker's case was tried in the 1950s at a state trial in an isolated backwater on the outskirts of civilization. My case was tried in the 1980s by a military tribunal at a remote post in the middle of Korea. Both cases were well judged and well litigated by both sides. The adversarial character of the trial was robust. The legal arguments were well considered and, in some cases, sophisticated. The juries acted with independence and their decisions reflected community values.

During the summer of 2018, I traveled to Marquette to conduct research for this book. While there, I stopped by the famous courthouse where the Peterson case was tried and *Anatomy of a Murder* was filmed. I saw that a trial was in session, and so I sat in the back of the gallery and observed. I immediately noticed that some things had changed since the 1950's. The gallery was practically empty; only about a half dozen people total were present, sitting on opposite sides to show support for the victim and the defendant. The courtroom had been retrofitted to accommodate an assortment of modern technology, most of which was unknown and perhaps unimagined decades earlier. The judge and the prosecutor were both women, a happy occurrence that would have been close to statistically impossible in American courtrooms at the time of the Peterson trial. But besides these few changes, I also noted that most things seemed undisturbed by the passage of time. The lawyers effectively examined and cross-examined witnesses. They were adversarial, raising well-considered objections that the judge correctly and fairly resolved. The jury seemed attentive. Decorum and ceremony were preserved and honored. All participants were respectful. Justice appeared to be sought.

My observations at this random trial confirmed for me that the most extraordinary aspect of the Peterson case and my trial in Korea is that they are, in fact, not so extraordinary. Quite to the contrary, I believe they represent the norm in American courtrooms. If this is true, they should be a source of comfort and pride for lawyers and lay persons alike. Comfort in that they provide reassurance that when a defendant is charged and tried for a criminal offense, he will likely receive a fair trial and might be acquitted if justice, however defined, requires this outcome even if this contravenes the strict letter of the law. A source of pride insofar as they are emblematic of the commitment and dedication, and acumen and skill, demonstrated by judges and lawyers on a daily basis throughout the legal system. The greater significance of these two cases is not that they are special, but rather that they are commonplace and what we have come to expect.

These cases also reflect that for all of its rules and formalities, the criminal justice system is a rather rudimentary endeavor in which juries and judges usually try to do the right thing. It is also a human endeavor, and thus invariably and unavoidably flawed. While *Anatomy of Murder* lays bare many of these shortcomings and raises important questions about the law and justice, it also reaffirms that defendants generally get a fair shake when they enter a criminal courtroom charged with a serious crime. Human history tells us that this is not an insignificant or modest achievement.

Notes

Foreword

[1] Garfield, Robert. Breaking the Male Code: Unlocking the Power of Friendship (Gotham Books 2015).

[2] Unburdened by the Male Code, women tend to excel, in comparison to men, at creating new "confidant" relationships throughout their lives. As a result, as they get older, men tend to feel lonelier, and to have fewer confidants compared to women. Joiner, T.E. Lonely at the Top: The High Cost of Men's Success (Palgrave Macmillan 2011).

[3] McPherson, Miller, Lynn Smith-Lovin and Matthew E. Brashears, "Social Isolation in America: Changes in Core Discussion Networks over Two Decades," 71 Am. Sociological Rev. 353 (Am. Soc. Ass'n 2006) ("Discussion networks are smaller in 2004 than in 1985. *The number of people saying there with no one with whom they discuss important matters nearly tripled. The mean network size decreases by about a third (one confidant), from 2.94 in 1985 to 2.08 in 2004.* The modal respondent now reports having no confidant; the modal respondent in 1985 had three confidants. Both kin and non-kin confidants were lost in the past two decades, but the greater decrease of non-kin ties leads to more confidant networks centered on spouses and parents, with fewer contacts through voluntary associations and neighborhoods.") (emphasis added).

Preface

[1] Traver, Robert. *Anatomy of a Murder* (1983) (Voelker's fond blessing when he released a fish caught after landing it with infinite skill and patience).

[2] After he became a "celebrity" due to his massive success with *Anatomy*, Voelker appeared on "See It Now," with host Fred Friendly, the then-President of CBS. Friendly asked "Lord Whosis," of the Queen's Bench, and Justice William O. Douglas, of the United States Supreme Court, if they enjoyed cooking. After each described some favorite dish they liked to prepare, Voelker recalled, "When he came to me, Friendly said, 'And what about you, Justice Voelker?' to which I replied, 'I do cook, after an old-fashioned.'"

[3] These concepts reflected his familiarity with an analysis technique referred to as the "Johari window." The idea of "unknown unknowns" was created in 1955 by two American psychologists, Joseph Luft (1916–2014), and Harrington Ingham (1916–1995), in their development of the Johari window—a technique to help people better understand their relationship with themselves and others.

[4] As Voelker once eloquently stated in *Huffman v First Baptist Church*, 355 Mich 437, 446 (1959):

> We are so often compelled to repeat this elementary proposition that we are moved to observe that it is probable that few trial judges, however experienced or learned, if given more time for meditation and research, would again give precisely the same jury instructions that they actually gave. Upon further reflection their instructions would doubtless be less halting and redundant, infinitely clearer and more cogent and more on target—much like the compelling jury arguments most lawyers make to their bedroom ceilings the night after the trial is over.

[5] Marquette Circuit Court Docket No. 15987 (1952).

[6] Traver, Robert. *Laughing Whitefish* (1965).

[7] Baker, Fred, and Vander Veen III, Richard. *Michigan Lawyers in History* (2001): 531 (quote attributed to CBS journalist Charles Kuralt).

Chapter 1 Endnotes

[1] Voelker, John. "John D. Voelker Papers." Central Upper Peninsula and Northern Michigan University Archives.

Chapter 2 Endnotes

[1] Chicago Tribune (*on file in the* John D. Voelker Papers, MSS-039, Central Upper Peninsula and Northern Michigan University Archives, Northern Michigan University).

[2] Delene, Elizabeth. *John Donaldson Voelker: Life's Influences On A Man's Writing Career* at 18 (Northern Michigan University Department of History, Thesis Submitted April 1997).

[3] *Anatomy '59: The Making of a Classic Motion Picture* (WMNU-TV Broadcast 2009).

[4] The population of Ishpeming is now about 6,000, *July 1, 2018, Ishpeming City Michigan*, Census, https://www.census.gov/quickfacts/fact/table/ishpemingcitymichigan/PST040218 (last visited Nov. 9, 2019). In 1950, the population and city totals were over 10,000, *1950 Census, Michigan*, Census, https://www2.census.gov/library/publications/decennial/1950/population-volume-1/vol-01-25.pdf (last visited Nov.9, 2019).

[5] Delene, *John Donaldson Voelker* at 4; Interview by Robert F. Lane with John D. Voelker, Justice of the Michigan Supreme Court (Oct. 1, 1990) (transcript available at https://archive.lib.msu.edu/AFS/dmc/court/public/all/Voelker/ASY.html).

[6] Hansen, Joan G. *Anatomy of "Anatomy" – The Making of a Movie* 17 (Globe Printing Inc. 1997 2d ed. 2013).

[7] Hansen, Anatomy of "Anatomy," at 17.

[8] Hansen, Anatomy of "Anatomy," at 17.

[9] Delene, John Donaldson Voelker, at 5.

[10] Delene, John Donaldson Voelker, at 3.

[11] Delene, John Donaldson Voelker, at 5.

[12] Delene, John Donaldson Voelker, at 5.

[13] Delene, John Donaldson Voelker, at 5.

[14] Noble, William T. *Voelker: An Anatomy of a Private Life*, Det. News Mag. 12, 35 (1967).

[15] *Anatomy of an Author*, Michigan Alumnus, Jan. 18, 1958.

[16] *Anatomy of an Author*, Michigan Alumnus, Jan. 18, 1958.

[17] Traver, Robert. *Troubleshooter: The Story of a Northwoods Prosecutor* (1943), at 22.

[18] Traver, Robert. *Troubleshooter*, at 61.

[19] Delene, *John Donaldson Voelker*, at 3.

[20] Delene, *John Donaldson Voelker*, at 3.

[21] Interview by Robert F. Lane with John D. Voelker, Justice of the Michigan Supreme Court (Oct. 1, 1990) (transcript available at https://archive.lib.msu.edu/AFS/dmc/court/public/all/Voelker/ASY.html).

[22] Interview by Eugene R. Milhizer with Richard Vander Veen III (Aug. 8, 2018).

[23] Delene, *John Donaldson Voelker*, at 6.

[24] Delene, *John Donaldson Voelker*, at 19.

[25] Fowler, G. William. *The Fishing Notes of John D. Voelker, Michigan's Mightiest Piscator*, 42 Am. Fly Fisher 2, 4–5 (Fall 2016).

[26] Delene, *John Donaldson Voelker*, at 51.

[27] Shaul, Richard D. *Backwoods Barrister*, Mich. Hist. Mag., Nov./Dec. 2001, at 84, http://www.superiorreading.com/pdf/anatomy.pdf.

[28] Interview by Eugene R. Milhizer with John Wirtanen (2019).

[29] Shaul, *Backwoods Barrister*, at 86.

[30] Interview by Eugene R. Milhizer with Ernest Woods (2018).

[31] *John Voelker (Alias Robert Traver): Anatomy of an Author*, Michigan Foundation for the Arts (1982), https://archive.org/details/johnvoelkeraliasroberttraveranatomyofanauthor.

[32] Delene, *John Donaldson Voelker*, at 20.

[33] Peters, John. *Robert Traver: Anatomy of a Fisherman*, Russell Kirk Ctr. (Nov. 30, 2008), https://kirkcenter.org/essays/robert-traver/.

[34] Delene, *John Donaldson Voelker*, at 19.

[35] Delene, *John Donaldson Voelker*, at 19

[36] Delene, *John Donaldson Voelker*, at 19.

[37] Delene, *John Donaldson Voelker*, at 50.

[38] Delene, *John Donaldson Voelker*, at 50.

[39] Delene, *John Donaldson Voelker*, at 5.

[40] Delene, *John Donaldson Voelker*, at 48–49.

[41] Delene, *John Donaldson Voelker*, at 48.

[42] Delene, *John Donaldson Voelker*, at 48.

[43] Delene, *John Donaldson Voelker*, at 49.

[44] Delene, *John Donaldson Voelker*, at 49.

[45] Delene, *John Donaldson Voelker*, at 49.

[46] Delene, *John Donaldson Voelker*, at 50.

[47] Delene, *John Donaldson Voelker*, at 50.

[48] Delene, *John Donaldson Voelker*, at 47.

[49] Traver, *Troubleshooter*, at 89

[50] Delene, *John Donaldson Voelker*, at 6.

[51] Delene, *John Donaldson Voelker*, at 9.

[52] Delene, *John Donaldson Voelker*, at 9.

[53] Interview by Eugene R. Milhizer with Ernest Woods (2018).

[54] Delene, *John Donaldson Voelker*, at 10.

[55] Delene, *John Donaldson Voelker*, at 11.

[56] Delene, *John Donaldson Voelker*, at 11.

[57] Delene, *John Donaldson Voelker*, at 12.

[58] Noble, *Voelker: An Anatomy of a Private Life*, at 35.

[59] *Northern's History,* N. Mich. U., https://www.nmu.edu/nmuhistory (last visited Sept. 8, 2019).

[60] Delene, *John Donaldson Voelker*, at 11.

[61] Noble, *Voelker: An Anatomy of a Private Life*, at 33.

[62] Acker, Steve. *Trout Stamp*, Mich. Nat. Resources, Mar./Apr. 1988, at 9.

[63] Acker, *Trout Stamp*, at 9.

[64] Delene, *John Donaldson Voelker*, at 17.

[65] *Anatomy of an Author*, Michigan Alumnus, Jan. 18, 1958.

[66] Voelker, "A Lawyer Graduates," *in* Delene, *John Donaldson Voelker*, at 16–17.

[67] Delene, *John Donaldson Voelker*, at 17.

[68] Voelker, "A Lawyer Graduates," *in* Delene, *John Donaldson Voelker*, at 17.

[69] Delene, *John Donaldson Voelker*, at 18.

[70] *Anatomy of an Author*, Mich. Alumnus, Jan. 18, 1958.

[71] Delene, *John Donaldson Voelker*, at 22.

[72] Voelker, John. Journal February 1, 1950, *in* Delene, *John Donaldson Voelker*, at 22.

[73] Delene, *John Donaldson Voelker*, at 21.

[74] Using poetic license, Voelker usually referred to the county office as "District Attorney" or "D.A." in a nod to the entertainment world. David Hacker, *John Voelker: 86 and Still A Storyteller*, Chicago Tribune (Oct. 24, 1989), https://www.chicagotribune.com/news/ct-xpm-1989-10-24-8901240953-story.html.

Voelker wrote in *Anatomy of a Murder* that "the simplest definition of a prosecuting attorney is a D.A. who lacks a comparable press and publicity; otherwise their jobs are the same." Traver, *Anatomy of a Murder*, at 8. Both terms—"prosecuting attorney" and "District Attorney (D.A.)"—will be used interchangeably in this book and treated as synonymous.

[75] Delene, *John Donaldson Voelker*, at 23.

[76] Shaul, *Backwoods Barrister*, at 84.

[77] Delene, *John Donaldson Voelker*, at 26.

[78] Delene, *John Donaldson Voelker*, at 26.

[79] Baker, Frederick. *An Anatomy of Anatomy of A Murder*, Jud. Fam. Inst., http://www.judicialfamilyinstitute.org/~/media/Microsites/Files/JFI/Resources/AN_A NATOMY_OF_ANATOMY_ OF_A_MURDER.ashx (last visited Sept. 7, 2019). Voelker uses the phrase "law-looking" *in* Traver, *Anatomy of a Murder*, at 247.

[80] Interview by Robert F. Lane with John D. Voelker, Justice of the Michigan Supreme Court (Oct. 1, 1990) (transcript available at https://archive.lib.msu.edu/AFS/dmc/court/public/all/Voelker/ASY.html).

Voelker's distaste for his job in Chicago should not be mistaken for his dissatisfaction with the legal system or the law as a profession. As Voelker writes in Anatomy of a Murder,

> The law, for all its lurching and shambling imbecilities, the law – and only the law – is what keeps our society from bursting apart at the seams, and becoming a snarling jungle. While the law is not perfect, God knows, no other system has been found for governing men except violence.

Traver, *Anatomy of a Murder*, at 63.

[81] Voelker, John. Journal, 1931 (*on file in the* John D. Voelker Papers, MSS-039, Central Upper Peninsula and Northern Michigan University Archives, Northern Michigan University).

[82] Voelker, John. Journal, 1931 (*on file in the* John D. Voelker Papers, MSS-039, Central Upper Peninsula and Northern Michigan University Archives, Northern Michigan University). He said that cities in general are "really uninhabitable." Noble, *Voelker: An Anatomy of a Private Life*, at 33.

[83] *Anatomy of an Author*, Michigan Alumnus, Jan. 18, 1958. *See also* Delene, *John Donaldson Voelker*, at 51.

[84] Baker, *An Anatomy of Anatomy of A Murder*.

[85] Traver, *Troubleshooter*, at 83.

[86] Delene, *John Donaldson Voelker*, at 51.

[87] Delene, *John Donaldson Voelker*, at 51.

[88] Traver, *Troubleshooter*, at 83.

[89] Delene, *John Donaldson Voelker*, at 52.

[90] Interview by Eugene R. Milhizer with Ernest Woods (2018).

[91] Delene, *John Donaldson Voelker*, at 52.

Chapter 3 Endnotes

[1] Noble, *Voelker: An Anatomy of a Private Life*, at 12. Voelker also liked to refer to mushrooms as big as "hamburger buns strewn across the forest floor." Katie Vloet, *Anatomy of an Alumnus*, 52 L. Quadrangle, Fall 2009, at 42.

[2] Letter from Voelker to his mother, Jan. 15, 1931 (*on file in the* John D. Voelker Papers, MSS-039, Central Upper Peninsula and Northern Michigan University Archives, Northern Michigan University).

[3] Interview by Robert F. Lane with John D. Voelker, Justice of the Michigan Supreme Court (Oct. 1, 1990) (transcript available at https://archive.lib.msu.edu/AFS/dmc/court/public/all/Voelker/ASY.html).

[4] Delene, *John Donaldson Voelker*, at 9.

[5] Noble, *Voelker: An Anatomy of a Private Life*, at 14.

[6] Woessner, Bob. *UP's John Voelker Continues Work He Loves in His Country*, Green Bay Press Gazette, Mar. 6, 1966, at 3.

[7] Interview by Eugene R. Milhizer with Frederick Baker (2018).

[8] Woessner, *UP's John Voelker Continues Work He Loves in His Country*, at 2.

[9] Noble, *Voelker: An Anatomy of a Private Life*, at 14. In *Anatomy of a Murder*, Biegler expresses the same bomb-the-bridge sentiments: "for years the straits stood as our English channel against invasion from the south." Traver, *Anatomy of a Murder*, at 335. The references to the Mackinac Bridge in the novel are anachronistic, as the Bridge did not open until after the Peterson trial had concluded.

[10] Noble, *Voelker: An Anatomy of a Private Life*, at 14.

[11] Voelker routinely kept a diary-like journal, often with daily entries, for several years. Voelker explained its purpose in an April 19, 1948, entry:

> I have been reading the Journals of Andre Gide and Henry James, and I have been impressed that the keeping of an informal daily journal is a good thing for a writer; that it is in itself a literary discipline; that it may become a sort of reservoir for ideas and impressions that might otherwise be lost.

Voelker, John. Journal, 1948-1950 (*on file in the* John D. Voelker Papers, MSS-039, Central Upper Peninsula and Northern Michigan University Archives, Northern Michigan University).

[12] "Yooper" is an endearing slang term that refers to residents of Michigan's Upper Peninsula. *Yooper*, Merriam-Webster, https://www.merriam-webster.com/dictionary/Yooper (last visited Sept. 8, 2019).

[13] *Anatomy of an Author*, Mich. Alumnus, Jan. 18, 1958.

[14] *Anatomy of an Author*, Mich. Alumnus, Jan. 18, 1958.

[15] *Student Profile, John D. Voelker*, Michigan Law, https://www.law.umich.edu/historyandtraditions/students/Pages/ProfilePage.aspx?SID=11113&Year=1928 (last visited Nov. 9, 2019).

[16] Baker, Jr., Frederick M. & Rich Vander Veen III, *Michigan Lawyers in History--John D. Voelker: Michigan's Literary Justice*, Mich. B. J. 530, 530 (2001).

[17] *Anatomy of an Author*, Mich. Alumnus, Jan. 18, 1958.

[18] Voelker's respect for Native Americans is perhaps best reflected in his novel *Laughing Whitefish*. Matthew L.M.Fletcher, *Laughing Whitefish: Justice and Anishinaabe Custom*, MICH. ST. U. C. L. 2008, at 2; Interview by Eugene R. Milhizer with Frederick Baker (2018).

[19] Voelker would go to great lengths to protect his privacy. He would hide his "fish car" in the woods and conceal the paths and trails he hiked, never revealing the location of his favorite fishing spots except to those closest to him. Fowler, *The Fishing Notes of John D. Voelker*, at 13–14.

[20] Noble, *Voelker: An Anatomy of a Private Life*, at 14.

[21] Fowler, *The Fishing Notes of John D. Voelker*, at 9.

[22] His quest for uranium was motivated by a desire for riches rather than a love for nature. Frederick Baker, *Reflections on the 50th Anniversary of Anatomy of a Murder*, Mich. Bar J. 50, 51 (Sept. 2008) (reviewing *Anatomy of a Murder* (1968)), https://www.michbar.org/file/barjournal/article/documents/pdf4article1405.pdf; Delene, *John Donaldson Voelker*, at 76–80. In fact, Voelker feared the prospect of nuclear war, writing in his journal that the "[f]uture can hold only disaster for all of us. The reason for my almost pathological drive to crowd everything into the present when searing light bursts upon the world. I want to have <u>lived</u> . . . ." John Voelker, Journal, 1947 (*on file in the* John D. Voelker Papers, MSS-039, Central Upper Peninsula and Northern Michigan University Archives, Northern Michigan University). Later, Voelker would campaign unenthusiastically and unsuccessfully for Congress. Baker, *Reflections on the 50th Anniversary*.

[23] Noble, *Voelker: An Anatomy of a Private Life*, at 32. Voelker occasionally hunted fowl but only to scout out rivers when fishing season had ended. Fowler, *The Fishing Notes of John D. Voelker*, at 9.

[24] Delene, *John Donaldson Voelker*, at 144.

[25] Fowler, *The Fishing Notes of John D. Voelker*, at 7.

[26] Noble, *Voelker: An Anatomy of a Private Life*, at 35.

[27] Noble, *Voelker: An Anatomy of a Private Life*, at 35.

[28] Fowler, *The Fishing Notes of John D. Voelker*, at 5.

[29] Ishpeming High School Yearbook, 1922.

[30] *Anatomy of an Author*, Michigan Alumnus, Jan. 18, 1958.

[31] Delene, *John Donaldson Voelker*, at 151.

[32] Delene, *John Donaldson Voelker*, at 19.

[33] *John Voelker (Alias Robert Traver): Anatomy of an Author*, Michigan Foundation for the Arts (1982), https://archive.org/details/johnvoelkeraliasroberttraveranatomyofanauthor.

[34] Voelker claimed he missed only a single day one season because of a "monumental hangover." Noble, *Voelker:An Anatomy of a Private Life*, at 14.

[35] Fowler, *The Fishing Notes of John D. Voelker*, at 9–10.

[36] Fowler, *The Fishing Notes of John D. Voelker*, at 9–10.

[37] Fowler, *The Fishing Notes of John D. Voelker*, at 9–10.

[38] Fowler, *The Fishing Notes of John D. Voelker*, at 13.

[39] Voelker named his favorite fishing spot and private refuge "Frenchman's Pond." It has been called "arguably . . . the most famous still-water fishery in America, its fame not because of the fish, but because of Voelker's writings. "Fowler, *The Fishing Notes of John D. Voelker*, at 14. Frenchman's cannot be found on a map; its real name was "Uncle Tom's Pond" – "Uncles" for short. Fowler, *The Fishing Notes of John D. Voelker*, at 10–11.

[40] Fowler, *The Fishing Notes of John D. Voelker*, at 13.

[41] Fowler, *The Fishing Notes of John D. Voelker*, at 13.

[42] Interview by Eugene R. Milhizer with John Wirtanen (2019).

[43] Shaul, *Backwoods Barrister*, at 84.

[44] Vloet, *Anatomy of an Alumnus*, at 41.

[45] Noble, *Voelker: An Anatomy of a Private Life*, at 14.

[46] Noble, *Voelker: An Anatomy of a Private Life*, at 14.

[47] *John D. Voelker*, Fresh Water Fishing Hall of Fame Inductees, https://www.freshwater-fishing.org/inductees-list-gallery/#(autogrid-grid-5c9bc65c17379|filter)=.S-T-U-V;(autogrid-grid-5c9bc65c17379|popup)=/wp-content/plugins/wp_auto_grid/galleries/inductees-letters-list//S%20T%20U%20V/Voelker,%20John%20D.jpg (last visited Nov. 9, 2019).

[48] Traver, Robert. *Trout Madness, Being a Dissertation on the Symptoms and Pathology of this Incurable Disease by One of Its Victims* (1960).

[49] Traver, Robert. *Anatomy of a Fisherman* (1978).

[50] Flick, Art. (*on file in the* John D. Voelker Papers, MSS-039, Central Upper Peninsula and Northern Michigan University Archives, Northern Michigan University).

[51] Voelker, John. Journal, Dec. 23, 1961 (*on file in the* John D. Voelker Papers, MSS-039, Central Upper Peninsula and Northern Michigan University Archives, Northern Michigan University).

[52] Fowler, *The Fishing Notes of John D. Voelker*, at 8.

[53] Voelker joked that Ishpeming had two seasons: "nine months winter and three months bad sleighing." John Peters, *Robert Traver: Anatomy of a Fisherman*.

[54] Voelker, John. Journal, 1948-1950 (*on file in the* John D. Voelker Papers, MSS-039, Central Upper Peninsula and Northern Michigan University Archives, Northern Michigan University).

[55] Voelker, John. Journal, 1948-1950 (*on file in the* John D. Voelker Papers, MSS-039, Central Upper Peninsula and Northern Michigan University Archives, Northern Michigan University).

[56] Voelker once said, "Fishing is such great fun, I have often felt, that it really ought to be done in bed." *Top 19 Quotes by John Voelker*, A-Z Quotes, https://www.azquotes.com/author/31314-John_D_Voelker (last visited Oct 26, 2018).

[57] Voelker, John. Journal, 1947 (*on file in the* John D. Voelker Papers, MSS-039, Central Upper Peninsula and Northern Michigan University Archives, Northern Michigan University).

[58] Voelker, John. Journal, 1953 (*on file in the* John D. Voelker Papers, MSS-039, Central Upper Peninsula and Northern Michigan University Archives, Northern Michigan University).

[59] Voelker, John. Journal, 1954 (*on file in the* John D. Voelker Papers, MSS-039, Central Upper Peninsula and Northern Michigan University Archives, Northern Michigan University).

[60] Voelker, John. Journal, 1954 (*on file in the* John D. Voelker Papers, MSS-039, Central Upper Peninsula and Northern Michigan University Archives, Northern Michigan University).

[61] Voelker once said "[i]t was better to starve in Ishpeming than to wear emeralds in Chicago." Lawrence P. Nolan, *Sacred Grounds and Holy Waters—Frenchman's Pond and Beyond*, Mich. Bar J. 12, 12–13 (Aug. 2017), http://www.michbar.org/file/barjournal/article/documents/pdf4article3186.pdf.

[62] Voelker, John. Journal, 1948-1950 (*on file in the* John D. Voelker Papers, MSS-039, Central Upper Peninsula and Northern Michigan University Archives, Northern Michigan University).

[63] Voelker, John. Journal, 1948-1950 (*on file in the* John D. Voelker Papers, MSS-039, Central Upper Peninsula and Northern Michigan University Archives, Northern Michigan University) (emphasis in original).

[64] Voelker, John. Journal, 1948-1950 (*on file in the* John D. Voelker Papers, MSS-039, Central Upper Peninsula and Northern Michigan University Archives, Northern Michigan University).

[65] Voelker, John. Journal, 1948-1950 (*on file in the* John D. Voelker Papers, MSS-039, Central Upper Peninsula and Northern Michigan University Archives, Northern Michigan University).

[66] Delene, *John Donaldson Voelker*, at 72.

[67] Voelker enthusiastically recorded in his Journal a secondhand account of a comment by a local judge who said that Voelker "was the best prosecutor [the Judge] had ever seen and that [Voelker] was prepared when [he] came in Court and that [he] prosecuted hard and intelligently." John Voelker, Journal, 1950 (*on file in the* John D. Voelker Papers, MSS-039, Central Upper Peninsula and Northern Michigan University Archives, Northern Michigan University).

[68] Krajicek, David J. *Justice Story: The Murder Behind the Movie*, Daily News (Jan. 17, 2009), https://www.nydailynews.com/news/killing-michigan-bar-owner-1952-inspired-film-anatomy-murder-article-1.423705?barcprox=true&print=.

[69] Voelker's notations in his fishing journal do reflect that he fished every day for a month preceding the trial, sometimes only in the afternoon after working on the case in the morning. Fowler, *The Fishing Notes of John D. Voelker*, at 3.

[70] Baker, *Reflections on the 50th Anniversary*.

[71] Baker, *Reflections on the 50th Anniversary*.

[72] Baker, *Reflections on the 50th Anniversary*.

[73] Baker, *An Anatomy of Anatomy of A Murder*.

[74] Shaul, *Backwoods Barrister*, at 85.

[75] Shaul, *Backwoods Barrister*, at 85.

[76] Delene, *John Donaldson Voelker*, at 7.

[77] Delene, *John Donaldson Voelker*, at 37.

[78] Peters, Stephen H. *Biographical Note* (*on file in the* John D. Voelker Papers, MSS-039, Central Upper Peninsula and Northern Michigan University Archives, Northern Michigan University).

[79] Delene, *John Donaldson Voelker*, at 38.

[80] Shaul, *Backwoods Barrister*, at 84.

[81] Delene, *John Donaldson Voelker*, at 38.

[82] Traver, Robert. *Danny and the Boys: Being Some Legends of Hungry Hollow* (1987). "Danny" has far less legal content than the D.A. books, but reflects his remarkable mastery of the now largely vanished Cornish, Finnish, Italian, and French-Canadian Upper Peninsula dialects that he absorbed as a boy listening to miners and lumberjacks in his father's saloon.

[83] Traver, Robert. *Small Town D.A.* (1954).

[84] *Anatomy of an Author*, Michigan Alumnus, Jan. 18, 1958.

[85] Traver, Robert. *The Traver Treatment,* Detroit News, June 25, 1967 (*on file in the* John D. Voelker Papers, MSS-039, Central Upper Peninsula and Northern Michigan University Archives, Northern Michigan University). As Delene notes, "Voelker wrote this column for the Sunday Magazine, from 1967-1969." Delene, *John Donaldson Voelker,* at 54.

[86] Interview by Eugene R. Milhizer with Richard Vander Veen III (Aug. 8, 2018).

[87] Voelker knew he drank too much and tried to quit on several occasions. Delene, *John Donaldson Voelker*, at 50–51.

[88] Grace said her husband was a "gracious man. In a tattered old hat and old boots he was gracious. Notice how carefully he listened and looked? He had a knack for storing things away in his head for future use." Delene, *John Donaldson Voelker*, at 208. He often wore a favorite garment until it was frayed, and more than once observed that "if you find something you like, buy as many as you can afford – it will not be there when you return to buy another." Interview by Eugene R. Milhizer with Frederick Baker (2018).

[89] "Voelker's 'recipe' for an old fashioned was very much 'to taste', but proceeded in a ritual order: in the glass first place two or three sugar cubes. Then add enough Angostora bitters to saturate the cubes without dissolving them. To the cubes then add a maraschino cherry (with stem, for later use as a handle). Then add the bourbon—he preferred Evan Williams, which he considered the equal of Jim Beam, Jack Daniels, or Wild Turkey ('the quality is in the bottle, not in the advertising')— though I know from personal experience that he was more than happy to receive a bottle of a more expensive brand as a gift from grateful visitors to Frenchman's Pond. To this, add cold spring water to the desired strength ('unless you are from the South, and know what branch water is,' he said, tongue in cheek). Finally, a single generous slice of orange—he preferred his unmuddled—and ice until the glass was full enough to require a careful, initial lift to the lips. Then let it sweat in the heat while playing cribbage. Heaven." Interview by Eugene R. Milhizer with Frederick Baker (2018).

[90] Voelker would often leave little love notes for his wife and daughters when he went away. Interview by Eugene R. Milhizer with Frederick Baker (2018). One note to his daughter read, "At the rainbow, call if you need anything." Delene, *John Donaldson Voelker,* at 68.

[91] Delene, *John Donaldson Voelker*, at 206.

[92] Interview by Eugene R. Milhizer with Frederick Baker (2018); Interview by Eugene R. Milhizer with Richard Vander Veen III (Aug. 8, 2018).

[93] Interview by Eugene R. Milhizer with Frederick Baker (2018).

[94] Noble, *Voelker: An Anatomy of a Private Life*, at 33 (quoting attorney Joseph Welch, who would portray the judge in the film *Anatomy of a Murder*).

[95] Volker interjected puns in his daily life and his writings. Baker described his friend Voelker's love of puns as "a test of his listener, that because I share the affliction, I passed with flying colors, making every effort to give as good as I got. If he said 'sprig is cubbing,' it was not because he had a head cold but because spring is when the black bears emerge from their dens with their young, and when sprigs of new life sprout from the ground." Frederick Baker, *John Voelker: Justice, Authority, Fisherman, Friend* (transcript available at http://www.micourthistory.org/wp-content/uploads/speeches_vignettes_pdf/john_voelker.pdf).

[96] Baker, *An Anatomy of Anatomy of A Murder*. For example, when the judge in *Anatomy of a Murder* asks whether counsel have any jury requests, Voelker lied whitely and replied "'Not quite yet, Your Honor.'" Traver, *Anatomy of a Murder*, at 196.

[97] Delene, *John Donaldson Voelker*, at 20. A fine example of this is found in *Children of Suomi*, in which he writes:

> I be walking down U.S. cement highvay dis morning an' one Fording car come down da road likeeverting—hit Tuano 'n nass, nass in da bush, Fording car go like hell down cement road—wifty miles hour!' He paused, 'What you goin' do for dat!'

Traver, *Troubleshooter*, at 125. Another dialect example is the dialog with Sulo Kangus, the jailer of Finnish extraction, in *Anatomy of a Murder*. Traver, *Anatomy of a Murder*, at 20.

[98] Interview by Eugene R. Milhizer with Frederick Baker (2018); Delene, *John Donaldson Voelker*, at 20–21. He also played the Italian clavietta and the mandolin. Fowler, *The Fishing Notes of John D. Voelker*, at 5. As a child, Voelker was prohibited from taking formal music lessons of any kind because his parents did not want a sissy or feminine boy. Voelker picked up playing the piano from observing his mother teaching music lessons at their home. Delene, *John Donaldson Voelker*, at 20-21.

[99] Baker & Vander Veen III, *Michigan Lawyers in History*, at 531.

[100] *Anatomy of a Writer*, Milwaukee J., June 2, 1959.

[101] Delene, *John Donaldson Voelker*, at 99–101.

[102] Delene, *John Donaldson Voelker*, at 204.

[103] Shaul, *Backwoods Barrister*, at 87.

[104] Hansen, *Anatomy of "Anatomy,"* at 16.

[105] Hansen, *Anatomy of "Anatomy,"* at 15–16.

[106] Hansen, *Anatomy of "Anatomy,"* at 16.

[107] Interview by Eugene R. Milhizer with Richard Vander Veen III (Aug. 8, 2018).

[108] Delene, *John Donaldson Voelker*, at 59.

[109] Delene, *John Donaldson Voelker*, at 59.

[110] Shaul, *Backwoods Barrister*, at 85.

[111] Noble, *Voelker: An Anatomy of a Private Life*, at 33.

[112] Interview by Eugene R. Milhizer with Richard Vander Veen III (Aug. 8, 2018);
Fowler, *The Fishing Notes of John D. Voelker*, at 3.

[113] Delene, *John Donaldson Voelker*, at 59.

[114] Traver, *Troubleshooter*, at 10.

[115] Traver, *Small Town D.A.*, at 11.

[116] He had also been defeated in 1942 but was re-elected in the next term. He served
a total of fourteen years as Prosecuting Attorney of Marquette County. Delene, *John
Donaldson Voelker*, at 59, 97.

[117] Baker, *Reflections on the 50th Anniversary*; Delene, *John Donaldson Voelker*, at
76–80.

[118] Traver, *Small Town D.A.*, at 253.

[119] Delene, *John Donaldson Voelker*, at 73.

[120] Delene, *John Donaldson Voelker*, at 73.

[121] Delene, *John Donaldson*, at 99. Voelker wrote in his journal, "It was like the
village gossip – let out after 6 months of lockjaw, the way he ran on after spending
time alone in his office." Delene, *John Donaldson Voelker*, at 99 (citing John
Voelker, Journal, 1948-1950 (*on file in the* John D. Voelker Papers, MSS-039,

Central Upper Peninsula and Northern Michigan University Archives, Northern Michigan University)).

[122] Traver, *Anatomy of a Murder*, "Preface" at i.

[123] Voelker, John. Journal, 1948-1950 (*on file in the* John D. Voelker Papers, MSS-039, Central Upper Peninsula and Northern Michigan University Archives, Northern Michigan University

[124] Traver, *Anatomy of a Murder*, "Preface" at i.

[125] Traver, *Anatomy of a Murder*, "Preface" at i–ii; Delene, *John Donaldson Voelker*, at 101.

Chapter 4 Endnotes

[1] Hunt, Mary Hoffman & Don Hunt. *Hunt's Guide to Michigan's Upper Peninsula* 212 (Midwestern Guides, 2d ed. 2001).

[2] Hunt, *Guide to Michigan's Upper Peninsula*, at 212.

[3] Heldreth, Leonard G. *Anatomy of a Murder From Fact to Fiction to Film, in A Sense of Place: Michigan's Upper Peninsula* 135 (Russell M. Magnaghi & Michael T. Marsden eds., 1994); Trial Tr., Mrs. Charlotte Anne Peterson's Test., at 249.

[4] *Anatomy '59: The Making of a Classic Motion Picture* (WMNU-TV Broadcast 2009).

[5] Interview by Marcus C. Robyns, University Archivist at Northern Michigan University with Max Muelle, Original Peterson Trial Jury Member, in Central Upper Peninsula and Northern Michigan University Archives LRC 126 (July 29, 2008) (audio transcript available at https://www.nmu.edu/voelker/interview.mp3).

[6] Interview by Robyns with Muelle (July 29, 2008).

[7] Interview by Robyns with Muelle (July 29, 2008).

[8] Traver, *Anatomy of a Murder*, at 112; Robert Traver, *The Traver Treatment,* Detroit News, June 25, 1967 (*on file in the* John D. Voelker Papers, MSS-039, Central Upper Peninsula and Northern Michigan University Archives, Northern Michigan University).

[9] Bergman, Shirley J. *The Real Trial*, Mich. Hist. Mag., Nov./Dec. 2001, at 91, http://www.superiorreading.com/pdf/anatomy_2.pdf.

[10] Trial Tr., Mrs. Charlotte Anne Peterson's Test., at 248.

[11] In the movie she played pinball. The tavern's original pinball machine has since been reacquired and is displayed at the Lumberjack. Interview by Eugene R.

Milhizer with Jack Borgeois (2018).

[12] Trial Tr., Mr. Adrian Wentzel's Test., at 218.

[13] According to Jack Borgeois, the owner of the Lumberjack Tavern, it was common knowledge among the local residents that Chenoweth had been dismissed from the state police because of misconduct. Interview by Eugene R. Milhizer with Jack Borgeois (2018).

[14] *Anatomy '59: The Making of a Classic Motion Picture* (WMNU-TV Broadcast 2009). Some sources claim instead that Chenoweth honorably retired from the Michigan State Police after eleven years of service. Ironically, he received a citation for helping to solve a shotgun murder downstate provoked by a lover's triangle.

[15] In an interview years after the trial, Voelker said that he had always believed that Chenoweth was "a terrific officer" who invariably obtained a confession. Voelker suggested that in retrospect he had become troubled about how these confessions may have been obtained.

[16] Daily Mining Journal, Oct. 13, 1982 (*on file in the* John D. Voelker Papers, MSS-039, Central Upper Peninsula and Northern Michigan University Archives, Northern Michigan University).

[17] Interview by Robyns with Muelle (July 29, 2008).

[18] Ticheleaar, Tyler R. *Timeline of Marquette History*, Marquette Fiction, http://marquettefiction.com/marquette-history-timeline.html (last visited Nov. 9, 2019).

[19] One juror said Chenoweth was a "sharpshooter." Another juror said he was over-rated. Bergman, *The Real Trial,* at 91.

[20] Trial Tr., Lieutenant Coleman A. Peterson's Test., at 306.

[21] Bergman, *The Real Trial*, at 91.

[22] *Anatomy '59: The Making of a Classic Motion Picture* (WMNU-TV Broadcast 2009).

[23] Jack Borgeois, who now owns the Lumberjack Tavern, also owns Chenoweth's engraved pistol, and showed it to me on my visit there. Interview by Eugene R. Milhizer with Jack Borgeois (2018).

[24] Years after the Peterson trial, Chenoweth's widow and daughter sued Voelker for defamation of character relating to his portrayal of Chenoweth and his family in *Anatomy of a Murder*. Voelker wrote to Robert Hendrickson, an attorney representing Voelker in the lawsuit, that Chenoweth's "wife came to me shortly before her husband was shot and wanted a divorce because he was such a bastard. I

declined the retainer. I may also add in a general way that I know of reasons, and the wife knows I know of reasons why she should be most reluctant to go to trial." Letter from John Voelker to Robert Hendrickson, New York, June 27, 1960 (*on file in the Wheeler Lawsuit File*, John D. Voelker Papers, MSS-039, Central Upper Peninsula and Northern Michigan University Archives, Northern Michigan University). One can only speculate whether these reasons included allegations of sexual misconduct by Chenoweth.

[25] Interview by Robyns with Muelle (July 29, 2008).

[26] Interview by Robyns with Muelle (July 29, 2008).

[27] Neither allegation was mentioned at the Peterson trial.

[28] Longtine, Sonny. *Murder in Michigan's Upper Peninsula* 111 (2014); Chicago Tribune (*on file in the* John D. Voelker Papers, MSS-039, Central Upper Peninsula and Northern Michigan University Archives, Northern Michigan University).

[29] Interview by Robyns with Muelle (July 29, 2008).

[30] 77th MP Criminal Investigation Detachment, Statement of Adrian N. Wentzel

[31] 77th MP Criminal Investigation Detachment, Statement of Adrian N. Wentzel.

[32] Interview by Robyns with Muelle (July 29, 2008).

[33] *Anatomy '59: The Making of a Classic Motion Picture* (WMNU-TV Broadcast 2009).

[34] *Anatomy '59: The Making of a Classic Motion Picture* (WMNU-TV Broadcast 2009).

[35] Chicago Tribune (*on file in the* John D. Voelker Papers, MSS-039, Central Upper Peninsula and Northern Michigan University Archives, Northern Michigan University); Interview by Eugene R. Milhizer with Jack Borgeois (2018).

[36] Interview by Eugene R. Milhizer with Jack Borgeois (2018). Borgeois told me that years later, while he was remodeling the Tavern, he found a bullet hole in the wall that had been masked by a tin surface. Also, Borgeois showed me Chenoweth's engraved pistol, and he also pointed out a black silhouette painted on the tavern floor where Chenoweth lay dead.

[37] Interview by Eugene R. Milhizer with Jack Borgeois (2018).

[38] Trial Tr., Mrs. Charlotte Anne Peterson's Test., at 266.

[39] Although Chenoweth was officially pronounced dead later, Wentzel testified that he immediately examined Chenoweth's body after the shooting and believed he had

already passed away. 77th MP Criminal Investigation Detachment, Statement of Adrian N. Wentzel.

[40] Trial Tr., Mr. Adrian Wentzel's Test., at 116.

[41] Trial Tr., Mr. Adrian Wentzel's Test., at 117.

[42] 77th MP Criminal Investigation Detachment, Statement of Adrian N. Wentzel.

[43] Trial Tr., Mrs. Charlotte Anne Peterson's Test., at 242.

[44] Milwaukee Sentinel, Sept. 18, 1952 (*on file in the* John D. Voelker Papers, MSS-039, Central Upper Peninsula and Northern Michigan University Archives, Northern Michigan University).

[45] Milwaukee Sentinel, Sept. 18, 1952 (*on file in the* John D. Voelker Papers, MSS-039, Central Upper Peninsula and Northern Michigan University Archives, Northern Michigan University).

[46] Interview by Robyns with Muelle (July 29, 2008).

[47] Interview by Robyns with Muelle (July 29, 2008).

[48] Interview by Robyns with Muelle (July 29, 2008).

[49] *See* Trial Tr., Mrs. Charlotte Anne Peterson's Test., at 248-50 (describing the Peterson's relationship with the Chenoweths before the alleged rape, including visits to the Peterson's trailer and the Tavern).

[50] 77th MP Criminal Investigation Detachment, Statement of Charlotte Ann Peterson.

[51] Heldreth, *Anatomy of a Murder From Fact to Fiction to Film*, at 140.

[52] Daily Mining Journal, Aug. 2, 1952 (*on file in the* John D. Voelker Papers, MSS-039, Central Upper Peninsula and Northern Michigan University Archives, Northern Michigan University).

[53] Wentzel, for one, never believed that Mrs. Peterson was raped. Still, he harbored no resentment toward Voelker, and they and their families even became close friends. During the filming of *Anatomy of a Murder*, Mr. and Mrs. Wentzel portrayed managers of the Big Bay Lodge. Delene, *John Donaldson Voelker*, at 122.

[54] Traver, *Anatomy of a Murder*, at 245.

Chapter 5 Endnotes

[1] *Marquette County, MI*, National Association of Counties, https://ce.naco.org/?county_info=26103 (last visited Nov. 9, 2019).

[2] Eckert, Kathryn Bishop. The Sandstone Architecture of the Lake Superior Region 131–32 (Detroit: Wayne State University Press 2000).

[3] Eckert, The Sandstone Architecture of the Lake Superior Region, at 131–32; Fedynsky, John. Michigan's County Courthouses 117 (Univ. of Mich. Press 2010).

[4] Eckert, The Sandstone Architecture of the Lake Superior Region, at 131–32.

[5] Eckert, The Sandstone Architecture of the Lake Superior Region, at 131–32.

[6] Fedynsky, Michigan's County Courthouses, at 117,

[7] Fedynsky, Michigan's County Courthouses, at 117,

[8] Fedynsky, Michigan's County Courthouses, at 117,

[9] Fedynsky, Michigan's County Courthouses, at 117,

[10] Interview by Eugene R. Milhizer with John (Tom) Burke (Nov. 2019).

[11] *Roosevelt Takes Marquette*, Mikel B. Classen, http://www.mikelclassen.com/Roosevelt_in_Marquette.php (last visited Sept. 8, 2019)

[12] *Roosevelt Takes Marquette*, Mikel B. Classen. Two days later, Taft was shot in the chest by a would-be assassin at a stop in Milwaukee.

[13] *Roosevelt Takes Marquette*, Mikel B. Classen.

[14] *Roosevelt Takes Marquette*, Mikel B. Classen.

[15] *Roosevelt Takes Marquette*, Mikel B. Classen.

[16] McCommons, James. *Roosevelt v. Newett: The Libel Trial of 1913*, 6 Upper Country: J. Lake Superior Region, Art. 2, 2018, at 19.

[17] *Roosevelt Takes Marquette*, Mikel B. Classen.

[18] *Roosevelt Takes Marquette*, Mikel B. Classen.

[19] *Roosevelt Takes Marquette*, Mikel B. Classen.

[20] Interview by Eugene R. Milhizer with John (Tom) Burke (Nov. 2019).

[21] Voelker, John. Journal, 1948-1950 (*on file in the* John D. Voelker Papers, MSS-039, Central Upper Peninsula and Northern Michigan University Archives, Northern Michigan University).

[22] Interview by Robert F. Lane with John D. Voelker, Justice of the Michigan Supreme Court (Oct. 1, 1990) (transcript available at https://archive.lib.msu.edu/AFS/dmc/court/public/all/Voelker/ASY.html).

[23] Interview by Robyns with Muelle (July 29, 2008).

[24] Voelker, John. Journal, 1948-1950 (*on file in the* John D. Voelker Papers, MSS-039, Central Upper Peninsula and Northern Michigan University Archives, Northern Michigan University).

[25] Voelker, John. Journal, 1948-1950 (*on file in the* John D. Voelker Papers, MSS-039, Central Upper Peninsula and Northern Michigan University Archives, Northern Michigan University).

[26] Voelker, John. Journal, 1948-1950 (*on file in the* John D. Voelker Papers, MSS-039, Central Upper Peninsula and Northern Michigan University Archives, Northern Michigan University).

[27] Delene, *John Donaldson Voelker*, at 102.

[28] *Anatomy '59: The Making of a Classic Motion Picture* (WMNU-TV Broadcast 2009).

[29] *Anatomy '59: The Making of a Classic Motion Picture* (WMNU-TV Broadcast 2009).

[30] The juror remembered that Voelker referred to "Boyne City" rather than "Marine City." There is no doubt that the juror was mistaken in his recollection. Interview by Robyns with Muelle (July 29, 2008).

[31] *Anatomy '59: The Making of a Classic Motion Picture* (WMNU-TV Broadcast 2009).

[32] Trial Tr., Mr. Adrian Wentzel's Test., at 122.

[33] Delene, *John Donaldson Voelker*, at 39.

[34] Trial Tr., Lieutenant Coleman A. Peterson's Test., at 319–20.

[35] The juror also called Voelker "damn good" and "sharp." Interview by Robyns with Muelle (July 29, 2008).

[36] *Anatomy '59: The Making of a Classic Motion Picture* (WMNU-TV Broadcast 2009). (Muelle Interview)

[37] Krajicek, *Justice Story: The Murder Behind the Movie*.

[38] Interview by Robyns with Muelle (July 29, 2008).

[39] Daily Mining Journal, Oct. 13, 1982 (*on file in the* John D. Voelker Papers, MSS-039, Central Upper Peninsula and Northern Michigan University Archives, Northern Michigan University). A juror said Voelker talked to the jury while opposing counsel tended to talk "at" them. Interview by Robyns with Muelle (July 29, 2008).

[40] Interview by Robyns with Mulle (July 29, 2008).

[41] Interview by Robyns with Mulle (July 29, 2008).

[42] Delene, *John Donaldson Voelker*, at 102. The jurors, of course, were well aware that Thomas had recently defeated Voelker in the election for prosecutor. Bergman, *The Real Trial*, at 90.

[43] Delene, *John Donaldson Voelker*, at 102.

[44] Delene, *John Donaldson Voelker*, at 102.

[45] Voelker, John. Journal, 1952 (*on file in the* John D. Voelker Papers, MSS-039, Central Upper Peninsula and Northern Michigan University Archives, Northern Michigan University).

[46] Incredibly, Voelker received word about a publisher's acceptance of *Anatomy of a Murder* during the same weekend that he received word that the Governor had appointed him to the Supreme Court. Rover Traver, *Anatomy of a Murder*, "Preface," iii.

[47] *See* Denise Noe, *The Murder In Michigan That Inspired A Culturally Significant Movie: 'Anatomy of a Murder,'* THOUGHT CATALOG (Nov. 2, 2015), https://thoughtcatalog.com/denise-noe/2015/11/the-murder-in-michigan-that-inspired-a-culturally-significant-movie-anatomy-of-a-murder/; *see also* Delene, *John Donaldson Voelker*, at 104.

[48] Traver, *Anatomy of a Murder*, at 45.

[49] In Michigan, the last apparent use of the "irresistible impulse" variant of insanity was in People v. Martin, 721 Mich. App. 280 (Mich. Ct. App. 2006).

[50] *Presenting*, The Collegian, March 6, 1945, at 1.

[51] Interview by Robyns with Mulle (July 29, 2008).

[52] Interview by Robyns with Mulle (July 29, 2008).

[53] Traver, *Troubleshooter*, at 11.

[54] Bergman, *The Real Trial*, at 90-91.

[55] Interview by Eugene R. Milhizer with John (Tom) Burke (Nov. 2019).

[56] Coverage by the local *Mining Journal* newspaper, as well as newspapers in Chicago, Detroit and Milwaukee, was extensive. For example, on August 8 and August 12, 1952, the *Mining Journal* reported that Mrs. Peterson had passed a lie detector test about being raped. The *Chicago Tribune* likewise reported this on September 12, 1952. Surely jurors were aware of this coverage, especially the reports that were published locally before trial began.

[57] Interview by Robyns with Mulle (July 29, 2008).

[58] Elizabeth Delene observed that at the time of the trial, "Voelker was known around the community as a good person and a fair attorney, liked even by Chenoweth's closest friends." Delene, *John Donaldson Voelker,* at 122. In fact, as noted, the Voelkers and the Wentzels developed a close and lasting friendship.

[59] Interview by Robyns with Mulle (July 29, 2008).

[60] *Anatomy '59: The Making of a Classic Motion Picture* (WMNU-TV Boradcast 2009).

Chapter 6 Endnotes

[1] Trial Tr. Opening Statement, at 11–12.

[2] Trial Tr. Opening Statement, at 12.

[3] Another example of Voelker's courtroom flair was his reference to Bolden as "big, red-faced nubby Bolden." Interview by Robyns with Muelle (July 29, 2008).

[4] Trial Tr., Norman Bolden's Test., at 85.

[5] Daily Mining Journal, Oct. 13, 1982 (*on file in the* John D. Voelker Papers, MSS-039, Central Upper Peninsula and Northern Michigan University Archives, Northern Michigan University).

[6] Trial Tr., Norman Bolden's Test., at 86.

[7] Much of the trial portrayed in the novel, including the precise verbal jousting of opposing counsel, is taken almost verbatim from the record of the Peterson trial. The novel diverges here, however, as Biegler's opening statement in the Manion case was described by Biegler as "one of the shortest … in the annuls of Michigan murder." Traver, *Anatomy of a Murder*, at 314.

[8] Trial Tr., Mrs. Charlotte Anne Peterson's Test., at 253.

[9] Trial. Tr., Dr. Warrant Lambert Test., at 289.

[10] Trial Tr., Lieutenant Coleman A. Peterson's Test., at 302–03.

[11] Trial Tr., Lieutenant Coleman A. Peterson's Test., at 300.

[12] Trial Tr., Lieutenant Coleman A. Peterson's Test., at 301.

[13] Trial Tr., Lieutenant Coleman A. Peterson's Test., at 301.

[14] Trial Tr., Lieutenant Coleman A. Peterson's Test., at 301.

[15] Trial Tr., Lieutenant Coleman A. Peterson's Test., at 302.

[16] Trial Tr., Lieutenant Coleman A. Peterson's Test., at 302.

[17] Trial Tr., Mrs. Charlotte Anne Peterson's Test., at 266.

[18] Trial Tr., Lieutenant Coleman A. Peterson's Test., at 319–20.

[19] Trial Tr., Lieutenant Coleman A. Peterson's Test., at 320.

[20] A juror later described Dr. Petty as a "fantastic" witness and the "most intelligent speaker [he] had ever heard." Interview by Robyns with Muelle (July 29, 2008).

[21] Trial Tr., Dr. Thomas A. Petty's Test., at 333–34.

[22] Trial Tr., Dr. Thomas A. Petty's Test., at 333–34.

[23] Trial Tr., Dr. Thomas A. Petty's Test., at 337.

[24] Trial Tr., Dr. Thomas A. Petty's Test., at 339.

[25] Trial Tr., Dr. Thomas A. Petty's Test., at 339.

[26] Trial Tr., Dr. Thomas W. Thompson's Test., at 365; *see* Chicago Tribune (*on file in the* John D. Voelker Papers, MSS-039, Central Upper Peninsula and Northern Michigan University Archives, Northern Michigan University).

[27] Trial Tr., Dr. Thomas W. Thompson's Test., at 370; *see* Chicago Tribune (*on file in the* John D. Voelker Papers, MSS-039, Central Upper Peninsula and Northern Michigan University Archives, Northern Michigan University).

[28] Trial Tr., Dr. Thomas W. Thompson's Test., at 368.

[29] Trial Tr., Dr. Thomas A. Petty's Test., at 341.

[30] Trial Tr., Dr. Thomas A. Petty's Test., at 341. The uninterrupted question would have been along the lines of whether an expert witness such as Dr. Thompson could offer a valid a psychiatric opinion based on the limited information that was available to him, which was a consequence of his failure to examine or conduct tests upon the defendant. As noted, Voelker did not finish his question as Beattie objected

and the judge sustained the objection. Trial Tr., Dr. Thomas A. Petty's Test., at 341.

[31] The disparity between the expert witnesses' interactions with the defendant apparently resonated with jurors. One juror said he even "felt sorry" for the prosecution expert because he was called upon to render an opinion about the defendant's sanity "without speaking one word to Lieutenant Peterson." Interview by Robyns with Muelle (July 29,2008).

[32] *Anatomy '59: The Making of a Classic Motion Picture* (WMNU-TV Broadcast 2009) (Muelle Interview).

[33] *See* Delene, *John Donaldson Voelker* at 114 (noting that the "judge's instructions to the jury are identical in the book and in the actual case"); Traver, *Anatomy of a Murder,* at 418 (quoting this instruction regarding insanity).

[34] Trial Tr., Jury Instructions, at 376–77.

[35] The closing arguments have not been preserved. We do know that one juror called Voelker's argument "another piece of art." Interview by Robyns with Muelle (July 29, 2008).

[36] Interview by Robyns with Muelle (July 29, 2008).

[37] Interview by Robyns with Muelle (July 29, 2008).

[38] Bergman, *The Real Trial*, at 90.

[39] Interview by Robyns with Muelle (July 29, 2008). Some later accounts incorrectly reported the initial vote was 8-4 in favor of guilty, rather than 8-4 in favor of acquittal. Muelle and another former juror had said it was just the opposite. Interview by Robyns with Muelle (July 29, 2008).

[40] Interview by Robyns with Muelle (July 29, 2008).

[41] Bergman, *The Real Trial*, at 90.

[42] Bergman, *The Real Trial*, at 90.

[43] Bergman, *The Real Trial*, at 91.

[44] Chicago Tribune (*on file in the* John D. Voelker Papers, MSS-039, Central Upper Peninsula and Northern Michigan University Archives, Northern Michigan University).

[45] Voelker, John. Journal, 1952 (*on file in the* John D. Voelker Papers, MSS-039, Central Upper Peninsula and Northern Michigan University Archives, Northern Michigan University).

[46] Interview by Elizabeth Delene with Millie Johnson Menze in Marquette, Mich. (June 1996); Delene, *John Donaldson Voelker*, at 104.

[47] Chicago Tribune (*on file in the* John D. Voelker Papers, MSS-039, Central Upper Peninsula and Northern Michigan University Archives, Northern Michigan University).

[48] Menze served as clerk of the circuit court for many years; she thought the world of John and left a bequest in herwill to the Voelker Foundation.

[49] Interview by Elizabeth Delene with Millie Johnson Menze in Marquette, Mich. (June 1996); *see* Delene, *John Donaldson Voelker* at 104 n.30.

[50] Interview by Robyns with Muelle (July 29, 2008).

[51] *Anatomy '59: The Making of a Classic Motion Picture* (WMNU-TV Broadcast 2009).

[52] Bergman, *The Real Trial*, at 91.

[53] Voelker, John. Journal. 1952 (*on file in the* John D. Voelker Papers, MSS-039, Central Upper Peninsula and Northern Michigan University Archives, Northern Michigan University).

[54] Heldreth, *Anatomy of a Murder From Fact to Fiction to Film*, at 136. At the hearing, Doctors Thompson and Petty agreed that Lieutenant Peterson was now sane. Daily Mining Journal, Sept. 24, 1952 (*on file in the* John D.Voelker Papers, MSS-039, Central Upper Peninsula and Northern Michigan University Archives, Northern Michigan University).

[55] They reportedly divorced about a year later. Krajicek, *Justice Story: The Murder Behind the Movie.*

[56] Delene, *John Donaldson Voelker,* at 104. Adding insult to injury, Lieutenant Peterson and his wife later sued Voelker to share in the profits of his novel based on the trial. The suit was dismissed. Baker, *An Anatomy of Anatomy of A Murder.*

[57] Noe, *The Murder In Michigan That Inspired A Culturally Significant Movie.*

[58] Noe, *The Murder In Michigan That Inspired A Culturally Significant Movie.*

[59] Voelker, John. Journal, 1952 (*on file in the* John D. Voelker Papers, MSS-039, Central Upper Peninsula and Northern Michigan University Archives, Northern Michigan University).

[60] Voelker, John. Journal, 1952 (*on file in the* John D. Voelker Papers, MSS-039, Central Upper Peninsula and Northern Michigan University Archives, Northern Michigan University).

[61] Bergman, *The Real Trial*, at 91.

[62] Bergman, *The Real Trial*, at 91.

Chapter 7 Endnotes

[1] Traver, *Anatomy of a Murder*, "Preface" at ii.

[2] Traver, *Anatomy of a Murder*, "Preface" at ii.

[3] Voelker, John. Journal, 1952 (*on file in the* John D. Voelker Papers, MSS-039, Central Upper Peninsula and Northern Michigan University Archives, Northern Michigan University).

[4] Voelker, John. Journal, 1952 (*on file in the* John D. Voelker Papers, MSS-039, Central Upper Peninsula and Northern Michigan University Archives, Northern Michigan University).

[5] Traver, *Anatomy of a Murder,* "Preface" at ii.

[6] Shaul, *Backwoods Barrister*, at 85.

[7] *Anatomy '59: The Making of a Classic Motion Picture* (WMNU-TV Broadcast 2009).

[8] *Anatomy '59: The Making of a Classic Motion Picture* (WMNU-TV Broadcast 2009).

[9] James, Laura. *John Voelker*, Legends True Crim. Rep., https://www.laurajames.com/clews/2006/09/legends_of_true.html (last visited Oct 28, 2018).

[10] Voelker, John. Journal, Sept. 11, 1953 (*on file in the* John D. Voelker Papers, MSS-039, Central Upper Peninsula and Northern Michigan University Archives, Northern Michigan University).

[11] Voelker, John. Journal, Sept. 11, 1953 (*on file in the* John D. Voelker Papers, MSS-039, Central Upper Peninsula and Northern Michigan University Archives, Northern Michigan University).

[12] Voelker, John. Journal, Sept. 11, 1953 (*on file in the* John D. Voelker Papers, MSS-039, Central Upper Peninsula and Northern Michigan University Archives, Northern Michigan University).

[13] Voelker, John. Journal, 1953 (*on file in the* John D. Voelker Papers, MSS-039, Central Upper Peninsula and Northern Michigan University Archives, Northern Michigan University).

[14] Voelker confirmed in a December 31, 1953 entry, "It is my plan, immediately after New Year, to get down to the writing of The Trial. I am afraid the incubation period has not been very fertile." John Voelker, Journal, 1953 (*on file in the* John D. Voelker Papers, MSS-039, Central Upper Peninsula and Northern Michigan University Archives, Northern Michigan University) (emphasis in original).

[15] Voelker, John. 1955 (*on file in the* John D. Voelker Papers, MSS-039, Central Upper Peninsula and Northern Michigan University Archives, Northern Michigan University).

[16] Voelker, John. 1955 (*on file in the* John D. Voelker Papers, MSS-039, Central Upper Peninsula and Northern Michigan University Archives, Northern Michigan University).

[17] Voelker, John. 1955 (*on file in the* John D. Voelker Papers, MSS-039, Central Upper Peninsula and Northern Michigan University Archives, Northern Michigan University).

[18] Voelker, John. Journal, 1956 (*on file in the* John D. Voelker Papers, MSS-039, Central Upper Peninsula and Northern Michigan University Archives, Northern Michigan University).

[19] Delene, *John Donaldson Voelker*, at 111.

[20] Shaul, *Backwoods Barrister*, at 84.

[21] Voelker once noted in a journal entry that he wrote Anatomy of a Murder with a "$1.95 ball point pen." John Voelker, Journal, 1956 (*on file in the* John D. Voelker Papers, MSS-039, Central Upper Peninsula and Northern Michigan University Archives, Northern Michigan University).

[22] Voelker once said, "There isn't any good writing; only rewriting." Fowler, *The Fishing Notes of John D. Voelker*, at 8.

[23] Christenson, Pam. *One Man's Life, Another Man's Quest: Collecting John D. Voelker*, MARQUETTE MONTHLY (AUG. 12, 2009), http://marquettemonthly.org/one-mans-life-another-mans-quest-collecting-john-d-voelker/.

[24] *Anatomy '59: The Making of a Classic Motion Picture* (WMNU-TV Broadcast 2009) (Snider Interview).

[25] Delene, *John Donaldson Voelker*, at 110.

[26] Delene, *John Donaldson Voelker*, at 110-11.

[27] Murder to Movie: Anatomy of a Murder (*on file in the* John D. Voelker Papers, MSS-039, Central Upper Peninsula and Northern Michigan University Archives,

Northern Michigan University).

[28] Voelker, John. Journal, 1956 (*on file in the* John D. Voelker Papers, MSS-039, Central Upper Peninsula and Northern Michigan University Archives, Northern Michigan University).

[29] Voelker, John. Journal, 1956 (*on file in the* John D. Voelker Papers, MSS-039, Central Upper Peninsula and Northern Michigan University Archives, Northern Michigan University).

[30] Voelker, John. Journal, 1956 (*on file in the* John D. Voelker Papers, MSS-039, Central Upper Peninsula and Northern Michigan University Archives, Northern Michigan University).

[31] Voelker, John. Journal, 1956 (*on file in the* John D. Voelker Papers, MSS-039, Central Upper Peninsula and Northern Michigan University Archives, Northern Michigan University).

[32] Delene, *John Donaldson Voelker*, at 111.

[33] Delene, *John Donaldson Voelker*, at 111.

[34] Baker, *Reflections on the 50th Anniversary*.

[35] *Anatomy of a Writer*, Milwaukee J., June 2, 1959.

[36] Krajicek, *Justice Story: The Murder Behind the Movie*.

[36] Delene, *John Donaldson Voelker*, at 111.

[38] Voelker, John. Journal, undated (*on file in the* John D. Voelker Papers, MSS-039, Central Upper Peninsula and Northern Michigan University Archives, Northern Michigan University).

[39] *Anatomy of an Author*, Michigan Alumnus, Jan. 18, 1958.

[40] *John D. Voelker Is Dead at 87: Author of 'Anatomy of a Murder'*, New York Times, Mar. 20, 1991.

[41] Delene, *John Donaldson Voelker*, at 112 (citing *The Case of Luscious Laura*, Time, Jan. 6, 1958). Crowther's review incorrectly states that the novel *Anatomy of a Murder* was sold to the movies before its publication. Preminger did read a copy of the manuscript before it was published but did not help settle pending lawsuits and purchase of the film rights until after the novel had been published. Richard Griffith, *Anatomy of a Motion Picture* 12 (1959).

[42] *Anatomy of an Author*, Michigan Alumnus, Jan. 18, 1958.

[43] *Anatomy of an Author*, Michigan Alumnus, Jan. 18, 1958.

[44] Baker, *Reflections on the 50th Anniversary*. The actual name of the title heroine in *Laughing Whitefish* was Black Carp. Voelker admitted to taking poetic license regarding her character: "History told me that this Indian woman was also married, graying, past middle age, remarkably intelligent, and built on the generous proportions of a Detroit Lions' fullback. But I waved my ball-point pen and, presto, she became a slender, beautiful, raven-haired slip of a girl." Delene, *John Donaldson Voelker*, at 181.

[45] Voelker, John. Journal, 1953 (*on file in the* John D. Voelker Papers, MSS-039, Central Upper Peninsula and Northern Michigan University Archives, Northern Michigan University).

[46] Delene, *John Donaldson Voelker*, at 114.

[47] Delene, *John Donaldson Voelker*, at 39. Another playwright, Elihu Winer, later obtained the rights to adopt the novel into a play. Delene, *John Donaldson Voelker*, at 39.

[48] Wheeler v. Dell Publ'g Co., 300 F.2d 372 (7th Cir. 1962).

[49] Delene, *John Donaldson Voelker*, at 39. Two of the suits were brought by Lieutenant Peterson and Chenoweth'swidow.

[50] Delene, *John Donaldson Voelker*, at 39.

[51] Interview by Robert F. Lane with John D. Voelker, Justice of the Michigan Supreme Court (Oct. 1, 1990) (transcript available at https://archive.lib.msu.edu/AFS/dmc/court/public/all/Voelker/ASY.html).

[52] "Paul Biegler" was Voelker's alter ego for years. The character's name was introduced in the 1939 novella *The Burning Earth*, an unpublished autobiographical work, and it appeared throughout his writings over his lifetime. In some journal entries, Voelker records imagined "conversations between Paul Biegler (the District Attorney), Robert Traver (the writer), and John Voelker (the voice of reason)." Delene, *John Donaldson Voelker*, at 48, 80.

[53] Mining Journal, Sept. 25, 1952 ((*on file in the* John D. Voelker Papers, MSS-039, Central Upper Peninsula and Northern Michigan University Archives, Northern Michigan University).

[54] Heldreth, *Anatomy of a Murder From Fact to Fiction to Film*, at 137.

[55] Hansen, *Anatomy of "Anatomy,"* at 17.

[56] Interview by Robert F. Lane with John D. Voelker, Justice of the Michigan Supreme Court (Oct. 1, 1990) (transcript available at

https://archive.lib.msu.edu/AFS/dmc/court/public/all/Voelker/ASY.html).

[57] *Anatomy '59: The Making of a Classic Motion Picture* (WMNU-TV Broadcast 2009).

[58] News accounts during the trial indicate that Wentzel said Chenoweth had been drinking more than usual and acting strangely for about two weeks before the shooting, and that Chenoweth had asked Wentzel to lock up three of his pistols. Heldreth, *Anatom of a Murder From Fact to Fiction to Film*, at 140.

[59] Heldreth, *Anatomy of a Murder From Fact to Fiction to Film*, at 140.

[60] Heldreth, *Anatomy of a Murder From Fact to Fiction to Film*, at 140.

[61] *See* Traver, *Anatomy of a Murder*, at 383-90.

[62] Voelker drives home this point through Biegler's closing argument, in which he rails against the prosecution's "studied and deliberate suppression of the *truth* ..." Traver, *Anatomy of a Murder*, at 394 (emphasis in original).

Chapter 8 Endnotes

[1] Traver, *Anatomy of a Murder*, Preface at ii-iv.

[2] In fact, Voelker even mentions in his novel that Biegler should "sell the plot to the movies." Traver, *Anatomy of a Murder,* at 174.

[3] Delene, *John Donaldson Voelker*, at 115.

[4] Delene, *John Donaldson Voelker*, at 115 (quoting Art Ferrell, Voelker's friend who was with Voelker when Preminger called and recounted the conversation to Delene).

[5] Delene, *John Donaldson Voelker*, at 115.

[6] Delene, *John Donaldson Voelker*, at 115.

[7] McCormick, Ken. *Justice Voelker? Call Him Johnny*, Detroit Free Press, Jan. 31, 1959. Once his financial ship came in, Voelker decided to resign from the Michigan Supreme Court and avoid urban life and the demands of the office. He delayed departing until after he was re-elected, which allowed the seat to remain in Democrat hands since Governor Williams would appoint his replacement. Interview by Eugene R. Milhizer with Richard Vander Veen III (Aug. 8, 2018).

[8] Delene, *John Donaldson Voelker*, at 116.

[9] LAURA (20th Century-Fox Pictures 1944).

[10] FALLEN ANGEL (20th Century-Fox Pictures 1945).

[11] THE MAN WITH THE GOLDEN ARM (Otto Preminger Films 1955).

[12] STALAG 17 (Paramount Pictures 1953).

[13] *Anatomy of a Murder* is widely recognized as "Hollywood's first attempt to deal with the subject of rape in frank terms." Gene D. Phillips, *Exiles in Hollywood: Major European Film Directors in America* 118 (1998).

[14] On one occasion, Voelker wrote to Van Druten that "he could see Henry Fonda as Paul Bieler. He was my first thought. And Thomas Mitchel as Parnell." Correspondence from John Voelker to John Van Druten, Nov. 11, 1957 (*on file in the* John D. Voelker Papers, MSS-039, Central Upper Peninsula and Northern Michigan University Archives, Northern Michigan University).

[15] *Notes* on *Anatomy of a Murder*, TURNER CLASSIC MOVIES, http://www.tcm.com/tcmdb/title/3737/Anatomy-of-a-Murder/notes.html (last visited Sept. 9, 2019).

[16] Griffith, *Anatomy of a Motion Picture*, at 12.

[17] Griffith, *Anatomy of a Motion Picture*, at 13. Preminger was a graduate of the University of Vienna Law School, but he never practiced law. Justin Philpott, *The Glory and Pitfalls of the Adversarial Justice System*, OBITER-DICTA(Jan. 20, 2018), https://obiter-dicta.ca/2016/01/20/anatomy-of-a-murder/. His father was a prosperous Viennese lawyer and a public prosecutor during the waning days of the Austro-Hungarian empire. Dave Kehr, *Mystery Endures After Verdict Is In*, N.Y. Times (Mar. 9, 2012), https://www.nytimes.com/2012/03/11/movies/homevideo/premingers-anatomy-of-a-murder-on-dvd.html.

[18] *Anatomy '59: The Making of a Classic Motion Picture* (WMNU-TV Broadcast 2009) (Hirsch Interview).

[19] Griffith, *Anatomy of a Motion Picture*, at 3.

[20] Letter from Voelker to Preminger, Dec. 4, 1958 (*on file in the* John D. Voelker Papers, MSS-039, Central Upper Peninsula and Northern Michigan University Archives, Northern Michigan University). Years later, Voelker wrote that he was "in love" with the movie and said "[i]t faithfully captured the spirit of my book." Stephen Winer, *Lettersfrom John: Getting to Know the Author of Anatomy of a Murder Criterion* (2012), https://www.criterion.com/current/posts/2153-dukie .

[21] Delene, *John Donaldson Voelker*, at 123.

[22] Papers (*on file in the* John D. Voelker Papers, MSS-039, Central Upper Peninsula and Northern Michigan University Archives, Northern Michigan University).

[23] Delene, *John Donaldson Voelker*, at 117.

[24] Hansen, *Anatomy of "Anatomy,"* at 49.

[25] Delene, *John Donaldson Voelker*, at 122.

[26] Hansen, *Anatomy of "Anatomy,"* at 31.

[27] Hansen, *Anatomy of "Anatomy,"* at 78.

[28] Hansen, *Anatomy of "Anatomy,"* at 78.

[29] Voelker Interview, Marquette Mining Journal, April 16, 1958 (*on file in the* John D. Voelker Papers, MSS-039, Central Upper Peninsula and Northern Michigan University Archives, Northern Michigan University).

[30] ANATOMY OF A MURDER (Otto Preminger Films 1959).

[31] Heldreth, *Anatomy of a Murder From Fact to Fiction to Film*, at 145.

[32] Phillips, Gene D. *Out of the Shadows: Expanding the Canon of Classic Film Noir* 162 (The Scarecrow Press, Inc., 2012) (quoting Richard Griffith, *Anatomy of a Motion Picture* 25–26, 28 (New York: St. Martin's Press, 1958)).

[33] Pepin, John. *A Silver Screen Classic: Otto Preminger's 'Anatomy of a Murder' Turns 60 This Month*, Mining J., June 29, 2019, at 9A.

[34] *Anatomy '59: The Making of a Classic Motion Picture* (WMNU-TV Broadcast 2009).

[35] *Anatomy '59: The Making of a Classic Motion Picture* (WMNU-TV Broadcast 2009).

[36] Lowe, Kenneth S. *Production of 'Anatomy' Pours Half Million Dollars in Area's Cash Registers*, Daily Mining Journal, Apr. 24, 1959 (*on file in the* John D. Voelker Papers, MSS-039, Central Upper Peninsula and Northern Michigan University Archives, Northern Michigan University).

[37] Lowe, Kenneth S. *Production of 'Anatomy' Pours Half Million Dollars in Area's Cash Registers*, Daily Mining Journal, Apr. 24, 1959 (*on file in the* John D. Voelker Papers, MSS-039, Central Upper Peninsula and Northern Michigan University Archives, Northern Michigan University).

[38] Interview by Eugene R. Milhizer with Robert Dossetto, Cir. Ct. Bailiff, Marquette, Michigan (Aug. 31, 2018).

[39] When Judge Weaver ducks into the library in the movie, this was actually a men's room with a library sign affixed over the doorway. Interview by Eugene R. Milhizer with Robert Dossetto, Cir. Ct. Bailiff, Marquette, Michigan (Aug. 31, 2018).

[40] Interview by Eugene R. Milhizer with Robert Dossetto, Cir. Ct. Bailiff, Marquette, Michigan (Aug. 31, 2018).

[41] Delene, *John Donaldson Voelker*, at 120.

[42] Delene, *John Donaldson Voelker*, at 120.

[43] Interview by Eugene R. Milhizer with Jack Borgeois (2018).

[44] *Anatomy '59: The Making of a Classic Motion Picture* (WMNU-TV Broadcast 2009).

[45] Delene, *John Donaldson Voelker*, at 123.

[46] Griffith, *Anatomy of a Motion Picture*, at 88.

[47] Hansen, *Anatomy of "Anatomy,"* at 38.

[48] Griffith, *Anatomy of a Motion Picture*, at 30.

[49] Kautz, Gabi. *60th Anniversary of Anatomy of a Murder*, VISIT THE WEST END (June 29, 2019), https://www.visitthewestend.com/blog/60th-anniversary-of-anatomy-of-a-murder.

[50] Hansen, *Anatomy of "Anatomy,"* at 18.

[51] Hansen, *Anatomy of "Anatomy,"* at 72–73.

[52] Interview by Eugene R. Milhizer with Grace Voelker (2019).

[53] Hansen, *Anatomy of "Anatomy,"* at 70–71.

[54] Hansen, *Anatomy of "Anatomy,"* at 74–75.

[55] Delene, *John Donaldson Voelker*, at 120.

[56] Delene, *John Donaldson Voelker*, at 120.

[57] THE PHILADELPHIA STORY (Metro-Goldwyn-Mayer 1940).

[58] *See* YOU CAN'T TAKE IT WITH YOU (Columbia Pictures 1938); MR. SMITH GOES TO WASHINGTON (Columbia Pictures 1939); IT'S A WONDERFUL LIFE (Liberty Films II 1946).

[59] *See* ROPE (Warner Bros. 1948); REAR WINDOW (Alfred J. Hitchcock Productions 1954); THE MAN WHO KNEW TOO MUCH (Paramount Pictures 1956); VERTIGO (Alfred J. Hitchcock Productions 1958).

[60] *See* WINCHESTER '73 (Universal International Pictures 1950); BEND OF THE RIVER (Universal International Pictures 1952); THE NAKED SPUR (Metro-Goldwyn-Mayer 1953); THE FAR COUNTRY (Universal International Pictures 1954); THE GLENN MILLER STORY (Universal Pictures 1954); THE MAN FROM LARAMIE (Columbia Pictures 955); STRATEGIC AIR COMMAND (Paramount Pictures 1955).

[61] *See* Brady, Patrick Trey. *The Celluloid Advocate: The Evolution of the Twentieth Century Cinematic Lawyer*, 27S. Cal. Interdisc. L. J. 165, 186 (2018).

[62] *The Feature Films of Jimmy Stewart*, The Jimmy Stewart Museum, https://www.jimmy.org/about-jimmy-biography/filmography-page-1-1935-1937/ (last visited Oct. 20, 2019).

[63] Van Druten, John. (*on file in the* John D. Voelker Papers, MSS-039, Central Upper Peninsula and Northern Michigan University Archives, Northern Michigan University).

[64] Interview by Eugene R. Milhizer with Frederick Baker (2018).

[65] Hansen, *Anatomy of "Anatomy,"* at 12.

[66] Delene, *John Donaldson Voelker*, at 208.

[67] Delene, *John Donaldson Voelker*, at 121.

[68] Stafford, Jeff. *Anatomy of a Murder*, TCM, http://www.tcm.com/this-month/article/85867%7C0/Anatomy-of-a-Murder.html (last visited Sept. 7, 2019).

[69] Pickard, Roy. *Jimmy Stewart: A Life in Film* 139 (St. Martin's Press 1992).

[70] Nolasco, Stephanie. *James Stewart Was 'Approached Several Times' To Pursue Senate Run But Chose To Stay Out Of Politics, Book Claims*, Fox News (May 15, 2018), https://www.foxnews.com/entertainment/james-stewart-was-approached-several-times-to-pursue-senate-run-but-chose-to-stay-out-of-politics-book-claims.

[71] *Facts By Film Anatomy of a Murder*, Classic Movie Hub, http://www.classicmoviehub.com/facts-and-trivia/film/anatomy-of-a-murder-1959/ (last visited Sept. 8, 2019).

[72] Crowther, Bosley. *Screen: A Court Classic*, N.Y. Times (Jul. 3, 1959), https://www.nytimes.com/1959/07/03/archives/screen-a-court-classic.html.

[73] Pickard, *Jimmy Stewart: A Life in Film*, at 143–44.

[74] Frischauer, Willi. *Behind the Scenes of Otto Preminger: An Unauthorized Biography* 173 (1974).

[75] Frischauer, *Behind the Scenes of Otto Preminger*, at 173.

[76] Hansen, *Anatomy of "Anatomy,"* at 47.

[77] Stafford, Jeff. *Anatomy of a Murder*, TCM, http://www.tcm.com/this-month/article/85867%7C0/Anatomy-of-a-Murder.html (last visited Sept. 7, 2019).

[78] A FACE IN THE CROWD (Newtown Productions 1957).

[79] Delene, *John Donaldson Voelker*, at 118.

[80] Delene, *John Donaldson Voelker*, at 118.

[81] Frischauer, *Behind the Scenes of Otto Preminger*, at 171.

[82] Delene, *John Donaldson Voelker*, at 118.

[83] Noe, *The Murder In Michigan That Inspired A Culturally Significant Movie*.

[84] ANATOMY OF A MURDER (Otto Preminger Films 1959).

[85] Voelker was infatuated with Remick. He took her for a ride in his fish car and they sipped bourbon from two of the four tin cups he kept in it for emergency libations. Interview by Eugene R. Milhizer with Frederick Baker (2018).

[86] Reeves, Thomas C. *Welch, Joseph Nye*, Am. Nat. Bio., https://www.anb.org/view/10.1093/anb/9780198606697.001.0001/anb-9780198606697-e-1100903 (last visited Dec.6, 2019).

[87] *Obituary of Joseph Nye Welch in Milestones*, Time, Oct. 17, 1960, at 72.

[88] Hansen, *Anatomy of "Anatomy,"* at 59.

[89] Longden, Tom. *Joseph Welch*, Des Moines Register News, http://data.desmoinesregister.com/famous-iowans/joseph-Welch (last visited Sept. 9, 2019).

[90] Griffith, *Anatomy of a Motion Picture*, at 18–23.

[91] *Cover of* Life Magazine (July 26, 1954).

[92] Daily Mining Journal (*on file in the* John D. Voelker Papers, MSS-039, Central Upper Peninsula and Northern Michigan University Archives, Northern Michigan University).

[93] Griffith, *Anatomy of a Motion Picture*, at 82.

[94] Hansen, *Anatomy of "Anatomy,"* at 21.

[95] Delene, *John Donaldson Voelker*, at 120.

[96] Lowe, Kenneth S. *Production of 'Anatomy' Pours Half Million Dollars in Area's Cash Registers*, Daily Mining Journal, Apr. 24, 1959 (*on file in the* John D. Voelker Papers, MSS-039, Central Upper Peninsula and Northern Michigan University Archives, Northern Michigan University).

[97] Lowe, Kenneth S. *Production of 'Anatomy' Pours Half Million Dollars in Area's Cash Registers*, Daily Mining Journal, Apr. 24, 1959 (*on file in the* John D. Voelker Papers, MSS-039, Central Upper Peninsula and Northern Michigan University Archives, Northern Michigan University). Those with speaking roles received $90 a day; Griffith estimated one thousand extras were used while the local paper had "a more conservative figure" of about 300. Delene, *John Donaldson Voelker*, at 120.

[98] Hansen, *Anatomy of "Anatomy,"* at 43.

[99] Delene, *John Donaldson Voelker*, at 124.

[100] Delene, *John Donaldson Voelker*, at 124.

[101] Delene, *John Donaldson Voelker*, at 124.

[102] Delene, *John Donaldson Voelker*, at 124.–125.

[103] Delene, *John Donaldson Voelker*, at 124–125.

[104] Hansen, *Anatomy of "Anatomy,"* at 48.

[105] That cannot account for *Anatomy*'s failure to garner the Best Picture Oscar, however: Ben-Hur, which, Voelker remarked, beat our *Anatomy* because the public preferred Charlton Heston's "oiled pecs" to a humble courtroom drama, ran 3 hours and 44 minutes.

[106] McCann, Dennis. *Marquette, Michigan Remembers 'Anatomy of a Murder'*, J. Sentinel (Nov. 7, 2008), http://archive.jsonline.com/features/travel/34099364.html.

[107] Delene, *John Donaldson Voelker*, at 120.

[108] Delene, *John Donaldson Voelker*, at 119.

[109] *Anatomy '59: The Making of a Classic Motion Picture* (WMNU-TV Broadcast 2009).

[110] Griffith, *Anatomy of a Motion Picture*, at 82.

[111] On August 2, 2018, I interviewed one of the last surviving cast members, Danny Abbott, who was a child extra seen playing on the lawn outside of the Thunder Bay Inn when Biegler arrives to talk with Paquette. Abbott told me about the jeep rides

with Stewart. Interview by Eugene R. Milhizer with Danny Abbott (2018).

[112] McCann, Dennis. *Marquette, Michigan Remembers 'Anatomy of a Murder'*, J. SENTINEL (Nov. 7, 2008), http://archive.jsonline.com/features/travel/34099364.html.

[113] O'Connell, Arthur. Anatomy of a Murder Bio Panels, N. Mich. U., https://www.nmu.edu/sites/DrupalBeaumierHeritageCenter/files/UserFiles/Files/Pre-Drupal/Documents/AnatomyofaMurder_bio_panels.pdf (last visited Dec. 15, 2019).

[114] Monaghan, John. *Freep Film Festival's 'Anatomy of 'Anatomy'' Revisits the Making of a Mich. Movie Classic*, Detroit Free Press (Apr. 13, 2019 8:00 AM), https://www.freep.com/story/entertainment/2019/04/13/anatomy- anatomy-revisits-making-mich-movie-classic/3443331002/.

[115] McCann, Dennis. *Marquette, Michigan Remembers 'Anatomy of a Murder'*, J. Sentinel (Nov. 7, 2008), http://archive.jsonline.com/features/travel/34099364.html.

[116] Interview by Eugene R. Milhizer with Richard Vander Veen III (Aug. 8, 2018).

[117] Hansen, *Anatomy of "Anatomy,"* at 36–37.

[118] Grant, Kathryn. Anatomy of a Murder Bio Panels, N. Mich. U., https://www.nmu.edu/sites/DrupalBeaumierHeritageCenter/files/UserFiles/Files/Pre-Drupal/Documents/AnatomyofaMurder_bio_panels.pdf (last visited Dec. 15, 2019).

[119] Arden, Eve. Anatomy of a Murder Bio Panels, N. Mich. U., https://www.nmu.edu/sites/DrupalBeaumierHeritageCenter/files/UserFiles/Files/Pre-Drupal/Documents/AnatomyofaMurder_bio_panels.pdf (last visited Dec. 15, 2019).

[120] Interview by Eugene R. Milhizer with John (Tom) Burke (Nov. 2019).

[121] Interview by Eugene R. Milhizer with John Wirtanen (2019); Interview by Eugene R. Milhizer with Roy Peterson (2019).

[122] Interview by Eugene R. Milhizer with Julie Voelker (2019).

[123] The 1960 Oscar nominations garnered by *Anatomy of a Murder* were Best Picture (Otto Preminger), Best Actor (James Stewart), Best Supporting Actor (George C. Scott as Claude Dancer and Arthur O'Connell as Parnell McCarthy), Best Adapted Screenplay (Wendell Mayes), Best Cinematography, Black-and-White (Sam Leavitt), and best film editing (Louis Loeffler). Ben Hur was the big winner that year with 10 Oscars. *Anatomy* was later selected for preservation in the United States National Film Registry by the Library of Congress as being "culturally, historically or aesthetically significant." *Preservation*, Los Angeles Times (Dec. 19, 2012), https://www.latimes.com/entertainment/la-xpm-2012-dec-19-la-et-mn-national- film-registry-20121217-story.html.

[124] *See Anatomy of a Murder – Awards*, IMDB, https://www.imdb.com/title/tt0052561/awards (last visited Oct. 20,2019). The Golden Globe nominations were Best Picture (Otto Preminger), Best Director (Otto Preminger), Best Actress (Lee Remick), and Best Supporting Actor (Joseph Welch). Susan King, *National Film Registry Selects 25 Films for Presevaton.*

[125] The three Grammy's were awarded to Duke Ellington included best sound track/background score. Thomas Cunniffe writes, "Ellington's music is used sparingly in the film, but it is very effective in enhancing the dramatic action." Thomas Cunniffe, *Anatomy of a Murder*, Jazz History Online, https://jazzhistoryonline.com/anatomy-of-a-murder/ (last visited Dec. 15, 2019).

> Despite being heard 'in bits and pieces' the score 'contains some of his most evocative and eloquentmusic … and beckons with the alluring scent of a femme fatale.' Including small pieces by Billy Strayhorn, film historians recognize it 'as a landmark — the first significant Hollywood film music by African Americans comprising non-diegetic music, that is, music whose source is not visible or implied by action in the film, like an on-screen band.' The score avoids cultural stereotypes which previously characterized jazz scores and 'rejected a strict adherence to visuals in ways that presaged the New Wave cinema of the '60s.'

Ellington, Duke. Discogs, https://www.discogs.com/Duke-Ellington-From-The-Soundtrack-Of-The-Motion-Picture-OttoPremingers-Anatomy-Of-A-Murder/master/243508 (last visited Dec. 15, 2019).

[126] *Anatomy of a Murder*, IMDB (1959), https://www.imdb.com/title/tt0052561/ (last visited Nov 2, 2018).

[127] *1959: Probable Domestic Take*, Variety (Jan. 6, 1960) (*on file in the* John D. Voelker Papers, MSS-039, CentralUpper Peninsula and Northern Michigan University Archives, Northern Michigan University).

[128] Verrone, Patrick M. *The 12 Best Trial Movies*, 75 ABA J. 96 (Nov. 1989).

[129] *See generally* Nina W. Tarr, *A Different Ethical Issue in Anatomy of a Murder: Friendly Fire from the Cowboy- Lawyer*, 32 J. Legal Prof. 137, 137 (2007) (discussing how *Anatomy of a Murder* is "used for teaching professional responsibility"); Patrick E. Longan, *Teaching Professionalism*, 60 Mercer L. Rev. 659, 668–669 (2009) (referring to using *Anatomy of Murder* for first-year law students); John Monaghan, *The Movie That Put Ishpeming on the Map*, Detroit Free Press, Jan. 20, 2009, https://forum.cinematour.com/cgi-bin/ubb/ultimatebb.cgi?ubb=get_topic;f=5;t=000190; *Theater to Present 'Anatomy of a Murder' at Historic Courthouse*, News-Dispatch, Jan. 3, 2015, https://www.thenewsdispatch.com/features/article_23be7c80-9375-11e4-b4b0-b7b505198e15.html.

[130] *Movies That Matter: "Anatomy of a Murder,"* Reel Change (July 9, 2014), https://reelchange.net/2013/07/09/movies-that-matter-anatomy-of-a-murder/.

[131] Turner, Adrian. *All Critics Anatomy of a Murder Reviews*, Rotten Tomatoes, (Nov. 6, 2013), https://www.rottentomatoes.com/m/anatomy_of_a_murder.

[132] Rosenbaum, Jonathan. *Top Critics Anatomy of a Murder Reviews*, Rotten Tomatoes (Oct. 23, 2007), https://www.rottentomatoes.com/m/anatomy_of_a_murder/reviews?type=top_critics.

[133] Crowther, Bosley. *Screen: A Court Classic*, N.Y. Times (Jul. 3, 1959), https://www.nytimes.com/1959/07/03/archives/screen-a-court-classic.html. Years later, Kim Newman of Empire wrote "Anatomy of a Murder is simply the best trial movie ever made . . ." Kim Newman, *Empire Essay: Anatomy of a Murder Review*, Empire (Jan. 1, 2000), https://www.empireonline.com/movies/reviews/empire-essay-anatomy- murder-review/.

[134] *Courtroom Drama*, American Film Institute, https://www.afi.com/afis-10-top-10/ (last visited Sept. 8, 2019).

[135] *The New Pictures*, Time Magazine, Jul. 13, 1959, at 70. Prior to the current rating system, the Motion Picture Association of American (MPAA) established a production code for movies. The MPAA reacted negatively to the film's frank courtroom discussions of rape and sexual intercourse, and its censors objected to the use of words such as "rape," "sperm," "sexual climax" and "penetration." Preminger made but one concession (substituting "violation"for "penetration") and the picture was released with the MPAA seal. The success of *Anatomy of a Murder* contributed to the eventual demise of the Code.

[136] General Correspondence, Hp-Jon (*on file in the* John D. Voelker Papers, MSS-039, Central Upper Peninsula and Northern Michigan University Archives, Northern Michigan University).

[137] Interview by Eugene R. Milhizer with Robert Dossetto, Cir. Ct. Bailiff, Marquette, Michigan (Aug. 31, 2018).

[138] Interview by Eugene R. Milhizer with Robert Dossetto, Cir. Ct. Bailiff, Marquette, Michigan (Aug. 31, 2018).

[139] Most of the crew stayed at the Landmark Hotel in Marquette. I visited both the former Mather Inn and the Landmark Hotel in 2018 and confirmed this.

[140] Delene, *John Donaldson Voelker*, at 123.

[141] Voelker and Duke Ellington would sometimes "go to the Crow's Nest restaurant and play duets together on the piano. John was a very good piano player." Vloet, *Anatomy of an Alumnus*, at 42.

[142] Hansen, *Anatomy of "Anatomy,"* at 51.

[143] Delene, *John Donaldson Voelker* at 123.

[144] *Anatomy '59: The Making of a Classic Motion Picture* (WMNU-TV Broadcast 2009).

[145] Interview by Eugene R. Milhizer with Kurt Gronvall, owner of Globe Printing Inc. (2018).

[146] Interview by Eugene R. Milhizer with Stacey Willey (Aug. 3, 2018).

[147] Interview by Eugene R. Milhizer with Kurt Gronvall, owner of Globe Printing Inc., (2018).

[148] *See* ANATOMY OF A MURDER (Otto Preminger Films 1959).

Chapter 9 Endnotes

[1] *Oxford Dictionary of Quotations* 717-22 (Elizabeth Knowles 6th ed. 2004) ("Democracy is the worst form of Government except all those other forms that have been tried from time to time.").

[2] *Burton's Anatomy of Melancholy*, The British Library, https://www.bl.uk/collection-items/burtons-anatomy-of-melancholy-1628 (last visited Oct. 20, 2019).

[3] Traver, *Anatomy of a Murder*, "Prologue" at 1.

[4] "Murder" is defined as "[t]he killing of a human being with malice aforethought." *Murder*, Black's Law Dictionary (7th ed. 1999).

[5] "Homicide" is defined as "[t]he killing of one person by another." *Homicide*, Black's Law Dictionary (7th ed.1999).

[6] "Malice aforethought" is defined as:

> The requisite mental state for common-law murder, encompassing any one of the following: (1) the intent to kill, (2) the intent to inflict grievous bodily harm, (3) extremely reckless indifference to the value of human life (the so-called "abandoned and malignant heart"), or (4) the intent to commit a felony (which leads to culpability under the felony-murder rule).

Malice Aforethought, Black's Law Dictionary (7th ed. 1999).

[7] A justification defense "arises when the defendant has acted in a way that the law does not seek to prevent." *Justification Defense*, Black's Law Dictionary (7th ed. 1999). As I have previously noted,

> Justification defenses focus on the act and not the actor. These defenses exculpate conduct that is 'otherwise criminal, which under the circumstances is socially acceptable and which deserves neither criminal liability nor even

censure.' Accordingly, an actor is justified if his conduct, taken in context, is judged to be proper, or at least to be warranted.

Eugene R. Milhizer, *Justification and Excuse: What They Were, What They Are, and What They Ought to Be*, 78 St. John's L. Rev. 725, 812 (2004) (*citing* Peter S.W. Heberling, Note, *Justification: The Impact of the Model Penal Code on Statutory Reform*, 75 Colum. L. Rev. 914, 916 (1975)).

For example, self-defense is a type of justification defense. If the defendant's actions would otherwise constitute murder but he acted in self-defense, then he did not commit murder and would be acquitted. *See* 1 Paul H. Robinson, *Criminal Law Defenses* § 24 (1984) (discussing justification defenses generally).

[8] Excuse defenses, like justification defenses, are affirmative defenses. "They exculpate even though the elements of the offense are satisfied. Excuses admit the deed may be wrong, but excuse the actor because conditions suggest that he is not responsible for his deed." 1 Robinson, *Criminal Law Defenses*, at § 25(a) (internal footnote omitted).

Excuse defenses focus on the actor and not the act. A defendant is excused when he is judged to be not blameworthy for his conduct, even though the conduct itself is improper and harmful. An excuse defense, in other words, "is in the nature of a claim that although the actor has harmed society, she should not be blamed or punished for causing that harm." Eugene R. Milhizer, *Justification and Excuse: What They Were, What They Are, and What They Ought to Be*, 78 St. John's L. Rev. 725, 812 (2004) (citing Joshua Dressler, *Justifications and Excuses: A Brief Review of the Concepts and the Literature*, 33 Wayne L. Rev. 1155, 1162–63 (1987)).

[9] *See generally* 2 Robinson, *Criminal Law Defenses*, at §173(a) (discussing the insanity defense in general).

[10] Of course the victim is just as dead. But murder is a legal term, not a factual term. The only exception to this proposition is where a jurisdiction authorizes a verdict of "guilty but insane." 2 Robinson, *Criminal Law Defenses*, at § 173(h) (discussing the verdict of "guilty but mentally ill" that is recognized in a minority of jurisdictions). This verdict is not authorized in Michigan, and Lieutenant Manion was found "not guilty by reason of temporary insanity."

[11] We know this for sure as Voelker defines first-degree murder in his novel thusly: "the deliberate, malicious and premeditated killing of a person without legal justification or excuse." Traver, *Anatomy of a Murder*, at 410.

[12] Murder to Movie: Anatomy of a Murder (*on file in the* John D. Voelker Papers, MSS-039, Central Upper Peninsula and Northern Michigan University Archives, Northern Michigan University) (emphasis added).

[13] Christenson, Pam. *One Man's Life, Another Man's Quest: Collecting John D. Voelker*, Marquette Monthly (AUG.12, 2009),

http://marquettemonthly.org/one-mans-life-another-mans-quest-collecting-john-d-voelker/.

[14] Traver, *Anatomy of a Murder*, at 1.

Chapter 10 Endnotes

[1] Canon 7-1 provides, "The duty of a lawyer, both to his client and to the legal system, is to represent his client zealously within the bounds of the law, which includes Disciplinary Rules and enforceable professional regulations." Model Code of Professional Responsibility Canon 7-1 (Am. Bar Ass'n 1969), https://www.americanbar.org/content/dam/aba/administrative/professional_responsibility/mrpc/mrpc_migrated/mcpr.pdf (last visited Oct. 20, 2019).

[2] Stephen Landsman defends the adversary system, writing:

> The central precept of the adversary process is that out of the sharp clash of proofs presented by adversaries in a highly structured forensic setting is most likely to come the information upon which a neutral and passive decision maker can base the resolution of litigated dispute acceptable to both the parties and society.

Stephan Landsman, The Adversary System: A Description and Defense 2 (1984). *See generally* Keith A. Findley, *Adversarial Inquisitions: Rethinking the Search for Truth*, 56 N.Y.L. Rev. 911 (2011/2012) (critiquing the assumption that the adversary system is an effective process for finding the truth).

[3] In *Anatomy of a Murder*, Parnell defends the truth-seeking benefits of the adversary system thusly: "criminal trials are from their very nature intensely partisan affairs— primitive, knock-down, every-man-for-himself combats—the very opposite of detached scientific determinations." Traver, *Anatomy of a Murder*, at 159.

[4] *See generally* Nina W. Tarr, *A Different Ethical Issue in Anatomy of a Murder: Friendly Fire from the Cowboy-Lawyer*, 32 J. Legal Prof. 137, 143–44 (2008) (discussing the "unwritten law" generally and the reference to it in *Anatomy of a Murder*).

[5] Traver, *Anatomy of a Murder*, at 36.

[6] Model Rule of Professional Conduct 3.4(b) provides, "A lawyer shall not falsify evidence, counsel or assist a witness to testify falsely, or offer an inducement to a witness that is prohibited by law." Model Code of Professional Conduct r. 3.4(b) (Am. Bar Ass'n 2018), https://www.americanbar.org/groups/professional_responsibility/publications/model_rules_of_professional_conduct/rule_3_4_fairness_to_opposing_party_counsel/ (last visited Oct. 20, 2019).

[7] Voelker uses the term "plausible legal peg" for this purpose. Traver, *Anatomy of a Murder*, at 43.

[8] Traver, *Anatomy of a Murder*, at 35. *See generally* Richard C. Wydick, *The Ethics of Witness Coaching*, 17 Cardozo L. Rev. 1, 26–27 (1995) (explaining that Biegler employs "the Lecture" to avoid being reported and disciplined, and to avoid the appearance of dishonesty); Erin C. Asborno, *Ethical Preparation of Witnesses for Deposition and Trial*, ABA, Dec. 13, 2011, http://apps.americanbar.org/litigation/committees/trialpractice/articles/121311- ethics-preparation-witnesses- deposition-trial.html (last visited Nov. 11, 2019) (referring to "the Lecture" as striking the "delicate balance between our duty to clients and our ethical obligations to the court").

[9] Professor Michael Asimov points out the subtle distinction between the novel and the film with regard to the issue of improper witness coaching. Michael Asimow, *Anatomy of a Murder—The "Lecture"*, USFCA (Feb. 1998), https://web.archive.org/web/20100303070430/http:/www.usfca.edu/pj/articles/anato my.htm. In the book, unlike the film, it is Biegler who explicitly suggests the insanity defense. Speaking in the first person, Biegler recounts the conversation with his client: "'Then, finally there's the defense of insanity.' I paused, and spoke abruptly, airily: 'Well, that just about winds it up.'" Traver, *Anatomy of a Murder*, at 45. Then Manion starts asking questions about insanity. Biegler plays dumb and answers the questions, but tells the reader:

> My naivete was somewhat excessive; it had been obvious to me from merely reading the newspaper the night before that insanity was the best, if not the only, legal defense the man had. And here I'd just slammed shut every other escape hatch and told him this was the last. Only a cretin could have missed it, and I was rapidly learning that Lieutenant Manion was no cretin.

Traver, *Anatomy of a Murder*, at 46. *See also* Richard C. Wydick, *The Ethics of Witness Coaching*, 17 Cardozo L. Rev. 1, 25-27 (1995) (arguing that Biegler went too far in witness coaching).

[10] Michael Asimow & Shannon Mader, Law and Popular Culture: A Course Book 35–36 (2d ed. 2013); *see also* J. Thomas Sullivan, *Defending the Guilty: Lawyer Ethics in the Movies*, 79 Mo. L. Rev. 585, 642 (2014) (referring to how *Anatomy of a Murder* portrays the "ill-defined line" between effective representation and coaching).

[11] Hoff, Timothy. *Anatomy of a Murder*, 24 Legal Stud. F. 661, 662 (1999).

[12] Applegate, John S. *Witness Preparation*, 68 Tex. L. Rev. 277, 301–304 (1989) (describing the "Lecture" as an "extreme example" of a lawyer discussing the law with his client).

[13] ANATOMY OF A MURDER (Otto Preminger Films 1959).

[14] Before introducing the possibility of an insanity defense, Biegler tells Lieutenant Manion, "The biggest reason I hesitate to take your case, as things now stand, is my fear of losing it. That is merely a negative form of advance face-saving." Traver, *Anatomy of a Murder*, at 42. *See generally* J. Thomas Sullivan, *Defending the Guilty: Lawyer Ethics in the Movies*, 79 Mo. L. Rev. 585, 637–643 (2014) (referring to *Anatomy of a Murder* and discussing the various causes that might motivate a lawyer to obscure the truth in order to win a case). Of course, Biegler is also motivated to avoid disciplinary sanctions.

[15] Voelker once observed that juries "frequently awarded the prize to the side that puts on the better show." Delene, *John Donaldson Voelker*, at 108.

[16] In the novel, Judge Weaver meets with Biegler after the jury verdict is announced. The judge congratulates Biegler his brilliant "prosecution" of the case. When defense counsellor Biegler looks confused, the judge tells him,

> I've known for years, of course, as you doubtless have, that murder juries invariably "try" the victim as well as the killer. Did the rascal deserve to be slain? Should we exalt the killer …? But this isthe first time in my legal career that I've seen a dead man successfully prosecuted for rape. This is a new one. Quite incidentally, I may add, you seem also to have acquitted a man called Manion.

Traver, *Anatomy of a Murder*, at 431.

[17] Voelker, John. Journal, 1948–1950 (*on file in the* John D. Voelker Papers, MSS-039, Central Upper Peninsula and Northern Michigan University Archives, Northern Michigan University).

[18] Voelker, John. Journal, 1948–1950 (*on file in the* John D. Voelker Papers, MSS-039, Central Upper Peninsula and Northern Michigan University Archives, Northern Michigan University).

Chapter 11 Endnotes

[1] Criminal Justice Standards for the Defense Function 4-1.2(b) (Am. Bar Ass'n, 4th ed.),
https://www.americanbar.org/groups/criminal_justice/standards/DefenseFunctionFourthEdition/ (last visited Oct.20, 2019).

[2] Criminal Justice Standards for the Prosecution Function 3-1.2(b) (Am. Bar Ass'n, 4th ed. 2018), https://www.americanbar.org/groups/criminal_justice/standards/ProsecutionFunctionFourthEdition/ (last visited Oct.20, 2019).

[3] Traver, *Troubleshooter*, at 41.

[4] Traver, *Small Town D.A.*, at 46.

[5] Traver, *Small Town D.A.*, at 250–51.

[6] Traver, *Anatomy of a Murder*, at 255.

[7] *See generally* Joshua Dressler, *Understanding Criminal Law* 7–10 (8th ed. 2018) (discussing jury nullification andthe arguments in favor of it and against it).

[8] Traver, *Small Town D.A.*, at 210.

[9] Traver, *Troubleshooter*, at 205.

[10] Voelker, John. Journal, 1948–1950 (*on file in the* John D. Voelker Papers, MSS-039, Central Upper Peninsula and Northern Michigan University Archives, Northern Michigan University).

[11] In the novel, the local prosecutor rejects Biegler's suggestion that the top charge be lowered to voluntary manslaughter because he could not "square that" with his constituents. Traver, *Anatomy of a Murder*, at 71.

[12] In the novel, Biegler explains to Lieutenant Manion, "All of us, everywhere, all the time, spend our waking hours saving face. This case is riddled with face. After all, one of the mute unspoken reasons you are being prosecuted is to save face, community face." Traver, *Anatomy of a Murder*, at 42.

[13] Traver, *Small Town D.A.*, at 246.

[14] Traver, *Small Town D.A.*, at 247.

[15] Model Code of Professional Conduct r. 3.8(c) (Am. Bar Ass'n 2018).

[16] Model Code of Professional Conduct r. 3.3(a)(2) (Am. Bar Ass'n 2018).

[17] Traver, *Anatomy of a Murder*, at 383.

[18] Traver, *Anatomy of a Murder*, at 385.

[19] Model Code of Professional Conduct r. 3.4(c) & (e) (Am. Bar Ass'n 2018).

[20] Henseler, Timothy B., *A Critical Look at the Admissibility of Polygraph Evidence in the Wake of Daubert: The Lie Detector Fails the Test*, 46 Cath. U. L. Rev. 1247, 1248 (1997).

[21] Henseler, Timothy B. *A Critical Look at the Admissibility of Polygraph Evidence in the Wake of Daubert: The Lie Detector Fails the Test*, 46 Cath. U. L. Rev. 1247, 1248 (1997).

Chapter 12 Endnotes

[1] ANATOMY OF A MURDER (Otto Preminger Films 1959).

[2] In *Anatomy of a Murder*, Parnell McCarthy lauds the "wonderful elasticity of the law," and he reminds Biegler that "[j]ustice, you know, lad, cannot be measured with calipers . . . criminals are from their very nature intensely partisan affairs . . . the very opposite of detached scientific determination." Traver, *Anatomy of a Murder*, at 159.

[3] Traver, *Troubleshooter*, at 132–33.

[4] Traver, *Anatomy of a Murder*, at 63.

[5] Fed. R. Evid. 803.

[6] Fed. R. Evid. 404.

[7] Biegler says, "I also guess that men will never devise a better system of determining their clashes with each other and society. At least our jury system, for all its absurdities and imperfections, achieves a sort of rough democracy inaction ..." Traver, *Anatomy of a Murder*, at 246.

[8] Traver, *Small Town D.A.*, at 212.

[9] Voelker, John. Journal, 1948–1950 (John D. Voelker Papers, MSS-039, Central Upper Peninsula and Northern Michigan University Archives, Northern Michigan University).

[10] Traver, *Laughing Whitefish*, at 63.

[11] *See* Kant, Immanuel. *The Philosophy of Law in Kant's Metaphysical Principles of the Science of Right* 198 (W.Hastie trans. 1887) (addressing the "desert of [a murderer's] deeds").

[12] Christopher, Russell L. *Deterring Retributivism: The Injustice of "Just" Punishment*, 96 NW. U. L. Rev. 843, 860 (2002).

[13] Fidler, John. *Anatomy of a Murder*, Senses of Cinema (Mar. 2013), sensesofcinema.com/2013/cteq/anatomy-of-a-murder/.

[14] Traver, *Small Town D.A.*, at 209–10.

[15] *See Oxford Dictionary of Quotations* 221–22 (Elizabeth Knowles 6th ed. 2004) ("Democracy is the worst form of Government except all those other forms that have been tried from time to time.").

[16] Traver, *Troubleshooter*, at 133.

Chapter 13 Endnotes

[1] *See generally* Asimow & Mader, Law and Popular Culture: A Course Book, at 36 (examining the application of the "unwritten law" to the jury's decision in *Anatomy of a Murder*).

[2] *Justice*, Black's Law Dictionary (7th ed. 1999).

[3] *Justice*, Black's Law Dictionary (7th ed. 1999).

[4] Traver, *Anatomy of a Murder*, at 396.

[5] Asimow & Mader, Law and Popular Culture: A Coursebook, at 31.

[6] "Manslaughter" is defined as "[t]he unlawful killing of a human being without malice aforethought." *Manslaughter*, Black's Law Dictionary (7th ed. 1999). "Voluntary manslaughter," a lesser-included offense charged at the Peterson trial, is defined as "[a]n act of murder reduced to manslaughter because of extenuating circumstances such as adequate provocation (arousing the "heat of passion") or diminished capacity." *Voluntary Manslaughter*, Black's Law Dictionary (7th ed. 1999).

[7] "Premeditated," in the context of premeditated murder, is defined as a murder "[d]one with willful deliberation and planning; consciously considered beforehand." Premeditated, Black's Law Dictionary (7th ed. 1999).

[8] Aquinas, Thomas. *2 Summa Theologica* Q. 58, Art. 11.

[9] Traver, *Troubleshooter*, at 133.

[10] *See generally* Dressler, Joshua. *Understanding Criminal Law* 7–10 (8th ed. 2018) (discussing traditional bases forjury nullification).

[11] In his novel, Voelker concedes that Biegler and the defendant "used" each other – "[the defendant] got his freedom and [Biegler] got whatever it is [he] got." Traver, *Anatomy of a Murder*, at 435.

[12] Barton, J. *Natural Law and Poetic Justice in the Old Testament*, 30 J. Theological Stud. 1, 13 (1979).

[13] THE TEN COMMANDMENTS (Cecil DeMille 1956).

Chapter 14 Endnotes

[1] Woessner, *UP's John Voelker Continues Work He Loves in His Country*, at 2.

[2] Woessner, *UP's John Voelker Continues Work He Loves in His Country*, at 2.

[3] Interview by Eugene R. Milhizer with Ernest Woods (2018).

[4] 76 Mich. 498 (Mich. 1889).

[5] *See, e.g.*, Lepczyk, Tim. *Review: Laughing Whitefish – Robert Traver*, Tim Lepczyk (Aug. 19, 2011), http://timlepczyk.com/2011/08/19/review-laughing-whitefish-robert-traver.html#mobile-foot.

[6] Voelker, John. Journal, 1981 (*on file in the* John D. Voelker Papers, MSS-039, Central Upper Peninsula and Northern Michigan University Archives, Northern Michigan University).

[7] Voelker, John. Journal, 1981 (*on file in the* John D. Voelker Papers, MSS-039, Central Upper Peninsula and Northern Michigan University Archives, Northern Michigan University).

[8] Delene, *John Donaldson Voelker*, at 195.

[9] Delene, *John Donaldson Voelker*, at 195.

[10] Interview by Eugene R. Milhizer with Frederick Baker (2019) (recalling a conversation with Grace Voelker).

[11] Delene, *John Donaldson Voelker*, at 195.

[12] Voelker, John. *Recollections and Ruminations on Law*, 64 Michigan Bar Jour. 16 (1985), at 17.

[13] Hansen, *Anatomy of "Anatomy,"* at 15.

[14] Shaul, *Backwoods Barrister*, at 85.

[15] Interview by Eugene R. Milhizer with Gary Walker (2019).

[16] Interview by Eugene R. Milhizer with Frederick Baker (2018).

[17] Delene, *John Donaldson Voelker*, at 208.

[18] Barone, Adam. *American Dream*, Investopedia (Nov. 21, 2019) https://www.investopedia.com/terms/a/american-dream.asp.

[19] *Oxford Dictionary of Quotations* 588 (Elizabeth Knowles 6th ed. 2004).

[20] *Leonardo da Vinci's Notebooks* (1452–1519).

[21] Voelker hated flying and would have continued to drive by car or commute by train to and from Lansing. As a young man on a fishing trip to Ontario, Voelker sat next to the door of a small plane that was held closed by a piece of bailing wire.

When the pilot banked sharply, Voelker tipped against the door. He was uninjured but terrified and rarely flew thereafter. In fact, he refused to fly back from Canada, hiking instead to a railroad track where he waved down a passing train and hitched a ride back to the UP. Shaul, *Backwoods Barrister*, at 85.

[22] Noble. *Voelker: An Anatomy of a Private Life*, at 35.

[23] Voelker, John. Journal, 1952 (*on file in the* John D. Voelker Papers, MSS-039, Central Upper Peninsula and Northern Michigan University Archives, Northern Michigan University).

Epilogue Endnotes

[1] *Leonardo da Vinci's Notebooks* (1452–1519).